ROUTLEDGE LIBRARY EDITIONS:
ACCOUNTING

Volume 57

PAPERS ON ACCOUNTING HISTORY

PAPERS ON ACCOUNTING HISTORY

R. H. PARKER

Routledge
Taylor & Francis Group
LONDON AND NEW YORK

First published in 1984

This edition first published in 2014
by Routledge
4 Park Square, Milton Park, Abingdon, Oxon OX14 4RN
605 Third Avenue, New York, NY 10017

Routledge is an imprint of the Taylor & Francis Group, an informa business

British Library Cataloguing in Publication Data
A catalogue record for this book is available from the British Library

ISBN: 978-0-415-53081-1 (Set)
eISBN: 978-1-315-88628-2 (Set)
ISBN: 978-0-415-71837-0 (Volume 57) (hbk)
eISBN: 978-1-315-86754-0 (Volume 57)

Publisher's Note
The publisher has gone to great lengths to ensure the quality of this book but points out that some imperfections in the original copies may be apparent.

Disclaimer
The publisher has made every effort to trace copyright holders and would welcome correspondence from those they have been unable to trace.

Papers on Accounting History

R. H. Parker

GARLAND PUBLISHING, INC.
NEW YORK & LONDON
1984

ACKNOWLEDGMENTS

The articles in this book are reprinted by permission of the following:

Pitman Books Ltd., "The Study of Accounting History." *Abacus*, "Lower of Cost and Market in Britain and the United States," "Bookkeeping Barter and Current Cash Equivalents in Early New South Wales," and "British Men of Account." *Journal of Accounting Research*, "Discounted Cash Flow in Historical Perspective," and "A Note on Savary's 'Le Parfait Negociant'." Philip Allan Publishers, Ltd., "History of Accounting for Decisions." D. M. Emanuel and I. C. Stewart, "The Want of Uniformity in Accounts." *Accountancy*, "Those First Councillors . . . A Golden Heritage." *The Accounting Review* and The American Accounting Association, "Memorial: Frank Sewell Bray, 1906-1979." *The Chartered Accountant in Australia*, "Australia's First Accountancy Body." *The Accountant's Magazine*, "The First Scottish Book on Accounting." Prentice-Hall International, "Reckoning, Merchants' Accounts, Book-keeping, Accounting or Accountancy?"

Library of Congress Cataloging in Publication Data

Parker, R. H. (Robert Henry)
Papers on accounting history.

(Accounting history and the development of a profession)
1. Accounting—History—Addresses, essays, lectures.
I. Title. II. Series.
HF5605.P37 1984 657'.09 83-49443
ISBN 0-8240-6310-4 (alk. paper)

The volumes in this series are printed on
acid-free, 250-year-life paper.

Printed in the United States of America

Contents

Introduction

The fourteen papers reproduced in this volume were written over a period of more than twenty years. They reflect my continuing interest in accounting history and the changing circumstances in which I have been able to contribute to its literature.

My interest in the subject was first aroused in the mid-1950s by Henry Rand Hatfield's "Historical Defense of Bookkeeping" (1924) as reprinted in the first edition of William Baxter's *Studies in Accounting* (1950). I also acquired at about the same time a copy of Littleton and Yamey's *Studies in the History of Accounting* (1956) which remains in my opinion one of the major publications in the subject.

In 1960 I was fortunate enough to be appointed a lecturer in accounting at the University of Adelaide in South Australia and to have Russell Mathews as my head of department. The modest article reprinted here on the Adelaide Society of Accountants dates from this period. Accounting education in Australian universities started to boom in the 1960s and Australia's first academic accounting journal, *Abacus*, was founded by Ray Chambers in 1965. I contributed two papers to the first volume, one of which was "Lower of Cost and Market in Britain and the United States: An Historical Survey" (1965). This article, written whilst I was at the University of Western Australia, suggests that the lower of cost and market rule has survived because it embodies the rival concepts of cost and value in a single rule. So long as accountants are unwilling or unable to decide on the objectives of financial accounting, such rules fulfil a need.

I spent most of 1966 as a P. D. Leake Research Fellow at the London School of Economics. One advantage of London was superior library facilities. It was these which enabled me to show in "A Note on Savary's 'Le Parfait Négociant'" (1968) how Littleton had been misled by a misprint. This two page paper is my entry in any competition for the most obscure article ever written on an accounting subject.

Most of my time at LSE was spent researching the history of accounting for decision making. The results of this research are represented in this volume by two papers. "Discounted Cash Flow in Historical Perspective" (1968) was later described, to my pleasure and surprise, by Levy and Sarnat in their text on *Capital Investment and Financial Decisions* (2nd ed., 1982, p.177n) as "informative and highly entertaining." (The editor of *The Journal of Accounting Research* had a rather different opinion of the first draft.) The second paper, "History of Accounting for Decisions" (1980), was written much later but represents an updating of material published in my book *Management Accounting: An Historical Perspective* (1969).

Late in 1966 I moved to the Manchester Business School which provided few opportunities for research into accounting history. The same was true of my period (1968-1970) at INSEAD in Fontainebleau. During this latter period, however, there were many opportunities to improve my knowledge of comparative accounting.

In 1970 I moved to the University of Dundee in Scotland and was able, in the birthplace of modern accountancy, to revive my interest in accounting history. I became the convenor of the Scottish Committee on Accounting History whose publications included *Accounting in Scotland: An Historical Bibliography* (2nd ed., 1976) compiled by Janet Pryce-Jones and annotated by me. It is included in the 1984 Garland series. The book owed much to the enthusiasm and help of Anna Dunlop, then Keeper of the Antiquarian Collection of The Institute of Chartered Accountants of Scotland. An article included in that book on "The First Scottish Book on Accounting: Robert Colinson's *Idea Rationaria* (1683)" (1974) was also published in *The Accountant's Magazine* and is included in the present volume. It is my only contribution to one way of writing accounting history: the detailed analysis of an early published text.

In 1976 I presented a paper (not included in the present volume but published in *The Accounting Historians Journal*, Fall, 1977) at the Second World Congress of Accounting Historians on "Research Needs in Accounting History." The paper called for more bibliographies and biographies, including collective biographies, more quantitative accounting history, and for research into the influence of the economic environment on accounting development, "scientific revolutions" in accounting, causes of changes in accounting practice, diffusion of accounting innovations, the development of international accounting firms and the development of academic accounting.

In the same year I moved to my present post at the University of Exeter, where the conditions for research, both in accounting history and comparative accounting, have been excellent. In my inaugural lecture at Exeter I tried to put into an historical context the continuing importance of the British accountancy profession to creditors, shareholders, taxpayers, managers, employees and other users. The lecture was later published in *Abacus* as "British Men of Account" (1978) and is included in the present volume.

Nineteen seventy-nine and 1980 were busy years. In 1979, as an encouragement and aid to teachers of British and American 19th and 20th century accounting history, Tom Lee and I produced a book of readings, included in the 1984 Garland series, on *The Evolution of Corporate Financial Reporting*. In 1979 also, the then editor of *The Accounting Review* asked me to write "Memorial, Frank Sewell Bray, 1906-1979." This was published in 1980, in the same year as my compilation *British Accountants: A Biographical Sourcebook*, which resulted from my conviction that to understand present-day accounting one needs to understand not only past accounting but also past accountants. The introduction to the book is reproduced in the present volume, together with a list of the biographies included. (The latter was inadvertently omitted in 1980.)

The centenary of the Institute of Chartered Accountants in England and Wales in 1980 and the Third International Conference of Accounting Historians held in London in the same year helped to keep me busy. I was one of the organizers of the conference and wrote an account of it which was published in the *Journal of European Economic History* (vol. 10, 1981, pp. 743-754).

I edited a Special Accounting History issue of *Accounting and Business Research* (no. 37A, 1980) and produced as a loose-leaf insert "An Accounting Historian's Guide to London." I enjoyed this task but have ever since had an increased respect for the stamina of the writers of guidebooks. Apart from *British Accountants*, the Arno Press also published my compilation *Bibliographies for Accounting Historians* (1980). "Those First Councillors . . . A Golden Heritage" (my entry in any competition for the worst title ever chosen by an editor for an author) was published in *Accountancy* in the English Institute's centenary month (May 1980) and looked at the very varying fortunes of the firms of the members of the first council of the Institute.

My main research contribution in the centenary year was a book I wrote jointly with Jack Kitchen: *Accounting Thought and Education: Six English Pioneers* (London: Institute of Chartered Accountants in England and Wales, 1980). The book, which is included in the 1984 Garland series, looked at the careers of Guthrie (who has a place in American accounting history as well as British), Pixley, Fells, Dicksee, Cutforth and de Paula.

Three of my recent papers on accounting history have been written for *Festschriften*. They are "The Want of Uniformity in Accounts: A Nineteenth Century Debate" (1980), prompted by the impending introduction into the UK of prescribed formats for published financial statements; "Bookkeeping Barter and Current Cash Equivalents in Early New South Wales" (1982); and "Reckoning, Merchants' Accounts, Book-keeping, Accounting or Accountancy? The Evidence of the Long Titles of Books on Accounting in English, 1543-1914" (1984).

The two last articles were conceived whilst I was on leave at the University of New South Wales in 1981/82. The starting point of the bookkeeping barter article, published in the special issue of *Abacus* in honor of Ray Chambers, was a visit to Old Sydney Town in Somersby, NSW. It was greatly improved by comments received when it was presented to a staff seminar at the University of Sydney. The long titles paper, rather than the bookkeeping barter paper, was originally intended for *Abacus*. It began as an extension of a footnote on page 343 of Chambers' *Accounting, Evaluation and Economic Behavior*. Library facilities in Australia proved inadequate, however, and it was completed in the UK in 1983 for a different *Festschrift*. The bookkeeping barter paper, on the other hand, could have been written nowhere else than in Australia. Academics need their travel grants!

Why study accounting history? What progress has been made so far, especially in Britain? How can research be encouraged in the future? These were some of the questions I tried to answer in a paper on "The Study of Accounting History" presented to a Social Science Research Council Conference at the London Business School in December 1979 and in a revised version at the 1980 conference of the European Accounting Association at the Free University of Amsterdam. The paper is included in Bromwich and Hopwood's *Essays in British Accounting Research* (1981) and reprinted in the present volume. I hope it will encourage others both to read and to write accounting history.

Accounting History

11 The study of accounting history

R H Parker
Professor of Accountancy, University of Exeter

The study of accounting history is beginning to flourish. Following the success of the first world congress of accounting historians held in Brussels in 1970, the newly founded (American) Academy of Accounting Historians organized, in 1976, a second international congress in Atlanta, Georgia and, in 1977, launched *The Accounting Historians' Journal*. The Arno Press of New York is reprinting accounting classics and producing numerous useful anthologies. In the U.K. the Accounting History Society organized the third international congress held at the London Business School in August 1980. Fifty papers from 14 countries were delivered. The Scottish Committee on Accounting History has published several useful books, e.g. Pryce-Jones and Parker (1976); Stewart (1977). The editors of such influential academic journals as *The Accounting Review, Abacus* and *Accounting and Business Research* number accounting history among their major research interests.

Accounting history, like accounting itself, is an international activity, but Britain has produced some notable accounting historians. Since this chapter is not a comprehensive survey of the field, not all of them receive here the attention they deserve, but mention must be especially made of the pioneering contribution of Brown (1905) and, more recently, Yamey (1978). A number of younger writers are making important contributions throughout the accounting history area. It is difficult to discern a specifically British approach, but in recent years there has been a natural tendency to concentrate on those periods when Britain was not only the leading industrial and commercial nation, but also the leading accounting nation. Both the industrial revolution and modern professional accountancy occurred in Britain first.

Why Study Accounting History?

Charles Waldo Haskins gave a brief answer in 1900: 'The better to understand our present and to forecast or control our future' (1904, p. 141). A detailed answer was attempted in 1970 by the Committee on Accounting History of the American Accounting Association:

> Accounting history is the study of the evolution in accounting thought, practices, and institutions in response to changes in the environment and societal needs. It also considers the effect that this evolution has worked on the environment.
>
> The ends of accounting history are both intellectual and utilitarian: *Intellectual*, for it illuminates the process by which accounting thought, practices, and institutions develop, identifying the factors in the environment that induce change and revealing how this change actually occurs. It also seeks to determine the effect on the environment of changes in accounting thought, practices, and institutions. Finally, it contributes to a better understanding of economic and business history. *Utilitarian*, for history throws light on the origins of concepts, practices, and institutions in use today, yielding insight for the solution of modern accounting problems. Given an understanding of the past interaction of the environment and changes in accounting practices and institutions, it may become somewhat easier to predict the consequences of currently proposed solutions. (1970, p. 52.)

A rather different view has been put forward by Goldberg:

> To sum up, the study of accounting history will help us to understand the past (in whatever sense we use the word 'understand'), it will give us appreciation of how our current practices and problems came into being and will help to put them into some sort of perspective. It should act as a caution against attempting to predict the future but it should help us to appreciate the complexity of the circumstances from which the future will unfold. It will give intellectual exercise and it should provide tools of thought for solving problems, not only by showing us how our predecessors solved or failed to solve some of their problems but also through its requirement for painstaking, meticulous accuracy in the examination of material. (1974, p. 410.)

It is an important function of the accounting historian to ask how well accounting and accounts satisfied the needs of *contemporary* users. If they failed to do so, what factors were responsible for the failure? One should not lightly assume, for example, that English medieval accounts would have been better kept by double entry than by charge and discharge (Jack, 1966). Vlaemminck (1956, p. 211) has asked, for example:

> Why in 3rd century Alexandrian Egypt did Zenon keep accounting records for salaries and entertainment expenses, and neglect the value of tools, seeds, transport costs and taxes, so numerous at that time? Quite simply, because, in the state of knowledge relative to the entity to be managed, it only appeared useful *to him* to record the former costs. Why, in early medieval commercial accounting, does one find only accounts of creditors and debtors? Once again, because they were the only facts which they believed useful to record.

This lesson from history is not, however, acceptable to Chambers (1966a, pp. 345–6):

> The development of accounting practice, the adoption and abandonment of principles or rules, merely on the basis of what was useful or justifiable at some time results in private usefulness (for concealment or other tactical effects) being accepted as equally good grounds with general informativeness. Communicative and uncommunicative practices alike may thus be justified.

Thus, although Littleton and Zimmerman (1962, p. 254) could find in accounting a discernible pattern of continuity in the midst of change, a tendency for the ideas that persist to be the useful ones, and a demonstrated capacity for accounting to make substantial contributions to society, Chambers sees only a tendency towards the diffuseness of ideas and diversity of practices (1966a, p. 359) and a series of disconnected episodes rather than a history of development (1966b, p. 38). Littleton's views have been characterized as 'accounting Darwinism': accounting is continually in evolution, and the elements that have withstood the succession of challenges have, at least thus far, earned a place in current practice (American Accounting Association, 1977, p. 9).

Watts and Zimmerman (1979), on the other hand, argue against such a public interest explanation. Their hypothesis is that much of accounting theory is the product of government intervention and that accounting theory satisfies a 'demand for excuses'.

The Committee on Accounting History accepts without argument that accounting theory, practice and institutions have *evolved*. Is there a case for saying that there has been revolution rather than evolution? No accounting historian has discerned revolutions in accounting practice (if the invention of double entry was a revolution it was a very long drawn out one) but Wells (1976) has suggested that financial accounting *thought* is undergoing a revolution.

To what extent have accounting historians achieved the objectives set out above? I shall attempt to answer this question by looking at four areas which have attracted their attention:

(i) double entry;
(ii) corporate financial reporting;
(iii) accounting institutions;
(iv) accounting history in relation to economic history and business history.

These four areas are illustrative only. There is no space, for example, to look at the important area of cost and management accounting (on which see Garner (1954); Solomons (1968); Parker (1969); Pollard (1965); Wells (1978)).

Double Entry

The reasons for studying the history of double entry (which not so long ago would have been regarded as forming the bulk, if not the entirety, of accounting history) are intellectual rather than utilitarian. The study of the double entry of the past has not led to any improvements in the present practice of double entry. It *could* have done, by demonstrating, for example, that such frills as 'To' and 'By' were only the vestiges of an historical development but it did not, in fact, do so. The dropping of 'To' and 'By' was, in fact, brought about mainly by the mechanization of book-keeping. On the other hand, researchers have tackled with some success the intellectual tasks of explaining where, why and how double entry originated, developed and spread and what influence, if any, double entry had on its environment.

The best account in English of the origins of double entry is still that by Raymond de Roover (1956). It needs to be supplemented by G. A. Lee (1973 and 1977). According to de Roover, double entry developed in Italy in response to the needs of nascent capitalism. Italian business organization was already so complex by the 14th century that merchants could not get along without an efficient system of book-keeping. The three factors which contributed most to its development were partnership (which led to the recognition of the firm as an entity distinct from its owners), credit and agency. Accounting, as actually practised, was far ahead of the rather simple system described in the early treatises from 1494 onwards. Until about 1500 double entry was a business technique known only to Italian merchants. Double entry did not penetrate the rest of Europe until the invention of printing aided its diffusion. The 14th and 15th centuries were perhaps the most brilliant and progressive period in the history of accounting. There followed a long period of stagnation until the 19th century.

Double entry was thus one of the products of capitalism. Can it be argued with the same force that capitalism could not have developed without the help of double entry? This view, associated with Sombart (1921, vol. 2.1, pp. 118–25) and others has been summarized by Yamey (who does not share it) as follows:

> . . . systematic or scientific accounting, identified with the double-entry system, played an important part in releasing, activating, stimulating or accentuating the 'rationalistic pursuit of unlimited profits', an essential element in the capitalistic spirit . . . by transforming assets into abstract values and by expressing quantitatively the results of business activities, double-entry book-keeping clarified the aims of acquisitive business; moreover, it provided the rational basis on which the capitalist could choose the directions in which to employ his capital to best advantage; and finally, it made possible the separation of the business firm from its

owners and hence the growth of large joint-stock businesses. (Yamey, 1962.)

Sombart's propositions have led to much fruitful discussion among accounting historians, notably by Yamey (1949, 1962, 1975), Most (1972) and Winjum (1972). Winjum attempted to test the hypothesis by assessing the role of accounting in the economic development of England from 1500 to 1750, a period in which economic development and the growth of accounting knowledge occurred simultaneously. He concluded that although double entry had the potential to accomplish what was attributed to it by Sombart it did not, in fact, do so. Its great practical contribution was instead that of a comprehensive record of past activities and present assets and liabilities.

Accounting history is a history of thought as well as practice and much effort has been devoted to a study of early books on double entry, beginning with Luca Pacioli's *Summa* of 1494. Researchers have interested themselves, especially, in the extent to which the early writers borrowed, almost always without acknowledgement, from each other. The writings of Jan Ympyn of Antwerp provide an example. The extent of Ympyn's debt to Pacioli is disputed; his book was the first text on double entry in both Dutch and French and the earliest to survive in English. The title of the English edition, which has been reproduced and discussed by Kojima and Yamey (1975), illustrates how 'the Italian method' spread throughout Europe:

> A Notable and very excellente woorke, expressyng and declarying the maner and forme how to kepe a boke of accomptes or reconynges . . . Translated with greate Diligence out of the Italian toung into Dutche, and out of Dutche, into French, and now out of Frenche into Englishe.

Double entry was still being diffused in the 19th century, e.g. into Japan after the Meiji restoration (Nishikawa, 1956).

A great deal of work has been done by historians and economists on the diffusion of techniques (Rogers, 1971). Accounting historians have discussed diffusion (Tritschler, 1970; Parker, 1977a) but no-one has yet looked at double entry in this context.

Corporate Financial Reporting: Predictions and Perspectives

Accounting historians have so far shown less interest in the development of corporate financial reporting than in double entry (Lee and Parker, 1979). Financial reporting is an area in which utilitarian ends can be argued to be as important as intellectual ones. Can one hope, as the AAA Committee 1970 suggests, that 'Given an understanding of the past interaction of the environment and changes in accounting practices and institutions it may become somewhat easier to predict the consequences of currently proposed solutions'? Goldberg (1974) has his doubts:

> For prediction in this sense implies a basically mechanistic view of the universe and all that happens in it—a view that was widely accepted a hundred years or so ago among scientists and many others but which, I believe, has been largely discarded by the thinkers of the century in which we happen to find ourselves living. A mechanistic view is appropriate to mechanical systems, of course, but not to everything in the universe, and, I suggest, certainly not to much that relates to human behaviour.

It is, in fact, difficult to find overtly predictive papers in the accounting history literature. Mumford (1979) is an exception. He discerns eight stages in two British inflation accounting cycles and finds the steps so predictable that they could be described as 'a blueprint for the next surge of inflation'. He believes the cycle could only be broken by a programme of research.

Moonitz (1974) has argued from historical evidence that a professional accounting body, acting by itself, cannot agree upon a set of accounting standards, much less enforce it in practice. Chatov (1975) has used the historical record to question why standards of corporate financial reporting, power over which was granted by the U.S. federal government to the Securities and Exchange Commission, are partly controlled by a private accounting group.

Other writers have placed more stress on the possibility of gaining perspective on current problems. Lee (1979) argues that:

> The upheaval of recent events in financial accounting may have persuaded many accountants that these are uniquely critical times for their profession. However, to do so would be to view the present too narrowly and without a relevant context. The problems of accounting must be placed within a wider perspective, otherwise they may appear to be more troublesome than they deserve. The most relevant context appears to be the historical one, in which the problems of today can be seen also to have been the problems of yesterday. In other words they are long-lasting problems, and may not lend themselves to permanent solutions.

Inflation accounting, for example, regarded by so many as a 'new' problem, has been discussed many times within the last sixty years (Zeff, 1976). Is any real progress being made, or is accounting thought merely moving in circles, rediscovering what was known a generation ago? Whittington (1980) concludes that progress has been made, even if the pace leaves something to be desired. He suggests that one should read earlier writers not in the hope of rediscovering ancient truths but 'to gain a perspective of how present-day ideas have evolved and, perhaps, by reading the original statements of important ideas, to see them more vividly and understand them more clearly'.

Accounting Institutions

Accounting institutions and their members attracted historical attention as early as the 1890s in Worthington's pioneer work *Professional Accountants: an Historical Sketch* (1895). Brown's *History of Accounting and Accountants* (1905), written to celebrate the first fifty years of chartered accountancy in Scotland, devotes much attention to this subject and is still well worth reading.

Worthington states in his preface that he 'whether to his disadvantage or otherwise, is in no way connected with any Association of Accountants'. Brown, on the other hand, was Secretary and President of the Edinburgh Society and very much an insider and most of the histories of the professional bodies (e.g. Garrett, 1961; Institute of Chartered Accountants of Scotland, 1954; Institute of Chartered Accountants in England and Wales, 1966; Carey, 1969 and 1970) and of particular firms (e.g. Cooper Brothers and Co., 1954; Winsbury, 1977) have been written, often not very critically, from the inside. A rather less loving account by a semi-outsider is Stacey's *English Accountancy: A Study in Social and Economic History, 1800–1954* (1954).

Table 11.1 shows how mightily accountants have grown in numbers in the British Isles not only since the granting of a charter to the Society of Accountants in Edinburgh in 1854, but also since Brown's fiftieth anniversary celebrations of that event. At the same time the larger firms have grown in size not only in absolute terms, but also relative to the size of the smaller (Briston, 1979). Professional accountancy has become international and has become dominated by such multinationals as Peat, Marwick, Mitchell & Co.; Price Waterhouse & Co.; Deloitte Haskins and Sells; Coopers & Lybrand and the rest—all familiar in our mouths as household words.

The questions to ask seem obvious. Why did a new profession grow up in the 19th century? Why has it been so successful? Who were the men who

Table 11.1

	1904	*1957*	*1977–79*	
Scottish chartered accountants	906	6,187	9,812	(8/9/78)
English chartered accountants	3,177	20,124	68,010	(5/6/79)
Irish chartered accountants	62	1,044	3,257	(31/7/77)
Incorporated accountants	2,068	11,335	—	
	6,213	38,690	81,079	

Sources: R. Brown (ed.), *History of Accounting and Accountants* (Edinburgh: Jack, 1905); A. A. Garrett, *History of the Society of Incorporated Accountants 1885–1957* (Oxford 1961); Lists of Members.

founded the new profession? Who was Peat? Who was Price? Were they typical? Why have their firms grown into multinationals?

According to Johnson (1972, p. 52):

> The conditions for professionalism developed in Britain in the second half of the nineteenth century in association with the rise to power of an urban middle class, which provided an expanding market for various services based largely on individual needs, whether private or entrepreneurial.

He sees the profession as at first subservient to business interests and as a 'prop of capitalism', subject to 'corporate patronage', but later also an instrument of the State in its role of mediating between producers and consumers. In such a situation, writes Johnson, 'The accountants could not lose' (Johnson, pp. 73–4). As their corporate patrons expanded multinationally so did the accounting firms.

Johnson, perhaps, treats accountants as more passive than they are and were. The British profession has shown a notable ability to adapt its skills to the changing needs of the consumers (users) of its services—at first creditors, later shareholders, managers, taxpayers and others (Parker, 1977b). The British legal profession, it could be argued, has shown less ability to adapt.

Johnson goes on to argue that the emerging urban middle class of 19th century Britain not only created an expanding demand for professional services, but also provided recruits for the growing ranks of professionals. 'Middle-class power provided the basis from which the expanding "professions" created their own autonomous organizations' (Johnson, 1972, p. 52). Insufficient detailed work has been done on the 'recruits' to the accountancy profession. In making a modest attempt at such work (Parker, forthcoming) I found it surprisingly difficult to obtain information about some of the early leaders (Price, for example).

Pixley (1852–1933), a self-proclaimed father of the accountancy profession (Kitchen and Parker, 1980), claimed in 1894 that:

> Those who have been articled to our members since the date of the charter (1880) come from the same class as do those who are now at Woolwich, Sandhurst, and the Inns of Court. They have been educated at the same class of schools . . . (Pixley, 1897, p. 128).

Such statements can only be checked by the compilation and analysis of collective biographies. Short, individual biographies of Scottish chartered accountants from 1854 to 1879 are already available (Stewart, 1977) and Kedslie of the University of Dundee is preparing a collective biography for the period 1854–1904 which shows that 60 per cent of Scottish chartered accountants went to fee-paying schools. Much larger numbers and the scattered nature of the sources make a collective biography of English chartered accountants much more difficult and none has been attempted.

Johnson (1972, Ch. 5) has used his corporate patronage model to explain the accountancy profession's approach to theory. He argues that a major criterion of theory in such a situation will be its applicability to the needs of the patron. Knowledge tends to be particularistic in content and local in orientation. Professional associations will be apathetic to the development of basic knowledge through research, since such knowledge appears to be less important than knowledge which is applicable to the current practical needs of the patron. Johnson's approach may be contrasted with that of Watts and Zimmerman (1979) already described. These 'theories about theories' can only be tested by looking at the historical evidence.

A study of the development of accounting institutions serves both intellectual and utilitarian ends. It emphasizes their changing rôle and the way in which accountants have responded to, or been moulded by, their environment. There is nothing inevitable in present institutional arrangements or accounting theories. Both have changed and are changing. To understand how and why is both a stimulating intellectual exercise and a guide to policy-makers.

Accounting History and Economic and Business History

How valid is the claim that a study of accounting history can contribute to a better understanding of economic and business history? For the economic or business historian, accounting is mainly a tool, a means to an end. Advice on how the historian can make use of accounting techniques is available from Yamey (1960). It is given to few to be equally renowned as economic historians and accounting historians. The shining exception is de Roover, as illustrated, for example, by his 'The Story of the Alberti Company of Florence 1302–48, as revealed in its Account Books' (1958). De Roover, it has been aptly said, studied mercantile capitalism through 'a close and hard examination of the merchant in his counting-house, an understanding of what he counted, how he counted and how he directed his complex affairs' (Herlihy, 1972).

Baxter's *House of Hancock* (1945) is a business history of 18th century Boston which could only have been written by an accountant. Looking at a very different period of American history, Johnson (1975a) has argued that accounting historians can contribute significantly to the understanding of the development of big business. He has illustrated this in his studies of E. I. du Pont de Nemours Powder Company, 1903–12 (1975b) and of General Motors in the 1920s (1978).

Sometimes, indeed, it is the mainstream historian not the accounting historian who is master of the necessary accounting skills. A recent example is Dom Hockey's edition of *The Account-Book of Beaulieu Abbey* (1975), a 13th century account-book described by Harvey (Hockey, 1974) as:

perhaps the most extraordinary monument to survive of the early history of accounting in England: a volume containing a specimen annual account not only for each of the abbeys, manors and granges, but also for every other officer or servant who had funds entrusted to his care, some fifty different accounts in all, interspersed with rules and tables for checking the accuracy of the accounts and the honesty of the officials.

No *accountant* historian is likely to acquire a deeper knowledge of the accounting methods of the medieval English Exchequer and the use of pipe rolls than is displayed by Charles Johnson in his edition (1950) of the *Dialogus de Scaccario*, or in his introduction to Stenton's edition (1925) of *The Great Roll of the Pipe for the Second Year of the Reign of King Richard the First*. What he can do, however, is to ask whether any lessons can be learned from these methods. Accounting historians trained in modern accounting techniques have too often uncritically assumed that the double entry, balance sheets and profit and loss accounts which they are so used to are necessarily 'better' than other forms of accounting.

Historians writing accounting history have had less narrow viewpoints. Jack, in 'An Historical Defence of Single-Entry Book-keeping' argues that:

> Medieval accounts . . . were public accounts, kept because it was necessary to settle affairs between one man and another whether the two were King and subject, man and servant, fellow servants or independent individuals.
>
> As such the method of auditing and the ethics and morality which developed around them in some ways more nearly anticipate mid-nineteenth century developments than do the practices associated with the mercantile book-keeping on which accountants have concentrated so much attention (Jack, 1966, p. 158).

Similarly, Ramsey has written of Tudor accounting that:

> . . . the distinction between business and private affairs would have seemed meaningless to a sixteenth-century merchant, who was not accountable to anyone but himself. The absence of the modern profit and loss account and balance sheet, in fact, mattered little before the advent of the modern shareholder and tax-collector. The experienced Tudor merchant undoubtedly had a perfectly clear idea of the progress of his affairs whatever the technical deficiencies of his book-keeping (Ramsey, 1956, p. 201).

And Clanchy (1979, p. 96) writes of the tallies used by the English Exchequer that they:

> were not a primitive survival from the preliterate past, but a sophisticated and practical record of numbers. They were more convenient to

> keep and store than parchments, less complex to make, and no easier to forge . . . the earliest records of the Exchequer were deliberately destroyed because they were in a medium, wood, which was too uncouth for scholars to appreciate.

These historical reflections should help us appreciate better the increasing modern dissatisfaction with the balance sheet and the profit or loss account as the only, or even the main, financial statements. The profit and loss account, in particular, embodies an important assumption about the dominant role of the shareholder.

Accounting records of little interest to those concerned with developments in accounting thought or practice can be of immense use even to the literary historian: for example, the life of Lord Byron has recently been illuminated through his accounts (Moore, 1974). Conversely, literary historians have found themselves researching the lives of accountants: for example, James Peele, the author of two of the earliest (1553 and 1569) English works on book-keeping and the father of the Elizabethan dramatist George Peele (Horne, 1952).

The benefits of collaboration between accounting and other historians are clearly reciprocal. Surprisingly, the marked trend towards a more quantitative approach to economic history has evoked little response from accounting historians. It is difficult to think of examples in the accounting literature other than Deakin's study (1976) of the effect of enforced increases in disclosure in the 1930s on the behaviour of securities returns. (There are related articles by Stigler (1964) and Benston (1973) in the economic literature.) The compilation and analysis of collective biographies will, of course, involve some statistics and a fair amount of computer time.

Encouraging Research into Accounting History

It is hoped that this paper has demonstrated that accounting history is a worthwhile activity. Most accountants, however, for reasons for which accounting history helps to provide an explanation, are not educated and trained in an environment which encourages them towards research. Also, the very success of the profession has meant that academic accounting has little financial appeal—and anyone suited to accountancy is unlikely to be completely indifferent to monetary reward.

What then should be done? It is suggested that in accounting history more co-operation between accountants and historians willing to work in fields of interest to accountants should be encouraged. There have, in fact, been several recent collaborations of this nature (e.g. Edwards and Baber, 1979).

What topics, in particular, should British accounting historians be encouraged to research? The following criteria (which take account of shortages of both money and manpower) may help us to make a choice:

(a) the research data should be available in the U.K.;
(b) the research should preferably have both intellectual and utilitarian objectives;
(c) any research assistants necessary need not be qualified accountants;
(d) the research results should be of interest to a wider audience than accounting historians alone, e.g. to accountants who are not historians or to historians who are not accountants;
(e) some moderate use of quantitative techniques.

Three topics in 19th and 20th century British accounting history which meet these criteria, and in the first two of which I must disclose a personal interest, are:

(a) the development of company financial reporting;
(b) a collective biography of English chartered accountants; and
(c) the development of cost and management techniques in relation to the development of large enterprises.

A research programme on these lines would prove of great value to accountants and historians alike.

References

American Accounting Association, Committee on Accounting History, *Accounting Review*, Supplement to vol. XLV (1970).

American Accounting Association, Committee on Concepts and Standards for External Financial Reports, *Statement on Accounting Theory and Theory Acceptance*. American Accounting Association (1977).

Baxter, W. T., *House of Hancock*. Harvard University Press (1945); reprinted Russell and Russell (1965).

Benston, G. J., 'Required Disclosure and the Stock Market: An Evaluation of the Securities Exchange Act of 1945', *American Economic Review* (March 1973).

Briston, R. J., 'The UK Accountancy Profession—the Move towards Monopoly Power', *Accountant's Magazine* (November 1979).

Brown, R. (ed.), *History of Accounting and Accountants* (Jack, 1905; reprinted Franklin, 1966).

Carey, J. L., *The Rise of the Accounting Profession* (American Institute of Certified Public Accountants, 2 vols. 1969 and 1970).

Chambers, R. J., 'A Theory of the Development of Accounting Practices', pp. 341–363 of his *Accounting Evaluation and Economic Behavior*. Prentice-Hall (1966a).

Chambers, R. J., 'The Development of Accounting Theory', pp. 18–35 of Chambers, R. J., Goldberg, L. and Mathews, R. L. (eds.), *The Accounting Frontier*. F. W. Cheshire (1966b).

Chatov, R., *Corporate Financial Reporting—Public or Private Control*. The Free Press (1975).
Clanchy, M. T., *From Memory to Written Record. England 1066–1307*. Edward Arnold (1979).
Cooper Brothers & Co., *A History of Cooper Brothers & Co. 1854 to 1954*. Privately published by B. T. Batsford (1954).
Deakin, E. B., 'Accounting Reports, Policy Interventions and the Behavior of Securities Returns', *The Accounting Review* (July 1976).
De Roover, R., 'The Development of Accounting Prior to Luca Pacioli according to the Account-Books of Medieval Merchants', pp. 114–174 of Littleton and Yamey (1956).
De Roover, R., 'The Story of the Alberti Company of Florence. 1302–1348, as Revealed in its Account Books', *Business History Review* (Spring 1958) 14–59; reprinted in his *Business, Banking and Economic Thought in Late Medieval and Early Modern Europe*. University of Chicago Press (1974).
Edwards, J. R. and Baber, C., 'Dowlais Iron Company: Accounting Policies and Procedures for Profit Measurement and Reporting Purposes', *Accounting and Business Research* (Spring 1979).
Garner, S. P., *Evolution of Cost Accounting to 1925*. University of Alabama Press (1954).
Garrett, A. A., *History of the Society of Incorporated Accountants 1885–1957*. Oxford University Press (1961).
Goldberg, L., 'The Future of the Past in Accounting', *Accountant's Magazine* (October 1974).
Haskins, C. W., *Business Education and Accountancy*. Harper (1904); reprinted Arno Press (1978).
Herlihy, D., 'Raymond de Roover, Historian of Mercantile Capitalism', *Journal of European Economic History* (Winter 1972).
Hockey, S. F. (ed.), *The Beaulieu Cartulary*. Southampton University Press, Southampton Records Series, v. 17 (1974).
Hockey, S. F. (ed.), *The Account-Book of Beaulieu Abbey*. Royal Historical Society, Camden Fourth Series, v. 16 (1975).
Horne, D. H., *The Life and Minor Works of George Peele*. Yale University Press (1952).
ICAEW, *The History of the Institute of Chartered Accountants in England and Wales 1880–1965 and of its founder accountancy bodies 1870–1880*. Heinemann (1966).
ICAS, *A History of the Chartered Accountants of Scotland from the Earliest Times to 1954*. ICAS (1954).
Jack, S. M., 'An Historical Defence of Single Entry Book-keeping', *Abacus* (December 1966).
Johnson, C. (trans. and ed.), *Dialogues de Scaccario*. Nelson (1950).
Johnson, H. T., 'Management Accountancy in an Early Integrated Industrial: E. I. du Pont de Nemours Powder Company, 1903–1912', *Business History Review* (Summer 1975b).
Johnson, H. T., 'The Role of Accounting History in the Study of Modern Business Enterprise', *The Accounting Review* (July 1975a).
Johnson, H. T., 'Management Accounting in an Early Multidivision Organization: General Motors in the 1920s', *Business History Review* (Winter 1978).

Johnson, T. J., *Professions and Power*. Macmillan (1972).
Kitchen, J. and Parker, R. H., *Accounting Thought and Education: Six English Pioneers*. ICAEW (1980).
Kojima, O. and Yamey, B. S. (eds.), *A notable and very excellente woorke*. Daigakudo Shoten (1975).
Lee, G. A., 'The Development of Italian Bookkeeping 1211–1300', *Abacus* (December 1973).
Lee, G. A., 'The Coming of Age of Double Entry: The Giovanni Farolfi Ledger of 1299–1300', *Accounting Historians Journal* (Fall 1977).
Lee, T. A., 'The Evolution and Revolution of Financial Accounting: a Review Article', *Accounting and Business Research* (Autumn 1979).
Lee, T. A. and Parker, R. H., *The Evolution of Corporate Financial Reporting*. Nelson (1979).
Littleton, A. C. and Yamey, B. S., *Studies in the History of Accounting*. Sweet and Maxwell (1956); reprinted Arno Press (1978).
Littleton, A. C. and Zimmerman, V. K., *Accounting Theory: Continuity and Change*. Prentice-Hall (1962).
Moonitz, M., *Obtaining Agreement on Standards in the Accounting Profession*. American Accounting Association, Studies in Accounting Research, No. 8 (1974).
Moore, D. L., *Lord Byron Accounts Rendered*. David Murray (1974).
Most, K. S., 'Sombart's Propositions Revisited', *The Accounting Review* (October 1972).
Mumford, M., 'The End of a Familiar Inflation Accounting Cycle', *Accounting and Business Research* (Spring 1979).
Nishikawa, K., 'The Early History of Double-Entry Book-keeping in Japan', pp. 380–387 of Littleton and Yamey (1956).
Parker, R. H., *Management Accounting: An Historical Perspective*. Macmillan (1969).
Parker, R. H., 'Explaining National Differences in Consolidated Accounts', *Accounting and Business Research* (Summer 1977a).
Parker, R. H., *Men of Account* (University of Exeter, 1977b) reprinted as 'British Men of Account', *Abacus* (June 1978).
Parker, R. H., *British Accountants: A Biographical Sourcebook*. Arno Press (forthcoming).
Pixley, F. W., *The Profession of a Chartered Accountant*. Henry Good and Son (1897); reprinted Arno Press (1978).
Pollard, S., *The Genesis of Modern Management*. Edward Arnold (1965).
Pryce-Jones, J. and Parker, R. H., *Accounting in Scotland. A Historical Bibliography* (2nd edn.), ICAS (1976).
Ramsey, P., 'Some Tudor Merchants' Accounts', pp. 185–201 of Littleton and Yamey (1956).
Rogers, E. M. with Shoemaker, F. F., *Communication of Innovations* (2nd edn.). Free Press of Glencoe (1971).
Solomons, D., 'The Historical Development of Costing' in his *Studies in Cost Analysis*. Sweet and Maxwell (1968).
Sombart, W., *Der Moderne Kapitalismus* (4th edn.). Duncker & Humblot (1921).
Stacey, N. A. H., *English Accountancy: A Study in Social and Economic History, 1800–1954*. Gee (1954).

Stenton, D. M. (ed.), *The Great Roll of the Pipe for the Second Year of the Reign of King Richard the First*. Publications of the Pipe Roll Society, vol 39, N.S., vol. 1 (1925).

Stewart, J. C., *Pioneers of a Profession*. ICAS (1977).

Stigler, G. J., 'Public Regulation of the Securities Markets', *Journal of Business* (April 1964).

Tritschler, C. A., 'A Sociological Perspective on Accounting Innovation', *International Journal of Accounting* (Spring 1970).

Vlaemminck, J. H., *Histoire et Doctrines de la Comptabilité*. Editions du Treurenberg (1956); reprinted Editions Pragnos (1979).

Watts, Ross L. and Zimmerman, Jerold L., 'The Demand for and Supply of Accounting Theories: The Market for Excuses', *The Accounting Review* (April 1979).

Wells, M. C., 'A Revolution in Accounting Thought?', *The Accounting Review* (July 1976).

Wells, M. C., *Accounting for Common Costs*. International Center for Education and Research in Accounting (1978).

Whittington, G., 'Pioneers of Income Measurement and Price-Level Accounting: a Review Article', *Accounting and Business Research* (Spring 1980).

Winjum, J. O., *The Role of Accounting in the Economic Development of England: 1500–1750*. Center for International Education and Research in Accounting (1972).

Winsbury, R., *Thomson McLintock & Co.—The First Hundred Years*. Thomson McLintock (1977).

Worthington, B., *Professional Accountants*. Gee (1895); reprinted Arno Press (1978).

Yamey, B. S., 'Scientific Bookkeeping and the Rise of Capitalism', *Economic History Review* (June 1949).

Yamey, B. S., 'Business Accounts', pp. 30–36 of Barker, T. C., Campbell, R. H. and Mathias, R., *Business History*. The Historical Association (1960).

Yamey, B. S., 'Notes on Double-Entry Bookkeeping and Economic Progress', *Journal of European Economic History* (Winter 1975).

Yamey, B. S., 'Accounting and the Rise of Capitalism: Further Notes on a Theme by Sombart', pp. 833–57 of *Studi in Onore di Amintore Fanfani* (Dott. A. Giuffre, 1962), reprinted in *Journal of Accounting Research* (Autumn 1964) and in Tucker, K. A., *Business History. Selected Readings*. Frank Cass (1977).

Yamey, B. S., *Essays on the History of Accounting*. Arno Press (1978).

Zeff, S. A. (ed.), *Asset Appreciation, Business Income and Price-Level Accounting: 1918–1935*. Arno Press (1976).

Accounting Problems

R. H. PARKER

Lower of Cost and Market in Britain and the United States: An Historical Survey

INTRODUCTION

And out of olde bokes, in good feith,
Cometh al this newe science that men lere
Geoffrey Chaucer (1340?-1400).
The Parlement of Foules.

THE SUBJECT of this article is the history of the lower of cost and market rule of inventory valuation in Britain and the United States. It is not possible to discuss the rule in isolation either from the progress of financial accounting theory in general, or from the economic environment in which practitioners of and writers on accounting have found themselves. Some attention has therefore been given to these matters.

All periods were once 'modern' and any terminal point in an historical essay is clearly arbitrary. Convenience demands, however, that one stops somewhere. The approximate date chosen for this essay is 1947, the year of publication of *Research Bulletin No. 29* on 'Inventory Pricing' by the American Institute of Accountants (as it then was). The first recommendation on the valuation of stock-in-trade of the Institute of Chartered Accountants in England and Wales was published two years before, in 1945.

The general plan of the paper is as follows:

(a) a short discussion of the views of early British writers;
(b) a longer look at the environment in which the lower of cost and market rule became traditional in nineteenth century England;
(c) a discussion of the influence, especially in the 1920s, of American academic accountants, especially Hatfield, Littleton and Paton;
(d) rules of inventory valuation as part of the search for accounting principles of the 1930s and 1940s, mainly in the United States, but with some reference to British developments; and
(e) some conclusions which can be drawn from an historical survey of the lower of cost and market rule of inventory valuation.

R. H. PARKER is Senior Lecturer in Commerce in the University of Western Australia.
This article is partly based on a paper, 'Inventory Valuation Historically Considered', presented at the May 1965 meeting of the Australasian Association of University Teachers of Accounting held at the University of Melbourne. The author is greatly indebted for the comments, constructive and destructive, on this previous paper, of Mr. R. P. Brooker of the University of Sydney and Mr. H. P. Hain of the University of Melbourne.

EARLY BRITISH WRITERS ON INVENTORY VALUATION

What's aught, but as 'tis valued?

William Shakespeare, *Troilus and Cressida*, Act II, Scene 2.

There was once a happy time when inventory valuation was not at all important. Raymond de Roover has written of medieval accounting that, 'Because of the prevalence of venturing, inventory valuation did not constitute a problem, and medieval merchants were accustomed to open a separate account for each lot or consignment and to leave it open until everything was sold.'[1]

It is not surprising therefore that there are very few references to the problem in early accounting literature. The early texts are in any case usually severely practical and devoid of theoretical discussion.

James Peele, citizen and salter of London, clerk of Christ's Hospital and father of George Peele the dramatist, wrote two books on double entry bookkeeping in the second half of the sixteenth century. In his second book, *The Pathwaye to Perfectnes* . . . (1569), there is an account of 'fine clothes' in which 'there is founde at takinge of the ballaunce, to remayne vii. clothes'. These are 'valewed as the cost'.[2]

In 1741 Richard Hayes stated that it was 'usual with Merchants, when they make a general Balance of their Books, to value the goods that they have by them at the Market Price they then go at, at the Time of their balancing; but some do not so'. His own advice is valuation at the market price 'or at the Price they cost you'.[3] In the same year John Mair recommended valuation 'at the prime Cost'.

1. R. de Roover, 'The Development of Accounting Prior to Luca Pacioli according to the Account-books of Medieval Merchants', in A. C. Littleton and B. S. Yamey (eds), *Studies in the History of Accounting*, London, Sweet & Maxwell, 1956, at p 117. In his recent book on the Medici bank, Professor de Roover writes:

> It was the custom of merchants, including the Medici, to open a separate account for each venture or lot of merchandise. Such accounts were charged with all outlays, costs, and expenses and credited with proceeds from sales. The difference remaining after conclusion of the venture represented either a profit or a loss and was usually transferred to an account, 'Profit and Loss on Merchandise' (*Avanzi e disavanzi di mercatantie*). Thus profits from trade and from exchange were kept separate. This system of opening a separate account to each venture has been called 'venture accounting' by accountants and students of the history of accounting. Venture accounting eliminated the necessity of inventory valuation. Since records were generally kept according to this system, it is not surprising that Luca Pacioli and other early authors on bookkeeping are silent on the subject of inventory valuation. Neither is it surprising that there are no examples of it in the Medici records.

R. de Roover, *The Rise and Decline of the Medici Bank 1397-1494*, Cambridge, Mass., Harvard University Press, 1963, p 148.

2. *The Patheway to Perfectnes* . . . (1569). The paragraph in which these phrases occur is reprinted in B. S. Yamey, H. C. Edey and H. W. Thomson, *Accounting in England and Scotland: 1543-1800*, London, Sweet & Maxwell, 1963, p 108. For a reprint in modern spelling of Peele's first book (1553) see P. Kats, 'James Peele's "Maner and Fourme"', *The Accountant*, Vol 82, 1930, pp 41-4, 88-91, 119-22. For further information on Peele and his books see Yamey, Edey and Thomson, op cit, pp 162-66; C. Gordon, 'The First English Books on Bookkeeping', *Accounting Research*, Vol 5, 1954, reprinted in Littleton and Yamey, op cit; and D. H. Horne, *The Life and Minor Works of George Peele*, New Haven, Yale University Press, 1952, Ch 1.

3. Richard Hayes, *The Gentleman's Complete Book-keeper* . . ., London, J. Noon, 1741, Ch 8. See Yamey, Edey and Thomson, op cit, p 116.

Alexander Malcolm (1731) preferred cost to using 'the current Rates' since 'it seems more reasonable to value goods as they cost you; for otherwise you bring in Gain or loss into your Accounts, which has not yet actually happened, and may, perhaps not happen'.[4]

Robert Hamilton (1743-1829), who was Professor of Natural Philosophy and later Professor of Mathematics at the University of Aberdeen, claimed in 1788:

> It is much more proper to value the goods on hand in conformity to the current prices, than at prime cost: For the design of affixing any value is to point out the gain or loss; and the gain is in reality obtained so soon as the prices rise, or the loss suffered as soon as they fall.[5]

The most complete discussion of the rule before the nineteenth century is to be found in a book by the French writer Jacques Savary (1622-1690).[6]

THE RISE OF A PROFESSION

> **The whole affairs in bankruptcy have been handed over to an ignorant set of men called accountants, which is one of the greatest abuses ever introduced into law.**
>
> **Mr. Justice Quain in 1875, quoted in A. H. Woolf, *A Short History of Accountants and Accountancy*, London, Gee & Co, 1912, p 177.**

It is doubtful if the writings discussed so far have had much influence on modern accounting theory and practice. The real beginnings of modern accounting are to be found in the nineteenth century. Sometime during that century the lower of cost and market rule appears to have become accepted as traditional. In 1862 Sawyer referred to the 'recognised principle that stock should be valued at cost price (unless depreciated in value) and that no profit should be estimated unless realised'.[7] George O. May tells us that the rule was well established when he entered the profession in England in 1892. He ascribes the rule to 'natural conservatism and a long period of falling prices'.[8]

One suspects that the conservatism and the falling prices were not unrelated. Was the conservatism of late nineteenth century accountants really 'natural' or was it a product of their environment? The English accountancy profession grew up because of the need for accounts and statements of affairs in connection with bankruptcies, failures, frauds and disputes. It was a profession which 'was born through bankruptcies, fed on failures and frauds, grew on liquidations and gradu-

4. John Mair, *Book-keeping Methodiz'd . . .*, Edinburgh, 2nd ed, 1741, p 77 (see Yamey, Edey and Thomson, op cit, pp 108-9); Alexander Malcolm, *A Treatise of Book-keeping . . .*, London, 1731, p 89, quoted in B. S. Yamey, 'Some Topics in the History of Financial Accounting in England 1500-1900', in W. T. Baxter and S. Davidson, *Studies in Accounting Theory*, London, Sweet & Maxwell, 2nd ed, 1962, p 35.
5. R. Hamilton, *An Introduction to Merchandise . . .*, Edinburgh, 2nd ed, 1788, p 285. This passage is reprinted in Yamey, Edey and Thomson, op cit, p 123. On Hamilton see D. Murray, *Chapters in the History of Bookkeeping, Accountancy and Commercial Arithmetic*, Glasgow, Jackson, Wylie & Co, 1930, p 49.
6. On Savary see A. C. Littleton, *Accounting Evolution to 1900*, New York, American Institute Publishing Co, 1933, p 152, and J.-H. Vlaemminck, *Histoire et Doctrines de la Comptabilité*, Brussels, Editions du Treurenberg, 1956, pp 128-30.
7. J. Sawyer, *Bookkeeping for the Tanning Trade*, London, 2nd ed, 1862, quoted in R. S. Edwards, 'The Nature and Measurement of Income', *The Accountant*, July-October 1938, reprinted in W. T. Baxter, *Studies in Accounting*, London, Sweet & Maxwell, 1950, p 259.
8. G. O. May, 'Concepts of Business Income and their Implementation', *Quarterly Journal of Economics*, Vol 68, 1954, p 16.

ated through audits'.[9] The Royal Charter granted on 11 May 1880 to the Institute of Chartered Accountants in England and Wales contains the following significant paragraph:

> . . . the Profession of Public Accountants in England and Wales is a numerous one and their functions are of great and increasing importance in respect of their employment in the capacities of Liquidators acting in the winding-up of companies and of Receivers under decrees and of Trustees in bankruptcies or arrangements with creditors and in various positions of trust under Courts of Justice as also in the auditing of the accounts of public companies and of partnerships and otherwise.

Auditing appears to be almost an afterthought and there is no mention of taxation, secretarial or management work, none of which was important at the time.

It is instructive to look at some figures relating to liquidations, bankruptcies and falling prices. According to H. A. Shannon,[10] 25.6 per cent of the companies formed 1856-65, 30.3 per cent of the companies formed 1866-74 and 33.4 per cent of the companies formed 1875-83 ended in insolvency. For the whole period 1856-83, the average is just over thirty per cent. Of the companies formed 1856-65 half of the liquidations took place within the first six years of existence; of the 1866-74 liquidations half took place within the first five years of existence; of the 1875-83 liquidations half took place within the first four years of existence.[11]

A. H. Woolf, writing in 1912, stated that the Companies Act of 1862 'offered new fields of lucrative employment for accountants and no doubt did much to attract many ambitious young men to seek their fortunes in the profession'. The attraction was section 92 which created the position of Official Liquidator, to which in most cases a professional accountant was appointed. The Act was spoken of as 'the accountant's friend'.[12] The Bankruptcy Act of 1869 abolished Official Assignees in Bankruptcy and provided for the appointment of trustees to distribute the debtor's estate; this also 'brought grist to the accountant's mill' as most of the trustees appointed were professional accountants.[13] The 1883 Act provided for Official Receivers in the place of trustees appointed by the creditors, thus transferring much work away from professional accountants. Nevertheless, the young George O. May, articled to Thomas Andrew of Exeter, 1892-97, was engaged during his articles almost entirely in bankruptcy work.[14]

It has been the aim of the above paragraphs to suggest that the environment in which the English accounting profession was born has much to do with the

9. H. W. Robinson, *A History of Accountants in Ireland*, Dublin, Institute of Chartered Accountants in Ireland, 1964, p 30.

10. H. A. Shannon, 'The First Five Thousand Limited Companies and their Duration', *Economic History*, Vol 2, 1932; H. A. Shannon, 'The Limited Companies of 1866-1883', *Economic History Review*, 1st ser, Vol 4, 1933, reprinted in E. M. Carus-Wilson, ed, *Essays in Economic History*, Vol 1, London, Edward Arnold, 1954. See also D. H. Macgregor, 'Joint Stock Companies and the Risk Factor', *Economic Journal*, Vol 39, 1929, and G. Todd, 'Some Aspects of Joint Stock Companies, 1844-1900', *Economic History Review*, 1st ser, Vol 4, 1932.

11. Carus-Wilson, ed, op cit, p 387.

12. A. H. Woolf, *A Short History of Accountants and Accountancy*, London, Gee & Co, 1912, p 176.

13. Woolf, op cit, p 177.

14. P. Grady, ed, *Memoirs and Accounting Thought of George O. May*, New York, Ronald, 1962, p 10.

accountants' conservatism, and does something to explain such rules as lower of cost and market. Their history has filled accountants, as Anthony Sampson has recently written, with 'a vivid sense of disaster'.[15]

The founders of our profession also lived in a period of almost continuously falling prices after the boom year of 1873. The Rousseaux overall index illustrates this well (see Table 1).

TABLE 1

ROUSSEAUX OVERALL PRICE INDEX, 1873-1900
(Average of 1865 and 1885 = 100)

Year		*Year*	
1873	127	1887	81
1874	121	1888	84
1875	117	1889	84
1876	115	1890	87
1877	110	1891	86
1878	101	1892	82
1879	98	1893	82
1880	102	1894	74
1881	99	1895	72
1882	101	1896	73
1883	101	1897	74
1884	95	1898	78
1885	88	1899	84
1886	83	1900	91

Source: P. Rousseaux, *Les Mouvements de Fond de l'Economie Anglaise*, 1800-1913, Brussels, 1938, as reported in B. R. Mitchell with the collaboration of P. Deane, *Abstract of British Historical Statistics*, London, Cambridge University Press, 1962, pp 471-473.

In such an atmosphere conservatism was perhaps inevitable. In the 1880s the lower of cost and market rule was recommended by J. W. Best;[16] and by C. R. Trevor in an address to the Manchester Accountants Students' Society which was described at the time as 'thoroughly orthodox from beginning to end'.[17] In 1904 the rule was endorsed by J. A. Walbank in his *Encyclopedia of Accounting* and by the influential Arthur Lowes Dickinson in a paper read to the first International Congress of Accountants at St. Louis.[18]

Dicksee, one of the leading English accountants of his day, has an interesting discussion of the general problem of asset valuation. Since it was the primary object of most ordinary undertakings to continue to carry on operations, 'it is but fair', he wrote 'that the assets enumerated in a Balance Sheet be valued with that end in view'. He recognized the necessity of valuation on a 'going concern basis', and concluded that 'As a general rule, the amount at which *all* assets are stated in the Balance Sheet—except where a special statutory provision to the contrary obtains—should be regulated by the realisable value of such assets on the basis of

15. A. Sampson, *Anatomy of Britain Today*, London, Hodder & Stoughton, 1965, p 525.
16. *Accountants' Journal*, 1 January 1886, cited in Littleton, *Accounting Evolution to 1900*, pp 310, 319.
17. S. Gilman, *Accounting Concepts of Profit*, New York, Ronald, 1939, p 439.
18. Gilman, op cit, p 440.

a going concern'.[19] On the valuation of 'floating assets' (as they were still called) in particular, he wrote as follows:

> It being the essential feature of these assets that the whole aim of the undertaking is to convert—or be able to convert—them into cash at the earliest possible opportunity, the element of immediate realisation is an important factor in their value. The only point to remember is that, while a manufacturing profit is earned only when the manufacture is completed, a trading profit is only made when the sale is completed. Neither profit must be anticipated, but it does not appear to be invariably essential that manufacturing profit should be held over until a sale has been effected. It may be added that, where a manufacture consists of several distinct processes, and separate accounts are kept of the manufacturing profit earned under each process, there seems to be no great objection to each process being considered as a separate manufacture, so long, of course, as the goods are readily saleable at the usual trade price.

With regard to what is a trading profit, a most ingenious argument was once advanced by Sir Richard Webster (now Lord Chief Justice) before the late Lord (then Mr. Justice) Field (in *Hordern v. Faulkner and others*), in which it was contended that the most scientifically correct method of valuing a stock-in-trade was to take it at selling prices, less the average trade profit; it being suggested that any profit realized in excess of the average was in reality a profit on buying, not on selling; and any profit realized less than the average a corresponding loss on buying. The argument passed muster at the time, appears to be plausible, and indicates a system that would doubtless prove very convenient in practice; but, unless the profit on different articles was very uniform, it would hardly be a safe one to adopt.[20]

Even Garcke and Fells, who were regarded by some as quite radical in their views,[21] were not free from the influence of conservatism:

> The right principle undoubtedly is that in a manufacturing business a profit should not be considered to have been made until a sale has been effected, or until a contract for the delivery at a future date of goods already manufactured is entered into. But in the case of the production of raw materials and in those exceptional cases in which the stock of manufactured articles could be put upon the market and realized at their normal price, a modification of this principle would seem to be necessary; for in that case the produce is generally saleable at an ascertained market price (or, at any rate, at an approximation to it), and it does not seem incorrect to say that the profit which that price leaves has been earned on the production of the commodity and not on its sale. *Nevertheless, even in this case, it would probably in the long run prove to be more judicious to price the commodity in the books at its cost, and only to credit profit and loss account with the profit when sales have been effected.*[22]

19. L. R. Dicksee, *Auditing*, London, Gee & Co, 7th ed, 1907, pp 197-201. The first edition was published in 1892.
20. Ibid, p 202.
21. A reviewer of the first edition of their book *Factory Accounts*, the most important early English work on cost accounting, in *The Accountant* of 5 May 1888, described their work as more theoretical than practical, and pedantic and involved 'in the nature of a work on political economy'. See R. S. Edwards, 'Some Notes on the Early Literature and Development of Cost Accounting in Great Britain', *The Accountant*, Vol 97, 4 September 1937, p 313.
22. E. Garcke and J. M. Fells, *Factory Accounts*, London, Crosby, Lockwood and Son, 4th ed, 1893, p 123. Emphasis added. The first edition was published in 1887. In the 6th edition (1911) the following sentence is added: 'In the exceptional case of the market price being lower than cost, the market price should be taken'. p 164.

Garcke and Fells were generally in favour of valuation at the cost of production (excluding 'standing charges' and interest on capital); but they considered that any deterioration undergone by the goods on hand 'should, of course, be periodically written off' and stocks which became entirely obsolete 'should be reduced to their scrap value'. 'Old' material on hand should be valued for stock-taking purposes 'at the market value of such old material or at the price at which similar old material was last disposed of, unless such price be higher than the market price, in which case the lower value should be taken'. They were not in favour of constant adjustments for 'fluctuations in the market price'. They did not, however, give unqualified approval to 'inordinate reduction in the value of assets' and they recognized the possibilities of distortion of profits by 'taking undue advantage of facilities and opportunities which may exist at particular periods for writing down the value of assets'.[23]

Garner is of the opinion that, whereas in England practically all authorities recommended the lower of cost and market rule, in the United States it was not very popular at this time, at least so far as factory inventories were concerned.[24]

THE COMING OF THE ACADEMICS

He was in logick a great Critick,
Profoundly skill'd in Analytick.
He could distinguish and divide
A hair 'twixt South and South-West side:
On either which he would dispute,
Confute, change hands, and still confute.

Samuel Butler (1612?-1680)
Hudibras, First Part, Canto I.

George O. May, writing in 1954, suggested that inventory accounting in Britain 'may be said to have had virtually no history for the last sixty years'.[25] Things were different in the United States; one reason may be the very dissimilar ways in which academic accounting developed in the two countries. The importance of the second half of the nineteenth century in the history of accounting has already been stressed. This was also the period in which most of the English civic universities were founded. The new universities were established in busy industrial and commercial centres but accounting failed to take root in them. At the beginning of the twentieth century only Birmingham University, where Dicksee was Professor of Accounting 1902-06, the London School of Economics and Manchester University provided courses in accounting. A number of other universities followed later, but even in the 1960s English academic accounting is still not very well developed by American (or even Australasian) standards.

The American experience has been very different. Joseph Wharton in the deed of gift, which made the Wharton School of Finance and Commerce at the University of Pennsylvania in 1881 the first school of business in the United States, specified that the staff should include 'One Professor or Instructor of Accounting or Book-

23. Ibid, pp 123-24.

24. S. P. Garner, *Evolution of Cost Accounting to 1925*, Montgomery, Ala., University of Alabama Press, 1954, p 321.

25. G. O. May, 'Concepts of Business Income and their Implementation', loc cit, p 16.

keeping, to teach the simplest and most practical forms of bookkeeping for housekeepers, for private individuals, for commercial and banking firms, for manufacturing establishments and for banks. . . .' During the rapid growth of collegiate business schools after the turn of the century every new school, without exception, provided instruction in accounting.[26] Thus, for over half a century now the United States has had a corps of academic accountants whose critical minds have not always been willing to accept such 'traditional' rules as the lower of cost and market.

One important group argued strongly that current market values had no place in accounting. A. C. Littleton of the University of Illinois was probably the most influential exponent of this school of thought.

> Assuredly (he wrote in 1929) value is a vague sort of thing, subject to all the whims of mankind and turned by the least wind of altered circumstances. . . . Whereas value is an estimate of what price ought to be, price itself is an established fact. . . . When accounting is loosed from this anchor of fact it is afloat upon a sea of psychological estimates which, however important they may be to business management, are beyond the power of accounting, as such, to express.[27]

Littleton therefore recommended that inventories be consistently and uniformly stated at 'cost', 'accompanied of course by any reserves the management and auditor may agree upon and such supplementary parenthetical figures or footnotes as may be thought necessary to supply bankers and others with the information they expect'.[28]

Not all writers were convinced of the superior objectivity of historical cost. Henry Rand Hatfield (1866-1945) of the University of California was concerned to point out some of the difficulties, especially in the case of self-manufactured articles.[29] Hatfield's views on inventory valuation can be found in his book *Accounting* published in 1927. He found contemporary practice 'curiously inconsistent and illogical',[30] but although he recognized the illogicality of the cost or market rule (he described arguments in favour of it as a 'brilliant . . . instance of flabby thinking'[31]) he recommended only means of improving disclosure. Inventories should be shown in the balance sheet at cost. Any significant decrease in value should be recognized by debiting Profit and Loss and crediting an account called Allowance for Decline in Inventory Value, the latter to be preferably shown in the balance sheet as a deduction from the cost figure of the inventory. A marked appreciation in value should be credited not to Profit and Loss but to a Reserve Due to Marking up Inventory, and the inventory should either be shown in the balance sheet simply at present market value or as made up of two items, cost

26. R. G. Cox, 'Accounting', Ch 14 of F. C. Pierson and others, *The Education of American Businessmen*, New York, McGraw-Hill, 1959, p 355.

27. A. C. Littleton, 'Value and Price in Accounting', *Accounting Review*, Vol 4, 1929, pp 149, 150.

28. A. C. Littleton, 'Value or Cost', *Accounting Review*, Vol 10, 1935, p 272.

29. 'A Symposium on Appreciation', *Accounting Review*, Vol 5, 1930, p 14.

30. H. R. Hatfield, *Accounting*, New York, Appleton-Century, 1927, p 99.

31. H. R. Hatfield, 'What is the Matter with Accounting?', *Journal of Accountancy*, Vol 44, 1927, reprinted in S. A. Zeff and T. F. Keller, *Financial Accounting Theory*, New York, McGraw-Hill, 1964, p 358.

price and estimated appreciation, with the sum extended. When the goods are sold, 'so much of the credit to Reserve Due to Marking up Inventory as is properly allocated to the goods sold should be transferred from this reserve to the general Profit and Loss Account or to Surplus.'[32]

Acceptance of either the lower of cost and market rule, or of the historical cost only doctrine implies acceptance of what we now call the realization convention. A number of academic writers were doubtful of the usefulness of this convention.

Hatfield, characteristically, cut through some of the more confused thinking on the subject:

> It is not always clear whether a writer considers that there are unrealized as well as realized profits, the latter only being of interest to the accountant, or whether there is no such thing as unrealized profit. If the latter is true the phrase realized profits is evidently tautological.
>
> Much of the discussion of realized profits is confused by an uncertainty as to whether the writer . . . means that profits are not in existence until realized, or that profits are not available for distribution unless they have been realized.[33]

Hatfield noted that probably the most generally accepted view was that profits were realized when a sale was made. This he ascribed largely to the fact that a contract of sale offered 'objective evidence of the correctness of the estimated profit.'[34] He regarded the view that profits are realized when assets appreciate, as 'logical' but not generally accepted because of the peculiar conservatism of accountants:

> The accountant transcends the conservatism of the proverb, 'Do not count your chickens before they are hatched', saying 'Here are a lot of chickens already safely hatched, but for the love of Mike, use discretion and don't count them all for perhaps some will die.'[35]

At this point Hatfield gives an example of the odd results of the 'realization convention' which in various guises has been repeated a number of times since.[36]

> One may have bought $10,000 Second Liberty Loan bonds and $10,000 Third Liberty Loan bonds when both issues were selling at 90. Somewhat later, when both have risen, he may sell his block of the third issue at par and buy, at the same figure, a block of the second issue. If this has been done, he is conventionally allowed to show that the more recently acquired bonds are worth par and that he has made a 10 point profit in the transaction. But the identical bonds which he bought at an earlier date, in accordance with the [conventional] rule, must still be valued at 90 showing no profit from appreciation.[37]

Hatfield also pointed out that it is inconsistent to deny that profit can exist without a sale and at the same time to recognize accrued interest as income:

> The exception in favour of accruing interest probably rests upon the idea that it is

32. Hatfield, *Accounting*, pp 102-3.

33. Ibid, p 251.

34. Ibid, p 255.

35. Ibid, p 256, note 13. The passage is indexed under 'Mike, love of,'!

36. Paton, in fact, gave a similar example five years before in 1922: W. A. Paton, *Accounting Theory*, New York, Ronald, 1922; and Chicago: Accounting Studies Press, 1962, p 467, note 5. Essentially the same point was later made by E. A. Heilman, 'Realized Income', *Accounting Review*, Vol 4, 1929, p 87; K. MacNeal, 'What's Wrong with Accounting?', *The Nation*, New York, 7-14 October 1939, reprinted in Baxter and Davidson, op cit, pp 60-61; and J. W. Bennett, J. McB. Grant and R. H. Parker, *Topics in Business Finance and Accounting*, Melbourne, Cheshire, 1964, pp 77-80.

37. Hatfield, *Accounting*, pp 256-57.

> definitely calculable, its amount may be accurately determined. But if this is a satisfactory basis of differentiation, the rule for recognizing profits should be expressed in terms of calculability or certainty rather than made dependent upon the existence of a contract.[38]

W. A. Paton of the University of Michigan has never seemed wholly convinced of the 'cost only' doctrine. In 1918 he argued strongly for taking the present market value rather than cost;[39] in 1924 he thought that 'actual cost furnishes the most satisfactory basis or starting point for the pricing of inventory in the trading field';[40] but he could still write in 1926 that 'there are undoubtedly many cases in which, everything taken into account, the most satisfactory method of inventory valuation involves the consistent use of market prices.'[41]

By 1934, however, he could state:

> . . . it seems to me that the matter of realizable values as associated with the preparation of a balance sheet has been unduly emphasized in the case of inventories. . . . Inventories, particularly in industrial plants, are substantially nothing more nor less than aggregates of cost factors which will be realized through the completion of the process of production. . . . When it is more fully appreciated that the conventional balance sheet includes a mass of costs which have little or no relation to realizable values and immediate liquid position . . . a long step toward better accounting practice will have been taken.[42]

Littleton, Hatfield and Paton all appeared to be agreed upon one thing: the illogicality and unreasonableness of the cost or market rule. Most academic writers probably agreed with them. DR Scott even went so far as to contribute in 1926 what he termed an obituary notice of the rule. E. J. Filbey, commenting on Scott's paper, claimed, however, that 'the reports of the death of this rule have been greatly exaggerated.'[43]

Filbey was right, of course. Accounting is practice as well as principle, and the practitioners were by no means willing to abandon the rule.

PRACTICE AND PRINCIPLE

> Sir, you are so grossly ignorant of human nature, as not to know that a man may be very sincere in good principles, without having good practice!
>
> Dr. Samuel Johnson as reported in James Boswell, *Journal of a Tour to the Hebrides*, 25 October 1773.

From the early 1930s onwards the accountants of the English-speaking world have increasingly concerned themselves with the search for accounting 'principles'. Most accountants have been convinced that they exist; but there has been plenty of disagreement about their nature and the way in which they should be found.

It is probably fair to say that practitioners have usually favoured an *inductive*

38. Ibid, p 257.

39. W. A. Paton and R. A. Stevenson, *Principles of Accounting*, New York, 1918, p 468, quoted in Hatfield, *Accounting*, p 102.

40. W. A. Paton, *Accounting*, New York, Macmillan, 1924, p 373.

41. *Accounting Review*, Vol 1, 1926, p 30 (part of a comment on a paper by DR Scott).

42. W. A. Paton, 'Aspects of Asset Valuations', *Accounting Review*, Vol 9, 1934, pp 123-24.

43. DR Scott, 'Conservatism in Inventory Valuations', *Accounting Review*, Vol 1, March 1926, pp 18, 24.

approach, whilst academics have tended to favour a *deductive* approach. Both approaches were tried in the 1930s.

The first use of the phrase 'accepted principles of accounting' and the first attempt at a formal statement of 'accounting principles' are to be found in the Report dated 22 September 1932 of the American Institute's Special Committee on Co-operation with Stock Exchanges.

The date is of interest. We have already discussed the environment of the English accounting profession during its early years. The environment of the first set of accounting principles may perhaps be best understood by looking at an index of common stock prices (Table 2).

TABLE 2

Index of Common Stock Prices (United States)

All stocks	1926 = 100
1926	100.0
1927	118.3
1928	149.9
1929	190.3
1930	149.8
1931	94.7
1932	48.6
1933	63.0
1934	72.4
1935	78.3
1936	111.0
1937	111.8

Source: United States Bureau of the Census, *Historical Statistics of the United States 1789-1945*, Washington, D.C., 1949, p 281.

In its Report, the Institute's Committee emphasized the need to 'bring about a better recognition by the public of the fact that the balance-sheet of a large modern corporation does not and should not be expected to represent an attempt to show present values of the assets and liabilities of the corporation' and to 'make universal the acceptance by listed corporations of *certain broad principles of accounting which have won fairly general acceptance*.'[44]

It was suggested that in the first instance the broad principles should be few in number. Five principles were set out which the Committee thought should 'presumably' be included. The first one is relevant to the present discussion. It states that 'unrealized profit should not be credited to income account . . . either directly or indirectly'. The Committee thought profit should be deemed to be realized 'when a sale in the ordinary course of business is effected'. It was perhaps an augury of the future that there were two qualifications: the collection of the sales price had to be 'reasonably assured'; and 'an exception to the general rule may be made in respect of inventories in industries (such as the packing-house

44. Report of the Special Committee on Co-operation with Stock Exchanges of the American Institute of Accountants to the Committee on Stock List of the New York Stock Exchange, dated 22 September 1932; reprinted in G. O. May, *Financial Accounting*, New York, Macmillan, 1943, pp 72-85. The quoted passages are from pp 79 and 80, emphasis added.

industry) in which owing to the impossibility of determining costs it is a trade custom to take inventories at net selling prices, which may exceed cost.'[45] No mention was made of the lower of cost and market rule in the suggested list of principles, but it was mentioned in the Report as 'the most commonly accepted method of stating inventories.'[46]

A further important step in the inductive derivation of principles was the work of T. H. Sanders of the Harvard Graduate School of Business Administration, H. R. Hatfield, and Underhill Moore of the Yale Law School. They were asked by the Haskins & Sells Foundation to 'formulate a code of accounting principles which would be useful in the clarification and improvement of corporate accounting and of financial reports issued to the public.'[47] In their letter of transmittal the three authors noted that since 1933 a large and increasing majority of auditors' certificates were using the terms 'accounting principles' or 'principles of accounting' and that the demand for a statement of accounting principles had become insistent.[48] The report which they produced has been recently described as 'the first relatively complete statement of accounting principles and the only complete statement reflecting the school of thought that accounting principles are found in what accountants do—the school which emphasizes the *accepted* part of "generally accepted accounting principles".'[49]

There is little doubt about what American accountants were *doing* in the 1930s. Writing in 1939, Gilman commented that the lower of cost and market rule had been so completely accepted that the great majority of all published balance sheets displayed inventories which had been so valued. Of 197 companies reported in the *N.A.C.A. Bulletin* of 15 March 1937, 172 or over eighty-seven per cent valued raw material inventories at the lower of cost and market.[50]

In their introductory chapter Sanders, Hatfield and Moore pointed out that accounting followed certain conventional procedures. Two very different classes of information were used: first, an historical record of transactions, and secondly, the adjustment of historical amounts to 'something nearer to practical present-day conditions.'[51] The difficulty with views such as these is that almost any valuation practice can be justified. The authors to some extent limited this by favouring conservatism. The sixth in their list of 'General Principles' reads as follows:

> The possible extent of unforeseen contingencies of adverse character calls for a generally conservative treatment of items to which judgment must be applied.[52]

45. Ibid, p 81.

46. Ibid, p 75. The five suggested principles were (with one addition) adopted as 'rules' by the American Institute in 1934. See *Accounting Research and Terminology Bulletins—Final Edition,* New York, American Institute of Certified Public Accountants, 1961, pp 11-12.

47. T. H. Sanders, H. R. Hatfield and U. Moore, *A Statement of Accounting Principles,* New York, American Institute of Accountants, 1938, p xiii (Letter of Invitation to the Committee).

48. Ibid, p xv.

49. R. K. Storey, *The Search for Accounting Principles,* New York, American Institute of Certified Public Accountants, 1964, p 31.

50. Gilman, *Accounting Concepts of Profit,* p 405.

51. Sanders, Hatfield and Moore, op cit, p 2.

52. Ibid, p 114.

The result was a set of principles which, *inter alia,* supported the lower of cost and market rule:

Only income realized by the sale of goods or rendering of service is to be shown in the income statement. Unrealized income should not be recorded,[53] nor utilized to absorb proper charges against earnings. . . . Cost and expenses must include . . . inventory losses of the period. . . . The proper showing of current assets requires . . . that the values in general be the lowest of cost, replacement, or realization, as may be applicable for the several items. . . .[54]

In 1936 development of accounting principles and standards became one of the objectives of the American Accounting Association.[55] Its aim was to prepare a statement of accounting principles 'which *might* be adopted as fundamental to sound accounting.'[56] It was recognized that such a statement 'must inevitably embody some conflict with existing accounting practice, since existing practice is in conflict with itself at a hundred points.'[57]

The Association's 'Tentative Statement of Accounting Principles affecting Corporate Reports' was published in June 1936. The Statement expressed belief in 'a single coordinated body of accounting theory' and took as a 'fundamental axiom' the view that accounting is not a process of valuation, but 'the allocation of historical costs and revenues to the current and succeeding fiscal periods.'[58] The lower of cost and market rule was not mentioned, but a way in which the rule could be 'reconciled' with a cost basis was provided:

Every business enterprise should eliminate from its accounts those costs which are applicable to assets no longer useful or salable, and should reduce the carrying values of assets in use or ultimately to be marketed to such amounts as may reasonably be expected to be recoverable in the course of future operations.[59]

There were now two ways in which the lower of cost and market rule could be supported. The first justification, perhaps becoming rather unfashionable, was an appeal to conservatism; the second justification was the newer doctrine of *recoverable cost,* which survived the first (1941) and second (1948) revisions of the 'Tentative Statement'.[60] In 1940 Paton and Littleton published 'an outline of

53. Compare Hatfield's views in 1927! (reference under footnotes 33-38 above).

54. Sanders, Hatfield and Moore, op cit, pp 114-15.

55. 'A Statement of Objectives of the American Accounting Association', *Accounting Review,* Vol 11, 1936.

56. Ibid, p 3.

57. Ibid.

58. 'A Tentative Statement of Accounting Principles affecting Corporate Reports', *Accounting Review,* Vol 11, 1936, p 188.

59. Ibid, p 189.

60. First revision, 1941:

Costs or productive factors or other resources which are no longer useful should be reduced to realizable value, if any; and in the case of resources to be continued in use or held for sale only such portion of their costs as may reasonably be assigned to future periods should be carried in the balance sheet. 'Accounting Principles Underlying Corporate Financial Statements', *Accounting Review,* Vol 16, 1941, p 135.

Second revision, 1948:

The portion of recorded cost [of an asset] to be reported in the balance sheet is the amount assignable to future periods. When an asset or asset group will be continued in use this amount is the portion of cost recoverable through the remaining useful services the asset is expected to yield. . . . The residual cost should be carried forward in the balance sheet for assignment in future periods except when it is evident that

the basic theory which underlies the Tentative Statement.'[61] They viewed inventories as 'essentially unrecovered costs . . . that portion of the stream of costs incurred in acquiring and producing goods which can reasonably be applied to revenues of the future.'[62] But they considered that this approach did not preclude the absorption in current charges to revenue of 'an appropriate portion of the cost of obsolete or damaged materials, work in process, or merchandise.'[63] They were at pains to point out that a clear distinction should be drawn between this kind of absorption and 'the substitution for recorded cost of figures designed to represent costs as they would be if the entire inventory were acquired or produced under the level of prices for the component factors obtaining at the inventory date.'[64] They regarded such a procedure as 'seriously objectionable.'[65] They did not support conservatism and clearly did not regard the deduction of an 'appropriate portion of the cost' as being connected in any way with the lower of cost and market rule.[66]

The American Institute's official statement on inventory valuation was published in 1947 as *Accounting Research Bulletin No. 29.*[67] It is described by Storey as 'a classic example of trying to please everyone'.[68]

The primary basis of accounting for inventories, states the Bulletin, is acquisition and production cost,[69] but

> A departure from the cost basis . . . is required when the utility of the goods is no longer as great as its cost. Where there is evidence that the utility of the goods, in their disposal in the ordinary course of business, will be less than cost, whether due to physical deterioration, obsolescence, changes in price levels, or other causes, the difference should be recognized as a loss of the current period. This is generally accomplished by stating such goods at a lower level commonly designated as *market.*[70]

'Utility' is to be thought of in terms of the equivalent expenditure which would have to be made at the balance sheet date to procure corresponding utility. 'Market' therefore usually means current replacement cost, by purchase or by reproduction as the case may be. But this is not appropriate when the net realizable value is lower or where it appears that cost will be recovered with an approximately normal profit upon sale in the ordinary course of business.[71] Exceptionally, inventories may be valued at more than cost, but this must be justified by inability to

60. (cont.)

> the cost of an item cannot be recovered, whether from damage, deterioration, obsolescence, style change, over-supply, reduction in price levels, or other cause. In such event the inventory item should be stated at the estimated amount of sales proceeds less direct expense of completion and disposal. 'Accounting Concepts and Standards Underlying Corporate Financial Statements', *Accounting Review,* Vol 23, 1948, pp 340-41.

61. W. A. Paton and A. C. Littleton, *An Introduction to Corporate Accounting Standards,* Menasha, Wis., American Accounting Association, 1940, p ix.

62. Ibid, p 77. 63. Ibid, p 80. 64. Ibid.

65. Ibid, p 81. 66. Ibid, pp 80-1, 126-29.

67. *Accounting Research Bulletin No. 29,* 'Inventory Pricing', New York, American Institute of Accountants, 1947; reproduced unchanged as chapter 4 of *Accounting Research Bulletin No. 43* in 1953 (pp 27-35 of American Institute of Certified Public Accountants, *Accounting Research and Terminology Bulletins. Final Edition,* op cit).

68. Storey, op cit, p 50.

69. American Institute of Certified Public Accountants, op cit, p 28.

70. Ibid, p 30. 71. Ibid, pp 31-2.

determine appropriate approximate costs, immediate marketability at quoted market price, and the characteristic of unit interchangeability.[72]

In Great Britain the cost or market rule was never seriously challenged; it was, indeed, hardly ever *discussed.* The following statements from an influential text book published in 1925 are typical:

> If all the assets were valued at the amount they are expected to realize if the business were closed down, a heavy loss would necessarily be shown. This method therefore is not adopted, but the valuation is made on the basis of a going concern . . . floating assets should not be valued above cost, as this would involve taking profit before it is realized; the proper basis of calculation being cost, market [i.e., replacement value] or realizable value, whichever is the lower [sic]. . . . In no case should the value [of stock-in-trade] be higher than cost, even though the market value has risen, as this would result in taking profit before the sale is effected and the profit earned. On the other hand, a fall in the market value, due to a fluctuation in the price, need not be considered if the value has since risen. A permanent fall in value, however, must be taken into account.
>
> Stock . . . is bought for the purpose of selling again at a profit, and if at the date of the Balance Sheet it cannot be sold at a profit, a loss has already been sustained which must be provided for by bringing such stock into account at a reduced value. This operation . . . must also be effected in cases where stock has become obsolete or spoilt.[73]

F. R. M. de Paula devoted a chapter of his standard work on auditing (first published in 1914) to inventory valuation and verification. He regarded it as a 'basic principle' that inventories should not be valued above cost and as 'an accepted and wise principle' that any possible or probable losses in connexion with unsold inventories should be anticipated.[74] As far as he could judge, stores and raw materials were usually valued at the lower of cost or replacement value, and work in process and finished goods at the lower of cost or net realizable value. This inconsistency he regarded as incorrect and he suggested that the lower of cost and net realizable value should be the rule in all cases.[75] He argued that if replacement value is below cost 'no loss has arisen, or is likely to arise, provided that there will be a margin of profit upon the ultimate sale of the finished products'.[76]

At least one academic voice was raised to criticize such views. R. S. Edwards could see no merit in the lower of cost and market rule. Against de Paula he argued that it would be ignoring plain facts to say that one's stock of goods was worth more than other stocks of the same goods which could be acquired in the market.[77]

The views of such writers as Edwards seem to have had practically no influence on accounting practice. *Recommendation on Accounting Principles, X,* of the Institute of Chartered Accountants in England and Wales, probably reflected faithfully the views of most British practising accountants when it was issued in June 1945. It recommended that the basis of valuation should normally be the

72. Ibid, p 34.

73. E. E. Spicer and E. C. Pegler, *Practical Auditing,* London, H.F.L. (Publishers) Ltd, 4th ed, 1925, pp 343-44, 168-69.

74. F. R. M. de Paula, *The Principles of Auditing,* London, Pitman, 8th ed, 1936, pp 96-7.

75. Ibid, pp 99-100.

76. Ibid, p 103.

77. Edwards, 'The Nature and Measurement of Income', loc cit, pp 265-66.

lower of cost and market value; the latter being interpreted to mean net realizable value. It was argued in the Recommendation that the fact that at the time of valuation the goods could have been acquired at a sum less than their cost 'only indicates that the expected profit is less than it might have been had it been possible to acquire them at the accounting date'. This is not a trading loss but 'only indicates that the ultimate results under other conditions might have been better.'[78]

No mention was made in the Recommendation of the concept of recoverable cost but it is not completely unknown in the British accounting and economic literature of the 1940s. Norris, for example, although defining assets as 'deferred costs to be carried forward'[79] thought that common practice in inventory valuation was 'probably not seriously wrong so far as resulting figures are concerned'. It was his opinion that the saleability of particular items should be taken into account 'for the purpose only of deciding how much cost is to be carried forward'. This process should not be thought of as providing for losses.[80]

The economist P. W. S. Andrews approved the lower of cost and market rule and claimed that its justification did not lie in conservatism. His argument was as follows:

> If market values have fallen . . . the costs expended on the stocks at the beginning of the next accounting year would be greater than the costs at which the business could *then* acquire similar goods. Now, it is essentially the purpose of the business to hold such goods for ultimate sale and to take the risks of the market. If they were carried at outlay-cost into the balance sheet at the end of the year, the next year would be saddled with what would be the consequences of financial risks which were really incurred in the earlier period, and the year in which the business acquired them would be avoiding one of the costs of its having done so—the fall in prices that has taken place. . . . To value at market prices when prices are rising would falsify the cost position and cause the following year to be charged with costs which had not been incurred in fact . . . the accountant's rule here is a strict application of the logic of his principle of charging as costs the money outlays that have been incurred during any period.[81]

CONCLUSIONS

> "Is that it?" said Eeyore.
> "Yes", said Christopher Robin.
> "Is that what we were looking for?"
> "Yes", said Pooh.
> "Oh!", said Eeyore. "Well, anyhow—
> it didn't rain," he said.
>
> A. A. Milne, *Winnie-the-Pooh*, Ch. viii.

The astonishing thing about the lower of cost and market rule is its ability to survive attack. G. O. May was probably right in suggesting that most accountants are 'content to regard the demonstrated practical wisdom of the rule as outweighing

78. Institute of Chartered Accountants in England and Wales, *Recommendation on Accounting Principles, X*, 'The Valuation of Stock-in-Trade', issued 15 June 1945.

79. H. Norris, *Accounting Theory*, London, Pitman, 1946, p 18.

80. Ibid, p 73.

81. P. W. S. Andrews, *Manufacturing Business*, London, Macmillan, 1949, pp 41-2.

any supposed illogicality.'[82] May embraced the doctrine of recoverable cost in order to 'avert the embodiment of the two rival concepts of cost and value in a single rule.'[83]

It might be suggested, however, that the lower of cost and market rule has survived precisely because it *does* embody the two rival concepts. Accountants are faced with a dilemma, as Littleton pointed out in 1929[84]: they are willing to accept neither a purely cost balance sheet, nor a purely appraisal balance sheet. In a purely appraisal balance sheet, they are worried about recognizing 'unrealized' profits; in a purely cost balance sheet, they are worried about showing an asset at a figure above that at which it could be currently sold or replaced. The 'practical' answer is obviously a lower of cost and market rule, without worrying too much about 'theoretical' illogicality.

To Littleton the rule is the result of 'convenience and expediency.'[85] Vance, on the other hand, regards it as having grown in response to the needs of businessmen.[86] It does fulfil a need so long as accountants are unwilling to decide on the *objectives* of financial accounting. They cannot really have it both ways: either a balance sheet is a historical record or it is a statement of current resources. The concept of recoverable cost is not convincing; it is, as an Australian writer has put it, 'a rationalization of accepted accounting practices rather than an attempt to discover fundamental principles on which practices should be based.'[87]

The search for accounting principles goes on. It is unlikely that there will be agreement on inventory valuation so long as the more general problem remains unsolved.

October 1965

82. May, *Financial Accounting*, p 180. 83. Ibid, p 184.
84. Littleton, 'Value and Price in Accounting', loc cit, p 148.
85. Littleton, 'A Genealogy for "Cost or Market"', *Accounting Review*, Vol 16, 1941, p 166.
86. L. L. Vance, 'The Authority of History in Inventory Valuation', *Accounting Review*, Vol 18, 1943, p 227.
87. J. R. Ballantyne, at p 129 of A. A. Fitzgerald, ed, *Accounting*, Sydney, Butterworths, 4th ed, 1963.

DISCOUNTED CASH FLOW IN HISTORICAL PERSPECTIVE

Discounted Cash Flow in Historical Perspective

R. H. PARKER*

The purpose of this paper is to survey the development of discounted cash flow criteria of investment evaluation before 1950. No attempt is made to discuss the problem of the cost of capital or the difficulties caused by risk and uncertainty.

The technique of discounted cash flow requires both an understanding of compound interest and an ability to set out the cash inflows and outflows likely to result from a particular decision to invest. Knowledge of compound interest goes back at least as far as the Old Babylonian period (c. 1800–1600 B.C.) in Mesopotamia.[1] Setting out the cash implications of an investment is more difficult. It is not surprising that the earliest applications of discounted cash flow were to loans where the cash outlays and receipts were known and to life insurance where probabilities could be calculated from historical evidence. The extension of discounted cash flow to investment in fixed assets came much later and was based on the work of engineers and economists. We therefore have to consider developments in three fields: actuarial science, engineering economy, and political economy. They will be discussed in the order stated.

Trenchant, Stevin, and the Birth of Actuarial Science

In spite of the medieval Christian Church's ban on usury, European books on mathematics from Leonardo of Pisa's *Liber Abaci* (1202) onwards

* Reader in Management Accounting, Manchester Business School. Much of the research on which this paper is based was carried out while the author was P. D. Leake Research Fellow in Accounting at the London School of Economics in 1966. The paper forms part of a forthcoming book, *Accounting in Historical Perspective*, to be published by Macmillan & Co. Ltd., London.

[1] O. E. H. Neugebauer, *The Exact Sciences in Antiquity* (Copenhagen: Ejnar Munksgaard, 1951), p. 33.

contained problems concerning compound interest.[2] Before the sixteenth century, however, interest tables were treated as highly confidential and existed only in manuscript. One of these early manuscript tables, composed about 1340, has been preserved in a copy made in 1472. It was prepared for the Florentine firm of the Bardi by Francesco Balducci Pegolotti as part of his *Pratica della Mercatura* which was not, however, published until 1766.[3] It is an interesting coincidence that the oldest accounting records definitely kept in double entry—those of the *massari* or stewards of the commune of Genoa—also date from 1340. Pacioli's *Summa de Arithmetica Geometria Proportioni et Proportionalità* (1494) does not contain any tables but includes a number of problems on simple and compound interest and sketches the way tables should be computed.[4]

It was at Antwerp and Lyons, the two great financial centers of Western Europe in the sixteenth century, that interest tables were first printed. Jean (or Jan) Trenchant in his *L'Aritmetique departie en troys livres*, published in Lyons in 1558, discussed geometric progressions and compound interest (Book 3, chapters 8 and 9, pp. 235–55). Tables were provided for $10^7\,(1.04)^n$, $n = 1, 2 \cdots 40$ and $10^7\, s_{\overline{n}|0.4}$, $n = 1, 2 \cdots 41$.[5]

Tables of Interest, the first book of Simon Stevin[6] (1548–1620), the famous Dutch mathematician, scientist, engineer, and accountant, was published in Antwerp in 1582. It is, in effect, a text on financial mathematics. Simple and compound interest are defined and explained, and illustrative problems are worked out. The tables used for the solution of the compound interest problems include: $10^7\,(1+i)^{-n}$, $i = 0.01, 0.02 \cdots 0.16$; $i = 1/15, 1/16 \cdots 1/22$; $n = 1, 2 \cdots 30$; $10^7 a_{\overline{n}|i}$, $i = 0.01, 0.02 \cdots 0.16$; $i = 1/15, 1/16 \cdots 1/22$; $n = 1, 2 \cdots 30$; $10^7\,(1 + 1/15)^n$, $n = 0, 1 \cdots 30$; and $10^7\, s_{\overline{n}|1/15}$, $n = 1, 2 \cdots 31$. Like Trenchant, Stevin used 10^7 as the base of his system in order to avoid decimal fractions.

In an appendix, Stevin describes "a general rule for finding which is the most profitable of two or more conditions, and by how much it is more profitable than the other." The rule is to find the present value of each proposed condition in respect to a given rate of interest, the difference between these present values showing by how much one condition is better

[2] B. Boncompagni (ed.), *Liber Abaci. Scritti di Leonardo Pisano*, Vol. 2 (1862), p. 267.

[3] A. Evans (ed.), *Francesco Balducci Pegolotti. La pratica della mercatura* (Cambridge, Mass.: The Medieval Academy of America, 1936), pp. ix, xiv, xi, xv, 301–2.

[4] Luca Pacioli, *Summa de Arithmetica Geometria Proportioni et Proportionalità* (Venice, 1494; 2d ed., Toscolano, 1523), 1st part, 9th distinctio, 5th tractatus. See D. J. Struik (ed.), *The Principle Works of Simon Stevin*, Vol. 11A, Mathematics (Amsterdam: C. V. Swets & Zeitlinger, 1958), p. 14.

[5] Neither Trenchant nor Stevin, of course, used this notation.

[6] On Stevin, see O. ten Have, "Simon Stevin of Bruges," in A. C. Littleton and B. S. Yamey (eds.), *Studies in the History of Accounting* (London: Sweet & Maxwell, 1956) and G. Sarton, "Simon Stevin of Bruges (1548–1620)," *Isis*, Vol. 21 (1934), reprinted in D. Stimson (ed.), *Sarton on the History of Science* (Cambridge, Mass.: Harvard University Press, 1962).

than the other. This is clearly the net present value criterion of choosing between alternative investments. As is to be expected, he applied it only to loans.[7]

An understanding of compound interest[8] was one of the preconditions for the development of scientific life assurance in England in the eighteenth century. So also were the theory of probability and statistics of mortality.

The essentials of the mathematical theory of probability were worked out in 1654 in a correspondence between the French mathematicians Pierre de Fermat (1601–65) and Blaise Pascal (1623–62) and were systematized by the Dutch physicist Christianus Huygens (1629–95) in his book *De Ratiociniis in Aleae Ludo* (1657). Shortly afterwards, John Graunt (1620–74), a friend of Sir William Petty, published his *Natural and Political Observations made upon the Bills of Mortality* (London, 1662) which contained a rudimentary life table. The way in which chances of death could be combined with allowance for compound interest to produce the value of a life annuity was first shown by the Dutch statesman Johann de Witt (1625–72). However, his report of 1671 to the States-General was not published and it was in fact the English astronomer Edmond Halley (1656–1742) who, using statistics from bills of mortality for Breslau for the years 1687–91, constructed the first mortality table computed from statistics.[9]

In 1756, James Dodson[10] (1710?–57), F.R.S., "Accountant and Teacher

[7] Simon Stevin, *Tafalen van Interest* (Antwerp: Christoffel Plantijn, 1582). The original is reprinted with a facing translation in Struik, *op cit.*, pp. 25–117. The passage quoted is on p. 107 of the translation. Struik's introduction (pp. 13–24) is very informative on the history of interest tables. See also G. W. Smith, "A Brief History of Interest Calculations," *Journal of Industrial Engineering*, 18 (1967), 569–74.

[8] The first English writer to include compound interest tables appears to have been Richard Witt in his book *Arithmeticall Questions, touching the buying or exchange of annuities* (London: Richard Redmer, 1613), 183pp.

[9] F. N. David, *Games, Gods, and Gambling* (London: Charles Griffin & Co., 1962) has chapters on Fermat and Pascal, Huygens, and Graunt, and also an English translation of the Fermat-Pascal correspondence. The original letters can be found in P. Tannery and C. Henry, *Oeuvres de Fermat* (Paris: Gauthier-Villars et fils, 1894), Vol. II, pp. 218–314; there is another translation in D. E. Smith, *A Source Book of Mathematics* (New York: McGraw-Hill, 1929), pp. 546–65. Graunt's book was reprinted in 1939 by The Johns Hopkins Press, Baltimore. Halley's paper, "An estimate of the Degrees of the Mortality of Mankind, drawn from curious tables of the Births and Funerals at the City of Breslaw; with an Attempt to ascertain the Price of Annuities upon Lives," was published in the *Philosophical Transactions of the Royal Society of London*, Vol. XVII, No. 196, 1693, pp. 596–610 and reprinted by The Johns Hopkins Press in 1942. See also, A. Armitage, *Edmond Halley* (London: Nelson, 1966), pp. 127–32. There are selections from Graunt and Halley in J. R. Newman, *The World of Mathematics* (London: Allen & Unwin, 1960), Vol. 3, Pt. VIII.

[10] His publications include *The Calculator: being correct and necessary Tables for Computation, Adapted to Science, Business, and Pleasure* (London: John Wilcox and James Dodson, 1747); *The Mathematical Repository* (London: John Nourse, 3 Vols., 1747–8, 1753, 1755); and the 18th and 19th editions of Edmond Wingate's *A Plain and Familiar Method for attaining the Knowledge and Practice of Common Arithmetic* (London, 1751 and 1760). All of these books include sections on compound interest

of the Mathematics," in his unpublished *First Lecture on Insurances*, made the first investigation into the principles of operation of a life assurance business and showed how premiums should be calculated. The general principles he set forth are still valid.[11]

The operations of the life assurance societies, notably the Equitable Life Assurance Society (founded 1762), gave rise to actuarial science. The first official reference to "professional actuaries" is to be found in the Poor Law Act of 1819; an Institute of Actuaries was established in England in 1848.[12] The first textbook published by the Institute listed and commented upon bond tables prepared by Charles Ingall (1862), Lt. Col. Oakes (1870), and Herbert Johnson (1881).[13] The earliest known set of such tables was prepared by the New York banker Joseph M. Price and published in that city in 1843.[14] The tables can be used to find the yield to maturity of a bond, i.e., that rate of interest which equates the issue or current market price with the stream of future cash receipts (periodic interest and redemption price). This is clearly a particular application of what was later to be named the marginal efficiency of capital or internal rate of return.

It is difficult to tell how much the writers on engineering and political economy who discussed the criteria for investment decisions owed to the writers mentioned so far. It is certain, however, that Irving Fisher (see p. 65 below) was familiar with the leading actuarial textbook of his day: Ralph Todhunter's *The Institute of Actuaries' Text-Book on Compound Interest and Annuities-Certain* (London: Layton, 1901).[15]

The Contribution of Engineering Economy

Discounted cash flow criteria were not applied to nonfinancial investments until the nineteenth century. This was probably due not only to the

---

and annuities with appropriate tables. Dodson was also the author of *The Accountant, or the Method of Book-keeping, Deduced from Clear Principles and Illustrated by a Variety of Examples* (London: John Nourse, 1750) which is one of the very few early works on book-keeping to deal with accounting for manufacturing operations. Extracts from this book are given in R. S. Edwards, "Some Notes on the Early Literature and Development of Cost Accounting in Great Britain—II," *Accountant*, 97 (August 14, 1937), 226–8. On Dodson, see Augustus de Morgan, "Some Account of James Dodson, F. R. S.," *Journal of the Institute of Actuaries*, Vol. XIV, No. LXXIII (October, 1868), pp. 341–64, M. E. Ogborn, *Equitable Assurances* (London: Allen & Unwin, 1962), and V. Snelling, "Two Respectable Accountants," *Accountant*, 151 (December 19, 1964), 782–3.

[11] Ogborn, *op. cit.*, pp. 30–1.

[12] Ogborn, *op. cit.*, pp. 198, 212; R. C. Simmonds, *The Institute of Actuaries 1848–1948* (London: Institute of Actuaries, 1948).

[13] W. Sutton, *The Institute of Actuaries' Text-Book of the Principles of Interest (including Annuities-Certain), Life Annuities, and Assurances and their Practical Application*, Part 1 (London: Layton, 1882), pp. 158, 160.

[14] See Robert M. Soldofsky, "A Note on the History of Bond Tables and Stock Valuation Models," *Journal of Finance* (March, 1966).

[15] He cites it on pp. 401 and 411 of his *The Nature of Capital and Income* (New York: Macmillan, 1906).

difficulties of forecasting the relevant cash flows but also because of the relatively small size of such investments. It was the coming of the railways that changed this. The building of railways entailed a massive capital outlay before any returns were received. Therefore, it is not surprising that in the second edition (1887) of his standard work on the location of railways, the American civil engineer A. M. Wellington, should anticipate some of the ideas of modern capital expenditure analysis.[16] In his chapter on the probable volume of traffic, he points out that it is rarely the case that a railway, especially in the United States, is built only for the existing traffic. But it is exceedingly dangerous for an average American corporation to look ahead for more than from three to at most ten years for the "rapidly increasing traffic" which is to justify an increase of present expenditure over what the prospects of the present and the immediate future will justify. He then continues as follows:

> Let us see why this is so. The theory of the subject is simple: In Table 18 is given the present value or present justifiable expenditure to save $1 (or one unit of any other value) at the end of a given period at any given rate of interest; that is to say, the sum which, if placed at compound interest now, will produce $1 at the end of the specified period. This fact given, it logically follows, that if the value of a given betterment for a given immediate traffic be $1, the present value of the same betterment for an equal traffic which is to exist only in the future will be that sum which at compound interest will produce $1 when the assumed traffic comes to exist.
>
> All this is undeniably correct in theory . . . [but] the indications of Table 18 are of value only as fixing a maximum which should never be exceeded.
>
> While it may be taken as a practical certainty that the traffic of any ordinary railway not only will grow, but that it will grow at an average rate of something like 5 to 8 per cent per annum east of the Alleghenies, and 7 to 10 or 15 or even 20 per cent per year west of there, yet . . . the rate of this growth of traffic is excessively variable and uncertain—liable to cease altogether at any time for many years.
>
> For this cause alone it is in general inexpedient to look forward more than at most five years for traffic to justify an increase of immediate expenditure.[17]

A present value approach was also used by Walter O. Pennell, Equipment and Building Engineer, Southwestern Bell Telephone System, in a paper[18] read to the Engineers' Club, St. Louis, Missouri, in April, 1914. He discussed the problem whether to install new machinery or to retain old machinery. In a curiously roundabout manner, he first calculates interest

[16] Compound interest and annuity factors have been used in mine valuation at least since the first edition of H. D. Hoskold's *Engineer's Valuing Assistant* (London: Longmans, Green, 1877).

[17] A. M. Wellington, *The Economic Theory of the Location of Railways* (New York: Wiley, 1887), Ch. IV; see also pp. 746–7. Wellington's book is discussed by M. B. Scorgie, "Rate of Return," *Abacus*, Vol. 1, No. 1 (Sept., 1965) and by R. J. Stephens, "A Note on an Early Reference to Cost-Volume-Profit Relationships," *Abacus*, Vol. 2, No. 1 (Sept., 1966).

[18] W. O. Pennell, " 'Present Worth' Calculations in Engineering Studies," *Journal of the Association of Engineering Societies* (Sept., 1914).

and sinking fund depreciation on the initial capital cost and then multiplies by an annuity factor to obtain present worth. This procedure may be shown symbolically as follows:

$$\left(Ci + \frac{C}{s_{\overline{n}|i}}\right) a_{\overline{n}|i} = P,$$

where C = the initial capital cost, i the rate of interest, $i/s_{\overline{n}|i}$ the sinking fund factor, $a_{\overline{n}|i}$ the annuity factor, and P present worth. But [19]

$$i + \frac{1}{s_{\overline{n}|i}} = \frac{1}{a_{\overline{n}|i}},$$

so the left-hand side is simply equal to C, i.e., the present value of C spent now is C! Pennell appears to have confused himself by including in the same calculation both the initial capital cost and the operating expenses. Pennell also failed to handle properly the abandonment of old machinery. Like many writers, he failed to realize the irrelevance of its historical cost.

Another engineering writer, John H. Van Deventer, gave the following advice in an article in *The American Machinist* in 1915: first, estimate the probable saving that an appliance will make; second, assign a probable length of life to it; third, estimate what the appliance will cost; fourth, decide on the minimum rate of return expected. The reader is then referred to a "Table of Maximum Permissible Investment to Accomplish a Given Saving." Unfortunately, as Wing has shown, the table does not make use of compound interest factors.[20]

O. B. Goldman of the Department of Mechanical Engineering, University of Arizona, shows a great advance on the work of Pennell and Van Deventer. He worked in terms of what he called "vestances," i.e., the present values of costs.[21] He defined depreciation vestance as the present worth of investments and reinvestments. If these are expected to go on forever, one obtains the simple formula $C/[1 - (1 + r)^{-n}]$, which (in notation not used by Goldman) is equal to $C a^{-1}_{\overline{n}|r}/r$, where C is the initial cost, r the rate of interest, n the length of life of the initial investment and of each reinvestment, and $a^{-1}_{\overline{n}|i}$ is the "capital recovery factor" (a phrase used later by Grant but not by Goldman). If operating costs, a, can also be regarded as constant and perpetual, then "operating vestance" will be a/r and "total vestance" (V) will be:

[19] The proof of the relationship between the sinking fund factor and the reciprocal of the annuity factor is given in many books, e.g., J. W. Bennett, J. McB. Grant, and R. H. Parker, *Topics in Business Finance and Accounting* (Melbourne: Cheshire, 1964), pp. 22–3.

[20] John Van Deventer, "Jigs and Fixtures in the Small Shop," *American Machinist*, XLII (1915), 807–9. See also George A. Wing, "Capital Budgeting, Circa 1915," *Journal of Finance*, 20 (1965), 472–9.

[21] O. B. Goldman, *Financial Engineering* (New York: Wiley, 1st ed., 1920, 2d ed., 1923), especially Ch. 2.

$$V = \frac{C}{1-(1+r)^{-n}} + \frac{a}{r}$$
$$= \frac{Ca^{-1}_{\overline{n}|r} + a}{r}.$$

If a finite life of *mn* years is assumed, then "total partial vestance" is:

$$V'_{mn} = \frac{C[1-(1+r)^{-mn}]}{1-(1+r)^{-n}} + \frac{a[1-(1+r)^{-mn}]}{r}$$
$$= V[1-(1+r)^{-mn}].$$

However, Fish and Grant, professors of engineering at Stanford University, preferred the "annual cost method." Fish explained that in deciding among alternative investments comparison should be made of:

(i) the equivalent uniform annual operation cost (excluding depreciation) which is found by reducing the series of actual annual costs to a convenient date and distributing the sum of the results uniformly over the whole period;

(ii) annual depreciation cost calculated by the sinking fund method and taking into account the salvage value;

(iii) interest on capital;

(iv) the equivalent uniform annual income.[22]

Grant[23] explains the use of "present worth" and "rate of return on extra investment" but, even in the revised fourth edition published in 1964, gives preference to the annual cost method on the grounds that people understand it more easily and that it is usually easier to compute.[24]

The Contribution of Political Economy

It is, however, in the discussions on capital theory by such economists as Marshall in England, Böhm-Bawerk in Austria, Wicksell[25] in Sweden and above all Fisher in the United States that the ultimate source of most of our present ideas on discounted cash flow can be found.

In his *Principles of Economics*, Marshall wrote of the accumulation of past and the discounting of future outlays and receipts. The balance of efforts and satisfactions involved in an investment may be made up to any day that is found convenient. But whatever day is chosen, every effort or satisfaction which dates from a time anterior to that day must have compound interest for the interval accumulated upon it; and every element

[22] J. C. L. Fish, *Engineering Economics* (New York: McGraw-Hill, 1st ed., 1915, 2d ed., 1923), Chs. II and IV.

[23] E. L. Grant, *Principles of Engineering Economy* (New York: Ronald Press, 1st ed., 1930, 2d ed., 1938, 3d ed., 1950, 4th ed. [with W. G. Ireson] 1960).

[24] Grant and Ireson (1964), p. 103.

[25] K. Wicksell, *Value Capital and Rent* (London: Allen & Unwin, 1954), Pt. II (German original published in 1893); and *Lectures on Political Economy*, Vol. I, Pt. II, Ch. 2 (London: Routledge, 1934) (Swedish original published in 1901).

which dates from a time posterior to that day must have compound interest for the interval discounted from it. Allowance should be made for the risk of failure. Difficulties may arise from changes in the general purchasing power of money. An alert businessman will push investment of capital in his business in each direction until what appears in his judgment to be the margin of profitableness has been reached, i.e., until there seems to him no good reason for thinking that the gains resulting from any further investment in that particular direction would compensate him for his outlay.[26]

Böhm-Bawerk also used a net present value approach. He gives as an example the problem of whether to buy a house offered for the payment of 20 annual installments of 1,000 florins each. The present value of the house should not, he says, be compared with the rate of sacrifice currently experienced (i.e., the first installment only) but with the value of the entire 20 installments entered at their present value.[27]

Fisher's work clearly owes something not only to his economist predecessors such as Böhm-Bawerk but also to the writers on actuarial science and finance already mentioned. This said, it is important to stress how far he was in advance of them and indeed of most of his successors until the 1950's. His most important work in this field was *The Rate of Interest* first published in 1907 and extensively revised and reissued as *The Theory of Interest* in 1930. In these books, he sets out four ways of choosing between investment options and claims that they all give the same result. Out of all eligible options, one should select (i) the one which has the maximum present value, reckoned at the market rate of interest (the principle of maximum present value); (ii) the one whose advantages (returns) over any other outweigh, in present value, its disadvantages (costs), when both returns and costs are discounted at the market rate of interest (the principle of comparative advantage); (iii) the one which, compared with any other option, yields a "rate of return on sacrifice" or "rate of return over cost" greater than the rate of interest (the principle of return over cost); or (iv) where options differ by continuous gradations, the one the difference of which from its nearest rival gives a rate of return over cost equal to the rate of interest (such a rate is called the *marginal* rate of return over cost).

These criteria are illustrated by examples of the alternative use of land. One example uses the following figures:

	Annual Value of Uses for		*Difference in Favor of Forestry*
	Forestry	*Farming*	
1st year	$000	$100	$−100
2nd year	210	100	+110
3rd year and each subsequent year	100	100	000

[26] A. Marshall, *Principles of Economics* (London: Macmillan for the Royal Economic Society, 9th [variorum] ed., 1961), Vol. 1, pp. 352–6, Vol. 2, pp. 368–71. The passage paraphrased first appears in the 5th ed., 1907.

[27] A. v. Böhm-Bawerk, *Recent Literature on Interest (1884–1899)* (New York: Macmillan, 1903), p. 36n. English translation by W. A. Scott and S. Feilbogen.

At a market rate of interest of 9%, the forestry use should be preferred because it has the greater present value ($1,112 as against $1,111 for farming) and because the rate of return over cost, 10%, is greater than the market rate. The rate of return over cost is computed from the difference column by solving for r in the equation, $100 = 110/1 + r$. At a market rate of interest of 10%, the two uses are equal, both having a present value of $1,000 and the rate of return over cost being equal to the market rate of interest. At a market rate of 11%, the farming use will be preferred since its present value is $909 as against $908 for forestry, and since the rate of return over cost (10%) is less than the market rate.[28]

Fisher's rate of return over cost is not the same as the internal rate of return or marginal efficiency of capital discussed by Boulding, Samuelson, and Keynes in the 1930's. This refers to a single investment only. Boulding pointed out that the internal rate of return could be calculated from the equation

$$V_0 = \frac{x_1}{(1+i)} + \frac{x_2}{(1+i)^2} + \cdots \frac{x_n}{(1+i)^n},$$

where V_0 = the value of the enterprise, i = the internal rate of return, n = the number of periods, and $x_1, x_2 \cdots x_n$ = a series of known net revenues (positive or negative). He noted that the solution was not mathematically a simple one, but he thought that in most practical cases a single solution could be found. He did not regard multiple rates of return as of much economic significance. In the context of the single investment which he was considering he was probably right.[29]

In *The General Theory*, Keynes defined the "marginal efficiency of capital" of an asset as being equal to that rate of discount which would make the present value of the returns expected from the asset during its life just equal to its current supply price and claimed that this was identical with Fisher's rate of return over cost.[30] He correctly quoted Fisher as stating that "the rate of return over cost is always that rate which, employed in computing the present worth of all costs and the present worth of all the returns, will make these two equal." But he omitted the sentences which follow:

> Or, as a mathematician would prefer to put it, the rate which, employed on computing the present worth of the whole series of differences between the two income streams (some differences being positive and others negative) will make the total zero.

If the rate, so computed, were taken for every possible pair of income streams

[28] I. Fisher, *The Rate of Interest* (New York: Macmillan, 1907), Ch. 8; *The Theory of Interest* (New York: Macmillan, 1930), Ch. 7.

[29] K. E. Boulding, "The Theory of a Single Investment," *Quarterly Journal of Economics*, Vol. 49 (May, 1949); "Time and Investment," *Economica* (May, 1936); C. A. Wright, "A Note on 'Time and Investment,' " *Economica* (November, 1936); K. E. Boulding, " 'Time and Investment'—A Reply," *Economica* (November, 1936).

[30] J. M. Keynes, *The General Theory of Employment, Interest, and Money* (London: Macmillan, 1936), pp. 140–1.

compared as to their advantages and disadvantages, it would authentically decide in each case which of the pair is to be preferred. That one which compared with the other shows a rate of return on sacrifice greater than the rate of interest would be preferred and the other rejected. By such preferences and rejections the individual would be led to a final *margin* of choice of the best option. This contrasted with its nearest rival would show a marginal rate of return over cost equal to the market rate of interest.[31]

When, at last, in the 1950's discounted cash flow methods started to become familiar, it was Keynes' misinterpretation which became best known.

The contributions made by Boulding and Keynes were discussed by Samuelson in *The Quarterly Journal of Economics* in 1937. He noted the essential equivalence of his own internal rate of interest, Boulding's internal rate of return, and Keynes' marginal efficiency of capital and pointed out quite clearly the possibility of no rate of return or of multiple rates. He rejected Boulding's view that it is the internal rate of return which a perfectly rational and foreseeing investor should maximize and claimed that, at least under ideal conditions, the proper principle was clear and was an old one in the literature of the subject:

Given an interest rate at which all can lend or borrow [r^0] *each entrepreneur will select that value of the variable under his control which maximizes the present value of the investment account, the present value being computed by capitalization of the income stream at the market rate of interest.* This follows from the fact that under our ideal conditions, the investment account necessarily has a market value equal to the capitalized value, and is equivalent to an equal money sum, *and a larger initial sum of money is always to be preferred to a smaller one.*[32]

J. B. Williams' book, *The Theory of Investment Value* (1938) was very much concerned with present values—one chapter was entitled "Evaluation by the Rule of Present Worth"—but in the context of financial assets and liabilities. It has an important place in the history of the concept of the cost of capital, which has been excluded from discussion in this paper.

An early use of the present value criterion was made by the South African Mining Industry Commission of 1907–8 in an attempt to measure the return of capital invested in the Witwatersrand gold industry. In later investigations of the same problem by Lehfeldt and Frankel (1923, 1935, 1967), the internal rate of return criterion was used. It is interesting to note that the use of these criteria was influenced by the fact that conventional accounting rates of return are difficult to calculate for companies which do not provide for depreciation on wasting assets.[33]

[31] Fisher, *The Theory of Interest*, pp. 168–9. Keynes' error was first pointed out by A. A. Alchian in "The Rate of Interest, Fisher's Rate of Return over Cost and Keynes' Internal Rate of Return," *American Economic Review* (December, 1955), reprinted in E. Solomon (ed.), *The Management of Corporate Capital* (New York: Free Press of Glencoe, 1959).

[32] P. A. Samuelson, "Some Aspects of the Pure Theory of Capital," *Quarterly Journal of Economics*, Vol. 51 (May, 1937), reprinted in J. E. Strighitz (ed.), *The Collected Papers of Paul A. Samuelson* (Cambridge, Mass.: M.I.T. Press, 1966), Vol. 1.

[33] See R. A. Lehfeldt, "Return to Capital Invested in the Witwatersrand," *Journal of the Chemical, Metallurgical and Mining Society of South Africa* (January, 1923);

There are very few references to making investment decisions in the accounting literature of the 1930's. The net present value method, however, was clearly described by the economist R. H. Coase in a series of articles in *The Accountant* in 1938.[34] His articles appear to have had very little impact on accounting theory and even less on accounting practice, although after being reprinted in 1952 they were quite widely used in university accounting courses.

On the actual practice of investment in the late 1930's, there is some evidence from surveys carried out at Oxford and Harvard about the effect of changes in rates of interest on the decisions of savers and borrowers. Sir Hubert Henderson of the Oxford Economists' Research Group reported in 1938 that frequently in response to the Group's question "the methods of calculation actually employed in weighing projects of capital expenditure were precisely explained; and these were such as to disregard altogether variations in interest rates." In a survey based on cases collected by the Harvard Business School, J. F. Ebersole reported that there was a strong presumption that the interest rate was seldom considered as a factor in the entrepreneurial decisions of business to expand or contract, and that it was a controlling factor in a negligible number of instances.[35] As late as 1950, Gort reported that discounting methods were not used in the U.S. electric power industry.[36]

Discounted Cash Flow in the 1950's and 1960's

It was not until the 1950's that interest in discounted cash flow methods began to quicken. Theoretical contributions of note were made by F. and V. Lutz, J. Hirshleifer, J. H. Lorie and L. J. Savage, F. Modigliani and M. H.

S. H. Frankel, "Return to Capital Invested in the Witwatersrand Gold-Mining Industry, 1887–1932," *Economic Journal* (March, 1935), *Capital Investment in Africa* (Oxford University Press, 1938), and *Investment and the Return to Equity Capital in the South African Gold-Mining Industry 1887–1965* (Oxford: Basil Blackwell, 1967).

I am indebted to Professor L. H. Samuels of the University of Witwatersrand for these references.

[34] R. H. Coase, "Business Organisation and the Accountant," *Accountant* (October 1–December 17, 1938), reprinted in D. Solomons (ed.), *Studies in Costing* (London: Sweet & Maxwell, 1952).

[35] H. D. Henderson, "The Significance of the Rate of Interest," *Oxford Economic Papers*, 1 (1938), 8–9, reprinted in T. Wilson and P. W. S. Andrews (eds.), *Oxford Studies in the Price Mechanism* (Oxford: Clarendon Press, 1951), p. 24; J. F. Ebersole, "The Influence of Interest Rates upon Entrepreneurial Decisions in Business—A Case Study," *Harvard Business Review*, Vol. 17, No. 1 (1938). See also Ruth P. Mack, *The Flow of Business Funds and Consumer Purchasing Power* (New York: Columbia University Press, 1941), Ch. 8, especially pp. 265–7. For a summary of these and other empirical findings on the influence of interest rates, see J. R. Meyer and E. Kuh, *The Investment Decision* (Cambridge, Mass.: Harvard University Press, 1957), pp. 25–6.

[36] M. Gort, "The Planning of Investment: A Study of Capital Budgeting in the Electric-Power Industry," *Journal of Business*, XXIV (July, 1951), p. 194.

Miller, and Ezra Solomon,[37] the last named editing, in 1959, a collection of important articles on the subject.[38] The internal rate of return rule was popularized by Joel Dean.[39]

There is some evidence of a growing practical application of discounted cash flow methods in the United States in the late 1950's. Eisner's study, *Determinants of Capital Expenditures* (1956), tells us something of the first half of the decade:

> Consideration of the various formal costs and earnings criteria reportedly used by business firms in deciding upon capital expenditures led into something of a wilderness where method was difficult to find. Rules of thumb appeared unduly crude and frequently internally inconsistent. Under probing questioning responsible officials indicated ignorance as to the specific nature of the calculations underlying their rules or they advised sagely that "judgment" was more important than rules.

Payback period and rates of return based on financial accounting procedures were used by many firms. Eisner found the handling of depreciation charges "downright offensive to one nurtured in the concepts of the marginal efficiency of investment."[40] In his book *Capital Expenditure Decisions: How They Are Made in Large Corporations* (1961), Istvan reported that of the 48 firms studied by him in the second half of the decade, five used some form of discounted cash flow criterion as a primary measure and nine used it in a supplementary manner. The accounting rate of return and payback were still the most popular methods.[41]

Discounted cash flow methods appear to have been used less extensively in the United Kingdom before the 1960's. In the early '60's, the surveys by Hart and Prussman, by Lawson, by Neild for the National Institute of Economic and Social Research, and by Williams and Scott for the Centre

[37] F. and V. Lutz, *The Theory of Investment of the Firm* (Princeton University Press, 1951); J. Hirshleifer, "On the Theory of Optimal Investment Decision," *Journal of Political Economy* (August, 1958); J. H. Lorie and L. J. Savage, "Three Problems in Rationing Capital," *Journal of Business*, XXVIII (October, 1955); F. Modigliani and M. H. Miller, "The Cost of Capital, Corporation Finance, and the Theory of Investment," *American Economic Review* (June, 1958); E. Solomon, "The Arithmetic of Capital-Budgeting Decisions," *Journal of Business*, XXIX (April, 1956).

[38] E. Solomon (ed.), *The Management of Corporate Capital* (Illinois: Free Press of Glencoe, 1959).

[39] J. Dean, "*Measuring the Productivity of Capital*," *Harvard Business Review* (January-February, 1954). See also his books *Capital Budgeting* (New York: Columbia University Press, 1951) and *Managerial Economics* (Englewood Cliffs; N.J.: Prentice Hall, 1951), Ch. 10.

[40] R. Eisner, *Determinants of Capital Expenditures* (Urbana, Illinois: Bureau of Economic and Business Research, University of Illinois, 1956), pp. 29–30. See also M. D. Brockie and A. L. Grey, Jr., "The Marginal Efficiency of Capital and Investment Programming," *Economic Journal*, 66 (December, 1956), pp. 662–75.

[41] D. F. Istvan, *Capital-Expenditure Decisions: How They Are Made in Large Corporations* (Bureau of Business Research, Graduate School of Business, Indiana University, 1961), p. 96.

for Business Research of the University of Manchester showed that D.C.F. was used by only a small minority of firms.[42] However, a number of large organizations, such as the Central Electricity Generating Board and Courtaulds, have adopted some form of D.C.F. criterion.[43] The recent writings of Alfred and Evans of Courtaulds and of Merrett and Sykes[44] have been very influential in spreading the use of D.C.F. techniques in the United Kingdom. The National Economic Development Council has also encouraged a wider use of discounted methods.[45]

Why has it taken so long for the application of discounted cash flow criteria to nonfinancial investments to gain acceptance in practice? The essential clue is surely to be found in the one group so conspicuously absent from our story: accountants. It is true that Pacioli in the 15th century, Stevin in the 16th century, and Dodson in the 18th century wrote on compound interest and actuarial problems as well as on accounting, but the accounting profession as it developed in the 19th century concerned itself much more with historical recording than with decision-making. Nevertheless, it was accountants in their role as financial experts who were in most cases consulted on capital expenditure decisions. Since their education did not include much economic theory, they naturally turned either to rates of return based on the traditional financial statements or to such simple and conservative techniques as the payback period. The relatively few economists who took an interest in accounting and who made recommendations based on economic theory were ignored. Such was the fate of R. H. Coase's excellent series of articles in *The Accountant* in 1938.[46]

It was not until the 1950's that economists began to play an important part as advisers in business. In the same decade accountants became more acquainted with economic ideas. In this new climate—whose coming in the

---

[42] H. Hart and D. F. Prussman, *A Report of a Survey of Management Accounting Techniques in the S.E. Hants Coastal Region* (Dept. of Commerce and Accountancy, University of Southampton, December, 1963) (mimeographed), p. 12; G. H. Lawson, "Criteria to Be Observed in Judging a Capital Project," *Accountants' Journal* (U.K.) (May, 1964), pp. 222–6, and (June, 1964), pp. 267–78; R. R. Neild, "Replacement Policy," *National Institute Economic Review* (November, 1964); B. R. Williams and W. P. Scott, *Investment Proposals and Decisions* (London: Allen & Unwin, 1965). See also D. C. Corner and A. Williams, "The Sensitivity of Business to Initial and Investment Allowances," *Economica*, 32 (February, 1965), p. 36, Table 1.

[43] F. H. S. Brown and R. S. Edwards, "The Replacement of Obsolescent Plant," *Economica* (August, 1961), pp. 297–302; A. M. Alfred, *Discounted Cash Flow and Corporate Planning* (Woolwich Economic Paper No. 3, 1964); A. M. Alfred and J. B. Evans, *Appraisal of Investment Projects by Discounted Cash Flow* (London: Chapman & Hall, 1st ed., 1965, 2d ed., 1967); A. M. Alfred, "Decision Taken," *Management Decision* (Summer, 1967), pp. 43–6.

[44] A. J. Merrett and A. Sykes, *The Finance and Analysis of Capital Projects* (London: Longmans, 1963) and *Capital Budgeting and Company Finance* (London: Longmans, 1966).

[45] National Economic Development Council, *Investment Appraisal* (London: H.M.S.O., 1st ed., 1965, 2d ed., 1967).

[46] See footnote 34 above.

U.K. was perhaps a decade later than in the U.S.A.—the practical use of discounted cash flow criteria became not only possible but, we may say with the advantage of hindsight, inevitable.

Summary

Discounted cash flow has its roots in compound interest, actuarial science, engineering economy, and capital theory. The net present value approach was applied to financial investments by Simon Stevin of Bruges as early as 1582. Bond tables incorporating the equivalent of the internal rate of return were in use by the second half of the 19th century by which time economists and engineers were beginning to discuss the application of discounting to nonfinancial investments. It was not until the 1950's, however, that interest in the use of D.C.F. techniques began to quicken and it is only in the 1960's that this use has become at all widespread. It is suggested that the bias towards historical recording in the education and training of accountants may have been partly responsible for this long delay.

13

History of Accounting for Decisions

R H PARKER

Professor of Accountancy,
University of Exeter

Introduction

In 1617 the Berkshire farmer Robert Loder wrote in his account book:

> It were my best course to sow halfe my lande with wheat for in this year if I had done so I judge I had gotton . . . xviij d or ther aboutes; besides I judge that for the carying of my wheat to Marquet I may reckon it to stand me in but little more then my manes labour that goeth with my horses and in selling it, because my charge in keping my horses is never the more or less (so long as I keep vj horses and a Teame) for they would be els idle in the stable: and the beannes or pese which they bring home at many times is more worth than my manes labour comes to, and sometimes lesse and sometimes nothing perhaps.

Nearly two centuries later in 1805–7, in the course of an *ex ante* comparison of the cost of coal gas as against candles to light the cotton mill of Phillips and Lee in Manchester, it was noted that:

> The cost of attendance upon candles would be as much, if not more, than upon the gas apparatus; so that in forming the comparison, nothing need be stated upon that score on either side.

A charge of £550 was made for 'the interest of capital sunk, and wear and tear of apparatus'. Loder also had made a charge for 'the use of my stocke [i.e. capital] which lay as dead'.

These two examples suggest that intelligent businessmen at an early date were aware intuitively of the notions of avoidable cost and opportunity cost, and of the irrelevance of costs which are the same under all alternatives.

But the examples are taken from practice, not from textbooks. There is no trace of such ideas in the literature of the time. When they did appear, which was not until the last three decades of the nineteenth century, they were to be found not in books on cost accounting, but in books on political economy. Moreover, although the last three decades of the nineteenth century were marked not only by a costing renaissance but also by the development of neo-classical economics, the interaction between cost accountants and economists was slight. The authors of the leading textbooks on cost accounting and economics, Emile Garcke and John Manger Fells, whose work *Factory Accounts* first appeared in 1887, and Alfred Marshall, whose *Principles of Economics* was first published three years later in 1890, quoted each other, but not on matters of central importance; and they made no attempt to reconcile their opposing viewpoints.

Garcke and Fells' text, excellent in many ways though it was, made only a small contribution to accounting for decisions. In it, they argued that all manufacturing costs fluctuated with the cost of labour and the price of material, and should therefore be allocated to products, whereas 'establishment expenses' (by which they meant administrative and selling costs) were, in the aggregate, more or less constant, and should not be so allocated because that would 'have the effect of disproportionately reducing the cost of each, with every increase, and the reverse with every diminution of business'. Such views did, of course, show some appreciation of the important distinction between fixed and variable costs.

In general, economists were not interested in accounting, because they believed, as Edward Cannan of the London School of Economics expressed it in his presidential address to the British Association for the Advancement of Science in 1902, that the practical usefulness of economic theory was not in private business but in politics.

W.J. Ashley, Professor of Commerce at the University of Birmingham, was not at all typical when he urged in an article in *The Economic Journal* in 1908 the enlargement of economics to include 'business economics', which frankly took for its point of view the interest of the individual businessman or business concern. The problem of cost accounts, he argued, was not how to get certain figures, but what figures to try to get, and how to combine them. Cost accounting could not, therefore, be left entirely to accountants.

Economic Concepts

But it was indeed so left and it was Stanley Jevons, first of the English neo-classical economists, not Garcke and Fells or their colleagues, who in a famous passage pointed out the irrelevance of past costs:

> A great undertaking like the Great Western Railway, or the Thames Tunnel, may embody a vast amount of labour, but its value depends entirely upon the number of persons who find it useful. If no use could be found for the Great Eastern steam ship, its value would be nil, except for the utility of some of its materials. On the other hand, a successful undertaking, which happens to possess great utility, may have a value for a time, at least, far exceeding what has been spent upon it, as in the case of the Atlantic cable. The fact is, that *labour once spent has no influence on the future value of any article:* it is gone and lost for ever. In commerce, bygones are for ever bygones; and we are always starting clear at each moment, judging the values of things with a view to future utility. (*The Theory of Political Economy*, London: Macmillan 1871; italics in the original)

It is worth noting that Jevons wrote it was in *commerce* (not in *economics* as it is usually misquoted) that bygones were for ever bygones. His examples were topical and well-chosen. Brunel's *Great Eastern* (launched 1858) was a disastrous failure; the successful Atlantic cable was laid by the *Great Eastern* in 1866. Garcke and Fells preferred Marx's view that machinery is 'congealed labour'. They quote Jevons on industrial partnership, but not on the theory of value.

By the turn of the century, 'marginalism' had triumphed in economics. In England its most avid exponent was Wicksteed, who in an address to the British Association explained that what a man will give for anything rather than go without it is determined by a comparison of the difference which he conceives its possession will make to him, compared with the difference that anything that he gives for it, or could have had instead of it, will or would make. The skill of a business manager consists in expanding and contracting his expenditure on the several factors of production so as to bring their differential significances to himself into coincidence with their market prices.

Meanwhile, Austrian and American economists were recognising and defining the concept of opportunity cost. 'To say that any kind of production involves cost', wrote von Wieser in 1889, 'simply implies that the economic means of production, which could doubtless have been usefully employed in other directions, are either used up in it, or are suspended during it'. 'As soon as we look more closely upon our varied resources and the individual activities of economic life', wrote Green in 1894, 'we discover that many of our good opportunities are limited in number and extent, so that before devoting the opportunity to a particular activity it behooves us to consider from what other uses we are thus withholding it. Such consideration gives rise to the concept of opportunity cost'. 'If', wrote Davenport in the same year, 'the choice lies between the production or purchase of two commodities, the value of one is measured by the sacrifice of going without the other'.

Accounting Practice

Early cost accounting practice, as developed by accountants and engineers, did not at all follow the ideas of Jevons and Wicksteed. Instead, the dominant ideas were that, firstly, cost accounting was mainly a matter of *ex post* recording rather than *ex ante* planning and, secondly, that all costs – fixed as well as variable – should be allocated to the product. The emphasis was thus on past allocations rather than future alternatives.

Cost accountants in fact convinced themselves that what was needed was the 'actual' cost of a manufactured product and increasingly concerned themselves with building up figures of total cost by means of overhead allocation. This philosophy was well expressed by Alexander Hamilton Church (an English electrical engineer who settled in the United States around the turn of the century) in his book *The Proper Distribution of Establishment Changes,* (New York: Engineering Magazine Co. 1916) (the italics are his):

> A production centre is, of course, either a machine or a bench at which a hand craftsman works. Each of these is in the position of a little shop carrying on one little special industry, paying rent for the floor space occupied, interest for the capital involved, depreciation for the wear and tear, and so on, *quite independently of what may be paid by other production centres* in the same shop. Then, in addition to this, there will be a separate debit representing those items of incidence which can only be treated as an average all-round charge . . . whatever else is done, *every dollar of charges must be burdened into some item of work.*

The ideas of Hamilton Church became the established orthodoxy of cost accounting, although a few accountants stressed the importance of distinguishing between fixed and variable costs. Two Scottish chartered accountants to do so were John Mann and Harold Judd, whose names have survived in the name of a leading British accounting firm. Mann helped to develop the break-even chart. Judd gave in 1914 the example of the manager of a business who goes down to the Exchange one day and is offered a contract of 500 tons of iron at 100s per ton. Before going to the Exchange, he has been told by his accountant that the cost is running at 105s a ton. What the manager should do is to go back to his accountant and ask how the cost of 105s has been arrived at. The accountant may explain that direct materials and labour cost 80s and oncost (i.e. indirect costs) 25s. If the latter figure is dissected, it may show that 10s is fluctuating oncost and 15s fixed oncost. Now, asks Judd:

> If that man gets a price of 100s per ton, what is the result? He has covered his Direct Cost and his Fluctuating Oncost, and he has got 10s over to account of his 15s of Fixed Oncost. If the manager knew that much at the time he would have known that

> in taking the contract at 100s he was getting a contribution of 10s a ton towards reduction of Oncost that is inevitably running on whether he gets work or not. The 'contribution to Oncost' is thus in reality 10s per ton, and not 20s per ton as first appeared; that is, he can without loss book orders down to 90s per ton, but anything below that is at an actual loss. With such information before him the manager knows how near he can sail to the wind without making undue leeway. (Fixed and fluctuating oncost, *Accountant's Magazine*, March 1914)

Why was it Hamilton Church's ideas which practising cost accountants preferred? One cannot be absolutely certain, but three reasons may be suggested. Firstly, cost accountants, whether from an engineering or an accounting background, did not often read economic theory (Garcke and Fells appear to have read it more than most) and when they did, they, like Cannan, did not expect to find anything of direct application to their own work. Secondly, a background of financial accounting, with its emphasis on past averages, was not conducive to a realisation of the importance of expected future increments. G. Charter Harrison, an Anglo-American accountant-engineer suggested in his book *Cost Accounting to Aid Production* (New York: Engineering Magazine Co. 1921) that the reason for the development of cost accounting along historical lines by professional accountants was that most of the work undertaken by them concerned past records and the investigation of past transactions. Thirdly, most accountants and engineers retained the idea, modified by the neo-classical economists, that value depends on cost. Economists had heavily qualified Adam Smith's contention that, if it costs twice the labour to kill a beaver as it costs to kill a deer, then a beaver will be worth two deer.

Cost Accounting after the First World War

The First World War greatly increased the need for cost accounts and both the UK Institute of Cost and Works Accountants and the US National Association of Cost Accountants (as they were then called) were established in 1919.

But it was not until 1923 that an economist took a hard

look at cost accounting. J. Maurice Clark's *Studies in the Economics of Overhead Costs* (University of Chicago Press 1923) was a major contribution. Cost accounting, wrote Clark, was still in its formative stage, but it already had a voluminous literature and at least one of the characteristics of a science – that of being inscrutable to the uninitiated. There were, he saw, great opportunities for the development of arbitrary and fictitious notions of cost, through the 'necessity' of apportioning items somehow, even if there was no scientific basis on which to do it. He coined the phrase 'different costs for different purposes' and pointed out that:

> If cost accounting sets out, determined to discover what the cost of everything is and convinced in advance that there is one figure which can be found and which will furnish exactly the information which is desired for every possible purpose, it will necessarily fail, because there is no such figure. If it finds a figure which is right for some purposes it must necessarily be wrong for others. (p. 234)

Clark's book was largely ignored by practising cost accountants and the mainstream practice and literature of the inter-war period reflects his ideas hardly at all. There were a few accounting academics, however, who understood the relevant economic theory and discussed how it could be applied to cost accounts. In the USA, W.J. Vatter re-examined cost accounting from a managerial viewpoint, as he put it, and stressed that the central idea of the concept of cost was that of giving up, parting with, or sacrificing, some thing or value to acquire some thing or value, but – '*There is no one cost* which will fit all purposes any more than there is a single wheel which will fit watches, motor trucks, and railway trains.' After a series of examples illustrating the practical importance of information concerning total-cost behaviour, differential costs, imputed costs, replacement costs, sunk and out-of-pocket costs, and opportunity cost, he concluded that the useful cost accountant,

> must be able and willing to secure the kind of data which management may require for the many and varied purposes cost data may serve. He must determine how total costs behave at various levels of production for the product. He must be able to determine differential costs where the situation demands their use. He must

> know when to use imputed costs and replacement costs; he must understand the difference between sunk and out-of-pocket costs; and he must recognise the need for the use of such concepts in attacking special problems. The mere grinding out of figures according to a stereotyped plan is not cost accounting and should not be referred to as such.

The cost accountant is thus called upon not only to find costs, but to know what costs to use.

Similar ideas flourished in the UK at the London School of Economics. The London tradition in the theory of cost has been discussed by J.R. Gould. He concludes that the main contribution of the tradition to accounting for decisions was to direct attention away from the standard conventions of accounting practice and towards the choice between alternative business plans, and that it may have played an important role in 'releasing cost accounting from its historical shackles'. Brought together at the LSE in a way not then common elsewhere were economic theorists, academic accountants and administrative theorists. The line between accounting and applied economics was deliberately blurred by writers such as R.S. Edwards, R.H. Coase and W.T. Baxter.

The most important thing about costs, argued Edwards (who had practised as an accountant before turning to economics) in a paper on 'The Rationale of Cost Accounting' (1937), was the extent to which they changed with output. Most textbooks were still prone to emphasise that cost accounting analysed past costs, not future estimates, and did not make clear that data about the past were useful only in so far as they were a guide to future costs. It is, wrote Edwards,

> future variable cost which is important . . . cost accountants can ignore expenses which are completely unchangeable . . . depreciation and every other expense must be examined in order to establish the relationship between changes in cost and output variations.

Profitability should be tested by comparing increments to cost with increments to revenue, rather than by totals and averages. Accountants have spent too much effort in trying to arrive at total cost 'by building up complicated and delicate oncost structures which depend on arbitrary assumptions'. In tendering for orders, knowledge of market conditions was more important than estimates of total cost; methods of computing oncost varied so much that it would be dangerous to suppose that one's competitors had allowed roughly for the same oncost as oneself.

Edwards pursued the same theme in two other papers: 'Cost Accounting and Joint Production', which criticised the orthodox methods of allocating joint costs, and 'The Approach to Budgetary Control' (1938).

Ideas similar to those of Edwards were developed at greater length by his colleague R.H. Coase in a series of articles on 'Business Organisation and the Accountant' in *The Accountant* of 1938. Coase stressed that attention ought to be concentrated on the variations in costs or receipts which would result if a particular decision were taken; costs and receipts which would remain unchanged whatever decision were taken should be ignored.

He gave as an example a department store whose managers were discussing whether or not to close a particular department. A decision could not be reached, because there was no agreement on the allocation to be made for rent to the department. Coase pointed out that, since in this case the amount of rent to be paid would remain the same whether the department was closed or not, the question of rent allocation was irrelevant. All that was necessary was to discover what changes in costs and receipts would occur if the department were closed down, including those of any other departments affected.

This conclusion was attacked by Bigg (author of a student text on cost accounting first published in 1932), who was clearly thinking in terms of net profit per department and thought that Coase's methods were 'inequitable' to the other departments. Bigg's views are interesting because they show how a background of financial accounting and auditing can lead to ways of thought wholly unsuitable for management accounting. For purposes of external reporting, a reasonable case can be made for the use of total unit costs and obviously in auditing the ideas of fairness and equity are fundamental, but such ideas are just not relevant when the problem is to maximise the profits of the business as a whole. The relevant theory for this problem was in fact clearly stated by W.T. Baxter in an article ('A Note on the Allocation of Oncosts between Departments') in the same volume of *The Accountant*.

Baxter pointed out that the reasons for preparing departmental statements were (i) to find out whether each department was sufficiently profitable to justify its continuance, (ii) to find out whether the heads of the individual departments were avoiding unnecessary expense, and (iii) (in some cases) to find suitable selling prices for the individual articles in which the department dealt. There was no point in allocating any overhead expenses, which would remain undiminished even if a department were abandoned and over which departmental heads had no control. A manager should ask, not whether the sale price of an article exceeded its average 'cost' (which might vary enormously by altering the method of allocation), but whether the business was making more profit by selling that article at that price than it could by adopting any other policy.

It was not until the 1960s that a different-costs-for-different-purposes approach entered the textbooks. Probably the earliest were two American books still well-known to students: G. Shillinglaw's *Cost Accounting: Analysis and Control* (first published in 1961) and C.T. Horngren's *Cost Accounting: A Managerial Emphasis* (first published in 1962).

Investment Decisions

In order to evaluate an *investment* decision, it is necessary not only to forecast the relevant cash inflows (revenues) and outflows (costs), but also to allow for the time value of money. In other words, a discounted cash flow approach is required. This in turn requires both an understanding of compound interest and an ability to set out the cash inflows and outflows likely to result from a particular decision to invest.

Compound interest calculations are included in the writings of both Luca Pacioli (c. 1445–c. 1523) and Simon Stevin (1548–1620), two mathematicians well known to accounting historians for their contributions to the early literature of double entry bookkeeping. Stevin was also the second writer to publish interest tables (the first being Jean Trenchant in a book published at Lyons in 1558).

Setting out the cash implications of an investment is more difficult. It is not surprising that the earliest applications of discounted cash flow were to loans, where the cash outlays and receipts could be forecast with some certainty, and to life assurance, where probabilities could be calculated from historical evidence. The extension of discounted cash flow to investment in fixed assets came much later.

Stevin's book *Tables of Interest*, published in Antwerp in 1582, included 'a general rule for finding which is the most profitable of two or more conditions, and by how much it is more profitable than the other'. (Antwerp and Lyons were the two greatest financial centres of Western Europe in the sixteenth century.) Stevin's rule was the first exposition of what is now known as the 'net present value' criterion. He applied it, of course, only to financial investments.

Among the successors of Stevin were the actuarial scientists, who developed scientific life assurance in England in the eighteenth century. They included James Dodson FRS (c.1710–1757), 'Accountant and Teacher of the Mathematics', who not only, in his unpublished 'First Lecture on Insurances' (1756), made the first investigation into the principles of operation of a life assurance business and showed how premiums should be calculated, but also wrote in 1750 one of the very few early works on bookkeeping to deal with accounting for manufacturing operations.

It was not, however, until the nineteenth century that discounted cash flow criteria were applied to non-financial investments. This was probably the result, not only of the difficulties of forecasting the relevant cash flows, but also of the relatively small size of such investments. The coming of the railways changed this; their building entailed a massive capital outlay before any returns were received.

The problems of capital expenditure analysis were discussed at some length by railway economists and engineers. A.M. Wellington, for example, wrote as follows in his book *The Economic Theory of the Location of Railways* (2nd edn, 1887):

> The theory of the subject is simple: In Table 18 is given the present value or present justifiable expenditure to save $1 (or one unit of any other value) at the end of a given period at any given rate of interest; that is to say, the sum which, if placed at compound interest now, will produce $1 at the end of the specified period. This fact given, it logically follows, that if the value of a given betterment for a given immediate traffic be $1, the present value

of the same betterment for an equal traffic which is to exist only in the future will be that sum which at compound interest will produce $1 when the assumed traffic comes to exist...

All this is undeniably correct in theory . . . but the indications of Table 18 are of value only as fixing a maximum which should never be exceeded . . .
. . . while it may be taken as a practical certainty that the traffic of any ordinary railway not only will grow, but that it will grow at an average rate of something like 5 to 8 per cent per annum east of the Alleghenies, and 7 to 10 or 15 or even 20 per cent per year west of there, yet . . . the rate of this growth of traffic is excessively variable and uncertain – liable to cease altogether at any time for many years . . .

For this cause alone it is in general inexpedient to look forward more than at most five years for traffic to justify an increase of immediate expenditure . . .

It is interesting to note, not only Wellington's application of the net present value rule, but the way he copes with uncertainty by limiting the potential life of the project.

The political economists were also aware of the relevant concepts. The greatest contribution was made by the American economist Irving Fisher in his book *The Rate of Interest* (New York: Macmillan), first published in 1907 and extensively revised and reissued as *The Theory of Interest* (New York: Macmillan) in 1930. In these books, he sets out four ways of choosing between investment options and claims that they all give the same result. Out of all eligible options one should select:

(i) the one which has the maximum present value, reckoned at the market rate of interest (the principle of maximum present value);
(ii) the one whose advantages (returns) over any other outweigh, in present value, its disadvantages (costs), when both returns and costs are discounted at the market rate of interest (the principle of comparative advantage);
(iii) the one which, compared with any other option, yields a 'rate of return on sacrifice' or 'rate of return over cost' greater than the rate of interest (the principle of return over cost); or
(iv) where options differ by continuous gradations, the one

the difference of which from its nearest rival gives a rate of return over cost equal to the rate of interest (the *marginal* rate of return over cost).

In his *General Theory* (1936), Keynes confused Fisher's rate of return over cost with his own 'marginal efficiency of capital' or, as most accountants now term it, 'internal rate of return'. When discounted cash flow methods started to become familiar in the 1950s, it was Keynes's mis-interpretation which became best known.

The accounting literature of the 1930s contained very few references to making investment decisions. The net present value method was, however, clearly described by the LSE economist R.H. Coase in his series of articles in *The Accountant* in 1938, to which we have already referred. His articles appear to have had very little impact on accounting theory and even less on accounting practice.

The 1950s saw a lively discussion in the economic and financial literature of the problems of choosing among mutually exclusive investments, of the possibility of multiple rates of return and of capital rationing. In the 1960s DCF was popularised in many books and courses.

Why did it take so long for the application of DCF criteria to non-financial investments to gain acceptance? The blame should perhaps be laid at the door of accountants. It is true that Pacioli in the fifteenth century, Stevin in the sixteenth, and Dodson in the eighteenth, all wrote on compound interest and actuarial problems as well as on accounting; but the accounting profession as it developed in the nineteenth century concerned itself much more with historical recording than with decision making. Nevertheless, it was accountants in their role as financial experts who were in most cases consulted on capital expenditure decisions. Since their education did not include much economic theory, they naturally turned, either to rates of return based on the traditional financial statements, or to such simple and conservative techniques as the payback period. The relatively few economists who took an interest in accounting, and who made recommendations based on economic theory, were ignored. Such was the fate of R.H. Coase's excellent series of articles in *The Accountant* in 1938.

It was not until the 1950s that economists began to play an important part as advisers in business. In the same decade, accountants became more acquainted with economic ideas. In this new climate – whose coming in the United Kingdom was perhaps delayed a decade compared with the USA – the practical use of discounted cash flow criteria became not only possible but, we may say with the advantage of hindsight, inevitable.

Conclusions

It is clear that accountants cannot claim to be the originators of the relevant concepts for accounting for decisions. These concepts were first formulated by the neo-classical economists at the end of the nineteenth century. The impact of their ideas on accounting thought and practice was delayed for two reasons: the fact that they were not writing for, and consequently tended not to be read by, practising accountants; and also the historical bias which most accountants derived from the nature of their daily work.

Similarly, the contributions of Irving Fisher's *The Rate of Interest* (1907) and J.M. Clark's *Studies in the Economics of Overhead Costs* (1923) were not realised until long after their dates of publication.

It was only in the 1960s that it could be claimed with any justification that incremental and related concepts of cost, and the concept of discounting cash flows, had become a generally accepted part of the theory and practice of accounting for decisions.

References and Guide to Further Reading

This chapter has concentrated on only one aspect of the history of management accounting. A wider view is taken by D. Solomons in his chapter, The historical development of costing, in his book of readings, *Studies in Cost Analysis*, 2nd edn, Sweet and Maxwell 1968. Closer to the present chapter are, R.H. Parker, *Management Accounting: an Historical Perspective*, Part One, Macmillan 1969, and M.C. Wells, *Accounting for Common Costs*, Center for International Education and Research in Accounting, Urbana, Illinois, 1978.

The quotation of 1617 comes from G.E. Fussell (ed.), *Robert Loder's Farm Accounts 1610–1620*, Camden 3rd Series, vol. LIII, Royal Historical Society, London, 1936, pp. 137–8. The Phillips and Lee example is taken from, T.S. Peckston, *A Practical Treatise on Gas-Lighting*, 3rd edn, Hebert, London, 1841, pp. 99–100.

The first edition of E. Garcke and J.M. Fells, *Factory Accounts* was published in London by Crosby Lockwood and Son in 1887. The fourth edition of 1898 was reprinted by Arno Press, New York, in 1976. The reference to establishment expenses is on p. 73 of this edition. Jevons is quoted on p. 145 of the same edition and p. 197 of the sixth (1911). The reference to Marx is in the sixth edition (p. 93n), but not the fourth.

The addresses by Cannan and Wicksteed to the British Association are reprinted in R.L. Smyth (ed), *Essays in Economic Method*, Duckworth 1962.

The quotation from F. van Wieser is on p. 168 of his *Natural Value*, Macmillan, London, 1893. The German original was published in Vienna in 1889. D.I. Green's definition of opportunity cost is from his article, Pain-cost and opportunity-cost, *Quarterly Journal of Economics*, vol. 8, 1893–4. The quotation from H.J. Davenport is from his article, The formula of sacrifice, *Journal of Political Economy*, vol. 2, 1893–4.

Mann's contribution to the development of the break-even chart can be found in, Oncost or expenses, in G. Lisle (ed.), *Encyclopaedia of Accounting*, vol. 5, William Green and Sons, Edinburgh, 1903–07.

The quotations from Vatter are taken from Chapter 29 of the first and second editions of J.J.W. Neuner, *Cost Accounting: Principles and Practice*, 1939, 1942.

Gould's paper, Opportunity cost: the London tradition, is in H. Edey and B.S. Yamey (eds), *Debits, Credits, Finance and Profits*, Sweet and Maxwell 1974. The articles by Edwards, Coase and Baxter are most easily to be found in D. Solomons, *Studies in Costing*, Sweet and Maxwell 1952. Bigg's comments were published in *The Accountant*, vol. 99, 1938, pp. 539 and 795.

Stevin's book *Tafalen van Interest* (Tables of Interest) is reprinted with an English translation in D.J. Struik (ed.), *The Principal Works of Simon Stevin*, vol. IIA, Mathematics, C.V. Swets & Zeitlinger, Amsterdam, 1958. The career of Dodson is discussed in M.E. Ogborn, *Equitable Assurances*, Allen & Unwin 1962.

Sufficient reference to other works cited is given in the body of the text.

THE WANT OF UNIFORMITY IN ACCOUNTS: A NINETEENTH CENTURY DEBATE

R.H. Parker

Among the many contributions to the accounting literature for which Trevor Johnston is likely to be remembered, pride of place must be given to *The Law and Practice of Company Accounting in New Zealand* [Johnston, Edgar and Hays, 1978] and *The Law and Practice of Company Accounting in Australia* [Johnston, Jager and Taylor, 1979].

Australasian company accounting has its origins in Britain. The entry of the UK into the EEC, however, and the latter's programme of company law harmonization will inevitably mean an increasing divergence between British and New Zealand and Australian company law. In particular, the EEC Fourth Directive, adopted in 1978 and to be embodied in British legislation in the early 1980s [Department of Trade, 1979], introduces prescribed formats for the balance sheet and the profit and loss account, based upon continental European practice, which are unlikely to be copied in Australasia.

Such formats are, however, by no means unknown in the history of British and Australasian company law. Trevor Johnston wrote on this subject as follows:

> The first draft of the United Kingdom Joint Stock Companies Bill of 1856, in keeping with Robert Lowe's submissions that the greatest publicity should be given to the affairs of companies, included clauses providing for filing with the Registrar and the annual presentation to members of an income and expenditure account and a balance sheet. The balance sheet was to have been in the prescribed form (set out in a schedule to the Bill) . . . and Lowe when introducing the Bill in the House of Commons made a feature of the ''uniform sheet'':
>
>> One thing, indeed, will be required . . . namely, that a balance sheet which shall contain certain items, shall be filed every year with the

> Registrar of Companies; . . . and as we prescribe a form, we shall at least succeed in obtaining a uniform sheet so that the shareholders will be able to compare the accounts of succeeding years and to gather information from them, which, from the practice too extensively prevailing of rendering a differently framed balance-sheet every year, they are now unable to collect: *Hansard* (UK) (1856) 140 p.134.

But in the second and subsequent drafts and in the Act itself (and in all Companies Acts which followed in other parts of the Commonwealth), the requirement relating to filing was omitted and the clauses relating to the presentation and form of the balance sheet were relegated to the optional set of articles in Table B; and in the optional set of articles they remained until 1896 in Victoria, 1928 in the United Kingdom and 1936 in New South Wales. There is no mention in the parliamentary debates of the removal of this particular clause; but there is constant mention of the deletion of certain "interferences" and "fetters" from the first draft. [Johnston, Jager and Taylor, 1979, pp.7, 10].

It may be added that, when the present writer arrived from the UK at the University of Adelaide in 1960, the South Australia *Companies Act* [South Australia 1934-1952] still contained a model balance sheet and it remained there until the Uniform Act of 1961.

The purpose of this paper is to review the 19th century British debate on the "want of uniformity in accounts" and prescribed formats. In Britain at least the subject has become of topical interest again.

The Context of the Debate

The September 1979 Green Paper on *Company Accounting and Disclosure* [Department of Trade, 1979, p.5] points out that the EEC Fourth Directive distinguishes, in the case of both medium and small companies, between accounts which are *drawn up* by a company and which must be circulated to shareholders and the information to be included in the accounts which are to be *published*. It claims that this distinction is new to the UK.

It is one, however, which would have been recognisable to participants in the nineteenth century debate on uniformity which was part of a large debate on company accounting generally. The participants were sometimes rather confused in their exposition but in essence four separate though linked questions were debated, viz:

(i) Should directors of companies be compelled by law to draw up accounts?

(ii) If so, should they be sent to shareholders only, or should they be made available to the general public as well?

(iii) Should a distinction be made between different types of companies?

(iv) If directors were to be compelled to draw up accounts for shareholders or to publish them generally, should the accounts have to be drawn up in a uniform manner?

Our concern in this paper is with the fourth question but, as we shall see, the answers reached depended to some extent upon the other three.

It is important to note that the debate was *not* explicitly about valuation and measurement problems or accounting standards in the present sense of the phrase.

The Beginning of the Debate: Railways Companies (1849)

Uniformity was first discussed, not in relation to companies generally, but in relation to railway companies, most of which were incorporated by private Acts of Parliament. The *Companies Clauses Consolidation Act* of 1845 provided (and, indeed, still provides) model clauses for the regulation of such companies. Audited balance sheets were to be presented to the ordinary meetings of shareholders, but their form and content were not specified.

As a result of the "railway mania" of the 1840s, a Select Committee of the House of Lords on Audit of Railway Accounts was established. In its Third Report (1849) the Committee explained as follows why the Legislature was justified in interfering in the affairs of railway companies [BPP, 1849]:

> It would be difficult to name any other branch of commercial enterprise with which a greater amount of public and private interest is now identified. It would, therefore, be an error to consider the British Railways as speculations important to the Shareholders only. They involve public interest, political and social, of the greatest magnitude. Nor have these great Companies been created by the unassisted efforts of individuals; on the contrary, they owe their origin to the will of the Legislature, as expressed in the several Acts of Incorporation. Their existence has depended upon the Legislature; and to that Legislature, therefore, they must be held in a peculiar degree responsible. They have been intrusted with principles and powers almost without precedent; and it behoves Parliament, from time to time, to consider how these powers have been exercised, and whether the Laws passed for regulating Railways may not require amendment.

The Select Committee reported, in a section entitled "Want of uniformity of Account", that almost all the witnesses they had examined agreed that the want of any prescribed and uniform system of account was a most serious omission in the law[1]. The Committee went on to explain that:

> Each Company is left, at its own will and pleasure, to adopt the form considered by them to be the most convenient, and to vary that form from time to time . . . The result is, that no adequate means are afforded by which to compare the financial affairs of any two Railways, or even to compare the Accounts of the same Railway from time to time; the form of the Balance-sheet submitted by one Railway to its Shareholders and Auditors has been found to vary in the very same year . . .

Such want of uniformity was, they argued, against the interest of investors, managers, shareholders, auditors and the public generally:

> It deprives capitalists, seeking investments, of all power of ascertaining the relative credit of the several Companies from a comparison of their Accounts. It deprives one Company of the means of profiting by the experience of another, by tracing in their Accounts the consequences of good and bad management. It leaves Shareholders without any check upon the governing body. It casts upon the public the necessity of learning a separate lesson every time the Balance-sheet of a different Company is taken up . . . It cannot fail, likewise, to render the examination of the Auditors more difficult, perplexing and uncertain.

The remedy was:

> a uniformity of Account prescribed by Law, on a specified model, so as to admit of easy comparison, and distinguishing the Cost of Formation, the Amount of Working Expenses, and the other great heads of disbursement . . .

Such a uniformity of account would instruct the public and guard the interests of the railways. It would make the accounts of more use to a potential purchaser wishing to determine the value of shares in any railway company.

The Committee went on to consider some possible objections to uniformity:

1. The accountant William Quilter, for example, stated that it was "necessary to the proper understanding of the relative merits of different Railways that there should be a uniform system" (Q.2228).

The Want of Uniformity

> Mr Russell (Chairman of the Great Western) suggests . . ., that the attainment of entire uniformity of Account would be difficult, and that some divergence from uniformity would go far to arrest improvements of which the system of Accounts may hereafter be susceptible. Giving full weight to this Evidence, it only leads to the inference that the uniform system of Accounts described may require modification hereafter, and that a certain discretionary power of variation should be allowed, to a competent authority, in peculiar and exceptional cases. In this opinion the Committee agree; it does not militate against a general rule of uniformity; and the great majority of the Witnesses examined agree in considering a uniform system of Account to be indispensable.
>
> Neither does it appear, according to the judgment of persons of the greatest experience, that there would be much difficulty in providing or enforcing such a uniform system . . .
>
> Conclusive as appear these reasons for prescribing and enforcing by Law a strict adherence to one regulated form of Account, this principle becomes still more important, when considered in relation to the primary object of preventing abuse, guarding against misapplication of funds, and giving certain means of detection where any irregularities have occurred.

The Committee recommended a form of account which was not only uniform but more detailed and more explanatory.

The Committee made out a strong case but its proposals did not bear fruit for almost another twenty years. They may well have influenced Robert Lowe, however.

Optional Uniformity

The *Joint Stock Companies Acts* of 1844 and 1855 included compulsory accounting and audit requirements but made no reference to uniformity. The 1856 Act abandoned the compulsory accounting and audit requirements, but included in a model set of articles of association (called Table A from the *Companies Act* 1862 onwards) optional accounting and auditing clauses considerably more advanced than those of 1844. Included also was the model balance sheet reproduced below. No model profit and loss account was included.

A number of points are worth noting:

(i) The "capital and liabilities" are on the left hand (debit) side; the "property and assets" on the right hand (credit) side.

(ii) Details have to be given of the amount paid per share, arrears of calls (including the names of defaulters!) and forfeited shares (these matters, which survived for so long into twentieth century textbooks, were of much greater practical importance in the nineteenth).

FORM of BALANCE SHEET referred to in TABLE B.
BALANCE SHEET of the Co. made up to , 18
Dr.

CAPITAL AND LIABILITIES.

		£ s. d.	£ s. d.
I. Capital	*Showing:* 1. *The total Amount received from the Shareholders; showing also:* *(a) The number of Shares* *(b) The Amount paid per Share* *(c) If any Arrears of Calls, the Nature of the Arrear, and the Names of the Defaulters.* *Any Arrears due from any Director or Officer of the Company to be separately stated.* *(d) The Particulars of any forfeited Shares.*		
II. Debts and Liabilities of the Company	*Showing:* 2. *The Amount of Loans on Mortgage or Debenture Bonds.* 3. *The Amount of Debts owing by the Company, distinguishing –* *(a) Debts for which Acceptances have been given.* *(b) Debts to Tradesmen for Supplies of Stock in Trade or other Articles.* *(c) Debts for Law Expenses.* *(d) Debts for Interest on Debentures or other Loans.* *(e) Unclaimed Dividends.* *(f) Debts not enumerated above.*		
VI. Reserve Fund	*Showing:* *The amount set aside from Profits to meet Contingencies.*		
VII. Profit and Loss	*Showing:* *The disposable Balance for Payment of Dividend, etc.*		
Contingent Liabilities	*Claims against the Company not acknowledged as Debts.* *Monies for which the Company is contingently liable.*		

206

Cr.

PROPERTY AND ASSETS.

		£ s. d.	£ s. d.
III. Property held by the Company	*Showing:* 4. *Immovable Property, distinguishing* *(a) Freehold Land* *(b) Freehold Buildings* *(c) Leasehold Buildings* 5. *Movable Property, distinguishing* *(d) Stock in Trade* *(e) Plant* *The Cost to be stated with Deductions for Deterioration in Value as charged to the Reserve Fund or Profit and Loss*		
IV. Debts owing to the Company	*Showing:* 6. *Debts considered good for which the Company hold Bills or other Securities.* 7. *Debts considered good for which the Company hold no Security.* 8. *Debts considered doubtful and bad* *Any Debt due from a Director or other Officer of the Company to be separately stated.*		
V. Cash and Investments	*Showing:* 9. *The Nature of Investment and Rate of Interest.* 10. *The Amount of Cash, where lodged, and if bearing Interest.*		

207

(iii) The debts owing by or owed to the company had to be analysed in some detail, with disclosure of doubtful and bad debts.
(iv) The reserve fund (the modern distinction between a reserve fund and a reserve did not then exist) and balance on the profit and loss account are shown at the foot of the balance sheet instead of being grouped with the share capital.
(v) The "property" (i.e. the non-monetary assets) is divided into immoveable property (freehold land, freehold buildings, leasehold buildings) and moveable property, the latter being subdivided into stock in trade and plant.
(vi) Property is to be shown at cost with deductions for deterioration in value.

Apart from the reversal of the sides, the model balance sheet bears more resemblance to modern French balance sheets than to modern British balance sheets.

But did companies actually prepare balance sheets in this form? There is conflicting evidence on this point. Edwards[1980, p.ix] believes that it is likely that most companies adopted Table A so that the legal abrogation of responsibility for company accounts was more apparent than real. William Turquand appears to indicate as much in his evidence (at Q.476) to the 1877 Committee [BPP, 1877]. David Chadwick, however, stated in evidence to the same Committee that he supposed that not 1 per cent of companies had adopted Schedule A (which contained the prescribed balance sheet), with the consequence that the form of account stated in the Act of 1862 was valueless for all practical purposes (Q.1947).

The Role of David Chadwick[2]

Chadwick was, in fact, the most enthusiastic champion of uniformity of account.

David Chadwick (1821-1895) was the son of John Chadwick, an accountant. Born in Macclesfield in 1821, the youngest of a family of nine, he was appointed borough treasurer of Salford in 1844 at the early age of 23, retaining the post for 16 years. He commenced practice as an accountant in Manchester in 1860, specialising in com-

2. *The Accountant's* obituary of Chadwick is reproduced in Parker [1980]. A full obituary was also published in the *Minutes of Proceedings of the Institution of Civil Engineers*, vol. 123, 1896, pp.448-451. See Cottrell [1980], especially pp.113-4.
I am indebted for information about Chadwick to the Principal Librarian of the Libraries and Museum Department, Cheshire County Council.

pany promotion. A London office was opened in 1865. He was responsible for the promotion as limited companies of many important enterprises [Cottrell, 1980, pp.113-4]. A Liberal in politics, he was a Member of Parliament for Macclesfield from 1868 to 1880. He was an Associate of the Institute of Civil Engineers, first president of the Manchester Institute of Accountants (formed in 1871 and absorbed into the Institute of Chartered Accountants in England and Wales, 1880) and a member of the first Council of the English Institute. His "Instructions for Audit" are reproduced in Dicksee's *Auditing* [1892, pp.3-5].

Chadwick had little early formal education and in later life took an active interest in further education and libraries. He presented a public library to Macclesfield in 1876 along with 10,000 books. He was president of the Manchester Statistical Society 1865-67 and the author in the 1850s of a series of pamphlets on the physical and social conditions of towns and their inhabitants. It was largely as a result of his advocacy that Manchester acquired the services of a Medical Officer of Health in 1868 [Ashton, 1934, pp. 55-6]. He was for a period an active campaigner for the reform of company law [Cottrell, 1980, ch.3] and in 1871, whilst Lowe was Chancellor of the Exchequer, moved for the appointment of a Select Committee on income and property tax. He died at Herne Hill in south London in 1895.

In 1867 Chadwick gave evidence to a Select Committee on Limited Liability Acts [BPP, 1867]. The Committee paid little attention to accounting matters. Chadwick stated:

> I think that in any alteration of the law, Joint Stock Companies under limited liability, ought to be compelled to make some near approach to that form of balance sheet which is included under Schedule A, in the Act; and that in fact, when a company does not choose to adopt the clauses of the Schedule A, which were intended to save them trouble and expense they should be required by the Registrar to make as near an approach to these regulations and to that form of account as possible . . .

He handed in to the Committee a proposed bill but it made no mention of accounts, nor did the Committee in its Report. The draft bill submitted to Parliament (which dealt with railway companies as well as limited companies registered under the 1862 Act) did contain Chadwick's suggestion, but the 1867 Act as passed contained no accounting provisions [Hein, 1978, pp. 193, 196].

Railways Again : the Legislation of 1868

Others, however, were concerning themselves with the narrower issue of railway accounts. In 1867 Sir William Hutt (a shareholder in the New Zealand Company whose name is commemorated in the Hutt Valley) introduced a Railway and Joint Stock Companies' Account Bill in the House of Commons. He gave it as his opinion that:

> Railway companies uniformly produced what they called a balance-sheet, but it was frequently such as no merchants or bankers would be satisfied with. With respect to companies formed under the Limited Liability Act the greater part of them were not in the habit of producing any balance-sheets at all, but were content with a report, whose chief purpose was that of mystifying their proprietors and the public. (*Hansard*, v.187, col. 1588).

In the debate on the second reading (April 29, 1868) Hutt stated that there were two important objects which would be gained by making it compulsory on companies to make out their accounts in a prescribed form:

> . . . there would be no dressing them up in order to make things pleasant, or to suit the interests of the company itself . . . there would be no payment out of borrowed money, and no money could be paid without passing through the books of the company . . . by compelling all companies to adopt the same form of accounts, the public and the shareholders would derive great advantage from being able to form some estimate of the respective value of the shares of the companies (*Hansard*, v.191, col. 1538).

In the same debate, Mr Stephen Cave, the vice-president of the Board of Trade, drew a "difference in principle between railway companies and ordinary limited companies":

> Very few of the latter had compulsory powers granted them by Parliament — a characteristic which alone would warrant Parliamentary interference in the internal concerns of railway companies. (*Hansard*, v.191, col. 1539).

He went on to argue that:

> There were many thousands of limited companies in the country, and the form of accounts suitable to one description of company would be quite unsuitable to another, so that it would be next to impossible to prescribe a form that would apply to all. (col. 1539).

Furthermore:

> . . . the business of the legislature was to give every facility to shareholders for protecting themselves, and not to bring about a state of things in which shareholders whenever they met with difficulty would go crying to the Government for assistance . . . it was quite impossible to control directors by Act of Parliament . . . if they were determined to cook the accounts, as it was called, they would do so. (col. 1540).

Meanwhile, on March 20, 1868 a Regulation of Railways Bill had been read a second time in the House of Lords. The Duke of Richmond, president of the Board of Trade, stated that it was proposed to insert in a Schedule a form of accounts which would be compulsory:

> He had not, however, as yet decided what the precise form should be, and he was in communication upon the subject with some most eminent accountants, who were specially connected with railway matters, in order that he might obtain, if possible, a system which would be approved by railway auditors, and which would at the same time secure the object which he had in view. He wished to establish such a form of accounts that any person looking at them could see at a glance what was the exact financial position of each company. At present one company had one form of account; a second another, and a third a form different from them both, so that it was impossible to compare the accounts of the various companies, as it was desirable to do, and as he hoped they would be enabled to do. (*Hansard*, v. 190, col. 1957).

In the short debate which followed Lord Redesdale stated that:

> It was exceedingly desirable to have one form of accounts; for all accounts were very difficult to be understood by persons not well acquainted with such matters. How could the position of railway companies be estimated when one company produced their accounts in one form and another in another? (*Hansard*, v.190, cols. 1961/2).

and Lord Westbury thought there was much truth in the allegations that railway companies "shuffled their charges, sometimes entering them to the capital account and sometimes to the revenue account; so that it was impossible to ascertain what was their actual expenditure, and still more impossible to say whether that expenditure was justified or not" (*Hansard*, v. 190, col. 1971).

The Railway and Joint Stock Companies Accounts Bill was withdrawn on June 24; the Regulation of Railways Bill received the royal assent on July 31, 1868.

Other "Public Companies"

After the 1868 legislation it appeared to be generally agreed that companies in which the public had a legitimate interest should publish their accounts not only to shareholders but also to the general public and that those accounts should be drawn up in a uniform manner. Other companies were still not compelled to publish accounts at all, even to their shareholders, unless so required by their articles of association.

Over the next few years, uniformity of account was extended to life assurance companies (1870) and gas companies (1871). The relevant sections of the Acts were reproduced in the pioneering audit text books of Pixley [1881] and Dicksee [1892].

The philosophy and practice was summed up by Cave in the debate on the second reading on the Life Assurance Companies Bill (February 23, 1870):

> I am one of those who have always been opposed to Government interference with private enterprise . . . I have always thought that perfect freedom and perfect publicity ought to be the motto of a legislator in such matters. I have endeavoured to carry out that principle in this Bill. It provides that assurance companies shall make simple uniform statements every year, according to the model form in the Schedule, which together with the actuarial report to be prepared at longer intervals will enable people to compare the position of one office with that of another, and to judge of the solvency of any particular company (*Hansard*, v. 199, col. 727).

He went on to state:

> I attach the greatest importance to uniformity of accounts. The Act of 1844, though not devoid of good results, was defective in two respects, it provided neither the form of the Returns, nor any means of enforcing compliance with its provisions (col. 729).

The Committee of 1877

Should those companies in which it might be argued the public did *not* have a legitimate interest also be compelled to publish their accounts and to do so in a uniform manner? These were questions which were to be debated before the 1877 Select Committee on the *Companies Acts* of 1862 and 1867 [BPP, 1877].

Chadwick (who, as we have seen, had been returned as a Liberal MP in 1868, too late to take part in the debates on the *Regulation of*

Railways Act) was both a member of, and a witness before, the Committee. Accounting matters were much more prominent than they had been ten years earlier. Those giving evidence included such leading accountants as William Turquand, Samuel Lowell Price and Robert Palmer Harding.

Chadwick introduced into the Commons a Companies Acts Amendment (No.2) Bill which was referred to the Committee on May 8, 1877. Clause 7 of the Bill proposed that a statutory form of balance sheet and profit and loss account should be required by all new joint-stock companies, in the same manner as was provided in the case of insurance, railway companies, and building societies. The text of clause 7 and the prescribed balance sheet and profit and loss account proposed by Chadwick are reproduced below:

BALANCE SHEET of ....Company, Limited, at ....18....
The total authorized capital of the Company is £.... in shares of £.... each, and £.... on mortgage, or in debenture bonds.
(State preference shares or any other authorized capital, and amount subscribed)

Dr. **CAPITAL AND LIABILITIES**	£. s. d.	Cr. **PROPERTY AND ASSETS**	£. s. d.
1. SHARE CAPITAL . . . Shares £.... called up Amount paid in advance of calls (The Amount of arrears on calls owing is £....) (Insert preference shares, &c., if any)		1. PROPERTIES Freehold and leasehold land and other properties (Insert principal items). Machinery and plant, including rolling stock (Insert principal items)	
2. MORTGAGES Amount owing on mortgages or debentures		2. STOCK-IN-TRADE, as per inventory and valuation (Insert principal items).	
3. DEBTS Amount owing on acceptances by the company. Do. for trade accounts (State special items separately, such as deposits, royalties, unclaimed interest or dividends, &c.)		3. DEBTS owing to the company, after deductions for bad and doubtful debts	
4 RESERVE FUND Balance of (State whether obtained from the general business operations, from share capital, or specially obtained, and if so how)		4. BALANCE OF CASH in bank; *viz* : Do. do. in hand: (Any other special assets or liabilities to be set forth). (Balance loss, if any, to be shown here)	
5 PROFIT Total gross profit for the year Less interest and dividends and portion of general expenses paid, as per profit and loss statement		Note: In case of Banks and other like Companies, the above Form to be used as far as practicable, and Assets in the nature of Loans to customers and Bills discounted, and Liabilities on Deposits, and on Acceptances, to be stated separately	

Chadwick's Balance Sheet (1877)

Profit and Loss Account of ....Company Limited, for the year (or half year) ending ....187.... showing the appropriation of the total Gross Profits on the Business of the Company

	£. s. d.		£. s. d.
To payments on liabilities on account of capital and management during the year, viz :		By gross profits for the year, as per Balance Sheet (being the result of the year's business after payments for materials, wages, current and working expenses)	
Interest on mortgage and debentures		(To be stated in one sum as above, or under various heads, showing results in each branch or department).	
General office and management expenses:		(Balance loss, if any, to be shown here)	
Directors and Auditors remuneration			
Amount proposed to be carried to reserve fund			
Interim dividend paid on share capital			
Do. on preference capital			
Further dividend proposed to be paid on share capital, making ....per cent. for the year			
Do. on preference share capital, making ....per cent. for year			
Balance proposed to be carried to next account			

Chadwick's Profit and Loss Account (1877)

The directors of every company formed and registered after the commencement of this Act, under the Companies Acts 1862 to 1877, and having a capital divided into shares, shall, at the general meeting of the shareholders, required to be held at least once in every year, submit to such meeting a report, with the names of the directors, managers, bankers, solicitors, auditors, and secretary of the Company, and a balance sheet and statement of profit and loss in the respective forms required by this Act; and a copy of every such report, balance sheet, and statement shall at least seven days before every ordinary meeting of the Company be, at the option of such company, either sent to the registered address of every member of the Company, or deposited at the Company's office, for the inspection of every member of the Company.
Every balance sheet issued by such Company shall be in the form marked A. in the schedule to this Act, or as near thereto as practicable, and there shall be annexed to every such balance sheet a profit and loss statement, in the form set forth in the same schedule and marked B., or as near thereto as practicable, and such balance sheet and statement shall be signed by two at least of the directors, and by an auditor or auditors appointed by the shareholders. [BPP 1877, I, 313].

Chadwick went further than the 1862 Act in proposing a balance sheet *and* a profit and loss account both of which were to be compulsory. His balance sheet was, however, as Hein [1978, p.213] points out, a retrogression from that of 1862 and his profit and loss account disclosed little. It was tactically unwise of him to substitute his own balance sheet. Both Price and Harding stated in evidence that they preferred the 1862 form. Chadwick was willing to give way to them on the balance sheet but did not accept their criticism of his profit and loss account (Q.1947).

Chadwick's proposals were supported by William Newmarch, the banker, who stated that "it certainly is convenient on many grounds that the accounts rendered by public companies should be in some uniform shape" (Q.258). Facts to be of any use, he claimed, must have some uniformity impressed upon them. The requirements for uniform railway and insurance accounts had worked well (Q.285 and 755). A prescribed form of accounts would fit most cases without difficulty (Q.286, 710).

Price was critical of Chadwick's proposed model balance sheet, preferring the one set out in the 1862 Act (Q. 1304 *et seq*). Harding agreed that there should be a prescribed balance sheet but he also preferred the form of 1862 (Q.1486, 1487, 1494). He agreed with the proposal for a profit and loss statement as well but found Chadwick's form "a little confused" (Q.1488).

Sir George Jessel, Master of the Rolls, strongly opposed Chadwick's clause 7. He could see the case for calling for the accounts of an insurance company, in which the whole public were interested, but could not understand why directors should be compelled to issue accounts to shareholders, which shareholders could call for themselves if they wished. He did not understand why the directors should prepare the accounts in a given form if the shareholders would like them in some other form. He believed the notion that any form of account would prevent fraud to be quite delusive : "Anybody who has had any experience of these things knows that a rogue will put false figures into an account, or cook it, as the phrase is, whatever form of account you prescribe" (Q. 2192). He was critical of Chadwick's balance sheet (Q.2195). He did not accept that fixed forms of balance sheet had worked well in relation to railways, insurance companies and building societies : "I know from evidence before me that you cannot compare the balance sheet of two railway companies, unless you know that they have been framed on the same theory" (Q.2241). It was not the same model in form but the same theory that was needed : "It is not sufficient to put it in form; it is the substance" (Q. 2242). He had an utter distrust of "these pieces of paper, called balance sheets" (Q.2253). In any case he did not see what right the Legislature had to interfere with the concerns of private companies as distinguished from companies which had some public privilege (Q.2256).

It was Jessel's views that prevailed with the Committee. The two essential points were that Parliament should not interfere between directors and shareholders unless the activities of the company were of public interest; and that uniformity of form was insufficient. Few British accountants would agree with the former proposition today; the second view is still widely held.

The *Companies Acts Amendment* (No.3) Bill which received the royal assent on July 23, 1877, dealt with the important subject of reduction of capital, also of interest to Chadwick [Cottrell, 1980, p.64], but contained no equivalent of clause 7.

The Accounts of Banks (1878-79)

In 1878 the City of Glasgow Bank failed disastrously both for its creditors and its shareholders (who did not have limited liability). In the *Companies Act* of 1879 which followed, the audit of banking but not of other companies was made compulsory [Tyson, 1974; text of Act in Anderson & Cottrell, 1974, pp. 312-6].

A clause in the Bill prescribed the form of the accounts of a bank, but this was withdrawn at the Committee stage (August 12, 1879) over the protests of Chadwick [Chadwick, 1883, p.8] who argued that:

> the present was the proper time to insist upon having uniform balance-sheets. These were already furnished by Railway and Insurance Companies; and it was most important, in the interest of the shareholders and the public, that all bank balance-sheets should have some general groundwork of uniformity. (*Hansard*, v. 249, cols. 855-6).

Other MPs argued, however, that a stereotyped system imposed by Act of Parliament would admit of no improvement and would inspire a false confidence on the part of the public (*Hansard*, v. 248, col. 1022) and that no forms could secure the credit of a bank, which rested upon the character of the directors (*Hansard*, v.249, col. 856).

After twelve years as an MP, divided equally between premierships of Gladstone and Disraeli, Chadwick lost his seat in 1880. In his comments on Guthrie's lecture of 1882 (see below) he was still optimistic of bringing about uniformity of account:

> In a bill that was passed in the House of Commons, and read a second time in the Lords, and only failed to become an Act of Parliament on the last day of the session by the illness of the Lord Chancellor I had intro-

> duced a fixed form of account, for all joint-stock companies accounts of every kind . . . if it ever comes to be my lot to be in Parliament again, the first thing I will do will be to introduce the Bill which was so nearly being passed and I feel quite sure I shall be able to carry it through [Guthrie, 4 November 1882, p. 12].

Chadwick never did get an opportunity again to introduce a companies bill into Parliament. Perhaps he might have succeeded, but bills introduced by others in 1884, 1887 and 1888, all of which contained, *inter alia,* prescribed balance sheets and profit and loss accounts all failed [Hein, 1978, p.199; Cottrell, 1980, p.64].

Guthrie's Lecture (1882)

On 20 October 1882, Chadwick attended a lecture given to the Manchester Society of Chartered Accountants by Edwin Guthrie on "The want of uniformity in the modes of stating accounts; the frequency of inconsistency between the title and subject-matter of published accounts, and the employment of non-correlative terms in accounts". The lecture was printed in *The Accountant* of 28 October [Guthrie, 1882] and aroused considerable interest and a lively correspondence.

Guthrie[3] was born in Bermondsey, south of London Bridge, in 1841. The family moved a few years later to Liverpool and in 1861 Guthrie was working as a bookkeeper to a general merchant. In the early 1870s he left Liverpool and went into practice in Manchester but he did not join the Manchester Institute of Accountants. In 1880, however, as an established practitioner, he was one of the signatories to the English Institute's Royal Charter and became a member of its first Council. He was president of the Manchester Society of Chartered Accountants in 1884-85 and 1898-99. He was also the catalyst in 1886 for the formation in New York of the American Association of Public Accountants. The firm he founded is now the Manchester office of Peat, Marwick, Mitchell & Co.

Like Chadwick, Guthrie was active as a Liberal in politics, although in his case more successful in local than central government. He was chairman of the Finance Committee of the Lancashire County Council from its formation in 1889 and a president of the Manchester Statistical Society (1888-90). He was the author of a number of pamphlets and articles. He died at Broughton Old Hall, Salford in 1904.

3. *The Accountant's* obituary of Guthrie is reproduced in Parker [1980]. See also Kitchen and Parker [1980], ch.2.

In his lecture, Guthrie was concerned with the lack of uniformity in naming and presenting the two principal financial statements. He saw this not as a matter of principle but of usage and convenience and argued that once an arbitrary election had been made "it will surely be most convenient and consistent that it be adhered to in all its reproductions". He therefore argued that published Profit and Loss Accounts should follow the form of the ledger account. He also asked: "On which side should the Assets appear on a Balance Sheet, and consequently on which side the Liabilities? Many English Accountants to whom I have put the question have answered without hesitation — the Liabilities on the Left and the Assets on the Right, and with this dismiss the question as beyond controversy". Guthrie noted, however, that the reverse form was almost universal in other countries and that uniformity was not complete in England. Again he argued that the balance sheet was a condensation of the ledger: "Why in the process of condensation, the balance should change sides is for someone else to explain. I cannot".[4]

The discussion and letters which followed Guthrie's paper concentrated largely on which side of the balance sheet the assets and liabilities should respectively be placed, and it was even suggested that a resolution should be passed on the subject. Chadwick, however, in his comments, thought this aspect of little importance:

> . . . I confess that I do not place anything like the same importance to the placing of liabilities and assets on the one side or the other, neither do I think it would be worthy of ourselves to pass a resolution on the subject . . . I rather take Mr [Adam] Murray's view — make your balance-sheet correct, and it does not much matter on which side you place your assets or your liabilities. [Guthrie, 4 November 1882, p.11]

He reiterated this view in a lecture to the Chartered Accountants Students Society for London in 1883:

> Whilst I recommend statutory uniformity, I do not think the "form" in such cases is of such consequence as the "substance", by which I mean the intelligent and correct classification under proper *heads* of all items of receipt and expenditure, and of assets and liabilities [Chadwick, 1883, p.9].

In his comments on Guthrie's lecture, he went on to praise the uniformity of railway accounts:

4. On the reason for the reversal of side see Yamey [1970].

> . . . the reform which was made in the statement of railway accounts, to which no reference has been made, is a model for any accountant to follow in any business or in any transaction; and if we could only force joint-stock companies and corporations to follow up the forms which are contained in the railway accounts that are now compulsory, we should have then no cause to complain of want of uniformity. There you have absolute conformity compulsorily made . . . Uniformity is the thing we ought to seek, and if we pass a resolution, as professional accountants, at this meeting, I hope it will not go further than an expression of opinion that in all accounts of a similar kind, in order to allow comparison to be made by the public and others, there should be uniformity in stating the accounts . . . [Guthrie, 4 November 1882, p.12].

Nobody in the discussion seriously disputed the desirability of uniformity, though they differed as to what uniform accounts should look like, and the debate ended with the unanimous resolution: "That it is desirable that the accounts of joint-stock companies and public bodies be stated in a uniform manner, which should be compulsory".

The debate was continued in a series of letters to *The Accountant* during 1882 and 1883. The most distinguished correspondent was George Walter Knox of Sheffield. "All will be agreed", he wrote in the issue of November 25, 1882 [Knox, 1882], "as to the desirability of uniformity in the presentation of statements of accounts so far as the form of the account is concerned". He brought out more clearly the implicit entity/proprietary distinction in the argument about which sides the assets and liabilities should be placed: "a distinction has to be made between A. B. the firm, viz, in his capacity of carrying on the particular business, and A. B. the individual who has capital in it".

The most striking feature of the debate is the lack of any doubt that although published accounts were not uniform they ought to be.

The Davey Committee (1895)

The next opportunity for major company law reform came with the appointment of the Davey Committee which reported in 1895 [BPP, 1895], the year of Chadwick's death. Evidence was heard on many matters, including uniformity of account. The Edinburgh Stock Exchange Committee, for example, suggested that the provisions of the *Regulation of Railways Act* 1868, might, with such modification as would be needful, be adopted for companies generally, adding that "The difficulty that one statutory form of accounts would not suit every kind of company could be met by providing classified sets, with power to the Board of Trade, as in the case of the *Railways Act* referred to, to modify them in exceptional cases'' (Davey Committee, Appendix, p.103). On the other hand, the London Chamber of Commerce (whose *Companies Acts* Committee included such leaders of the accountancy profession as Frederick Whinney and the then President of the Institute of Chartered Accountants in England and Wales, Charles Fitch Kemp) argued that it was ''undesirable and probably impracticable, in consequence of the varied circumstances of so many companies, to lay down any form of the balance sheet'' (Appendix, p.110).

The Davey Committee accepted the latter view, stating in its Report that it had ''not attempted to settle a statutory form of balance-sheet for general purposes'', as it was thought that ''the character of the business and the different circumstances of the various companies would render such a general form inapplicable'' (Report, para. 51). The Committee adopted the view, ''tersely expressed by the Wakefield Chamber of Commerce'', that ''the true financial position of the company should be honestly disclosed to shareholders but not for public use'' (Report, para. 52 and Appendix, p.133), at the same time *not* adopting the Wakefield Chamber's view that uniformity of balance sheets was most desirable (Appendix, p.137).

Into the Twentieth Century

The recommendations of the Davey Committee relating to disclosure were not adopted by Parliament and at the turn of the century, except for public utilities and insurance companies, directors were still not compelled to draw up and send accounts to shareholders or to the Registrar of Companies. Whilst many voluntarily did so, there was little uniformity. The position was authoritatively summed up by Dicksee in the first edition of his *Advanced Accounting* [1903, pp.248-9]:

> It is usual for the annual, or other, accounts of [a] Company to be printed and circulated among the shareholders, although in the case of Companies registered under the Companies Acts there is no statutory provision to this effect, and the matter is accordingly regulated by the Articles of Association of each individual Company. The Articles also to some extent determine the amount of information that shall be given in the published accounts, although this is a matter that is in all cases very largely within the discretion of the directors, who, within very wide limits, have power to determine the form that the accounts shall take.
>
> This question of form is one upon which it would be difficult to lay down any hard and fast rules of universal application. The varying cir-

> cumstances determining the position of different undertakings renders the adoption of any stereotyped form practically impossible, although concerns carrying on similar classes of business might, as a rule, have their accounts framed upon very much the same lines. Opinions, however, vary greatly as to the amount of information which it is desirable to publicly disclose, and the precise form that the information should take, with the result that in practice the published accounts of almost every concern present some points of difference. Doubtless some nearer approach to uniformity would from most points of view be desirable, and in the case of clearly defined industries would be by no means impracticable, as is shown by the fact that Railways, Gas Companies, Life Assurance Companies, Building Societies and certain other undertakings are required to publish their accounts in the form prescribed by the Legislature, and are enabled to adhere very closely to that form without inconvenience.

Dicksee did not express himself very strongly one way or the other and avoided stating a firm preference: no doubt a suitable attitude for the author of a text book! Looking back over the debate, the arguments for and against uniformity can be seen to have been put most forcefully by, respectively, the 1849 Select Committee in its Third Report and by Sir George Jessel in his evidence to the 1877 Committee; the one stressing above all that only uniformity could ensure the comparability which was so necessary to investors and managers in their decision-making and as a safeguard to the public; and the other arguing against interference with a private contract between shareholders and directors and placing much less faith in uniformity of form and in financial statements generally.

In the event, those who argued for uniformity were successful only for certain classes of companies, notably the railways. But this may have been, as David Chadwick claimed, an accident. Then as now companies bills were not always given a sufficient share of scarce Parliamentary time.

It is not the intention in this article to pursue the debate into the twentieth century, if only because no new arguments were added and whilst more and more was required to be published (balance sheets in 1908, profit and loss accounts in 1929, group accounts in 1948, turnover in 1967), there were relatively few calls for uniformity of account.[5]

By the 1970s, when uniformity again became an issue, via a draft

5. Proposals for uniformity from 1900 to 1962 are noted by Hein [1978]. None of them succeeded.

EEC directive inspired mainly by German practice, the earlier debate had been forgotten. British accountants have striven hard and successfully for rather more flexible balance sheet and profit and loss account formats than originally envisaged but it is noteworthy that there has been no outcry against the uniformity soon to be imposed.

The want of uniformity of account which worried Chadwick and Guthrie will soon be remedied but to find out how and why would require an excursion into German accounting history rather than British.

REFERENCES

Anderson, B.L. and Cottrell, P.L., *Money and Banking in England* (David & Charles, 1974).

Ashton, T.S., *Economic and Social Investigations in Manchester, 1833-1933* (P.S. King and Son, 1934).

British Parliamentary Papers, *Reports of Select Committee on Audit of Railway Accounts*, vol. 10, 1849.

British Parliamentary Papers, *Report from the Select Committee on Limited Liability Acts*, vol. 10, 1867, p.393.

British Parliamentary Papers, *Report from the Select Committee on the Companies Acts, 1862 and 1867*, vol. 8, 1877, p.419.

British Parliamentary Papers, *Report of the Departmental Committee on Amendments to the Companies Acts, 1862 to 1890*, vol. 88, 1895, p.151.

Chadwick, D., "Duties of a Professional Auditor", *Accountant* (29 September, 1883), pp.8-10.

Cottrell, P.L., *Industrial Finance 1830-1914* (Methuen, 1980).

Department of Trade, *Company Accounting and Disclosure*, Cmnd. 7654 (HMSO, September 1979).

Dicksee, L.R., *Advanced Accounting* (Gee & Co, 1903; Arno Press, 1976).

Dicksee, L.R., *Auditing* (Gee & Co, 1892; Arno Press, 1976).

Edwards, J.R., *British Company Legislation and Company Accounts, 1844-1976* (Arno Press, 1980).

Guthrie, E., "The Want of Uniformity in the Modes of Stating Accounts", *Accountant* (28 October 1882), pp.8-12; debate, (4 November, 1882), pp.10-14.

Hein, L.W., *The British Companies Acts and the Practice of Accountancy 1844-1962* (Arno Press, 1978).

Johnston, T., Edgar, G.C., and Hays, P.L., *The Law and Practice of Company Accounting in New Zealand* (Butterworths, 5th ed, 1978).

Johnston, T.R., Jager, M.O., and Taylor, R.B., *The Law and Practice of Company Accounting in Australia* (Butterworths, 4th ed., 1979).

Kitchen, J., and Parker, R.H., *Accounting Thought and Education: Six English Pioneers* (Institute of Chartered Accountants in England and Wales, 1980).

Knox, G. Walter, "Want of Uniformity in Accounts", Letter to the Editor, *Accountant* (25 November 1882), p.5.

Parker, R.H., *British Accountants: A Biographical Sourcebook* (Arno Press, 1980).

Pixley, F.W., *Auditors: Their Duties and Responsibilities* (Effingham Wilson, 1881; Arno Press, 1976).

South Australia, *Companies Act, 1934-1952*, s.143 and Fifth Schedule.

Tyson, R.E., "The Failure of the City of Glasgow Bank and the Rise of Independent Auditing", *Accountant's Magazine* (April 1974), pp.126-131.

Yamey, B.S., "Closing the Ledger", *Accounting and Business Research*, 1970, pp.71-77.

R. H. PARKER

Bookkeeping Barter and Current Cash Equivalents in Early New South Wales

Introduction

Although Australia has produced accounting historians of some eminence, they have paid relatively little attention to the accounting history of their own country. In particular they have, with the exception of Goddard (1938), Goldberg (1956) and McCredie (1960), ignored the first forty years or so of European settlement in Australia. The purpose of the present paper is twofold: to demonstrate that accounting, in the guise of bookkeeping barter, played an essential role in the economic life of early New South Wales; and to show that the teaching of bookkeeping in Australia can be traced back to at least the early 1800s.

Barter and Bookkeeping Barter

Bookkeeping barter can be distinguished from pure barter in that whilst the latter requires the use of money neither as a unit of account nor as a means of payment, the former requires money as a unit of account but can, if need be, dispense with money as a means of payment.

Barter, although seemingly simple, suffers from three serious inconveniences (Jevons, 1883, Ch. 1): a want of coincidence of needs, a want of a measure of value, and a want of a means of subdivision. If, for example, as illustrated by the ledger account reproduced in Appendix A, a soldier wishes to exchange kangaroo meat for rum, he has to find a storekeeper who needs kangaroo meat and who possesses a quantity of rum which can be agreed to be equivalent to the quantity of kangaroo meat on offer. These difficulties can be overcome by using money as a unit of account even if money is not available as a means of payment. The result can be termed 'bookkeeping barter':

> Barter became plain sailing when traders could appraise goods in common terms, and still more could stretch the exchange over a long time. Money — even though it was too scarce to be always available as the unit of exchange — provided the common unit of value; and book-keeping gave the means for remembering and proving the details of a lengthy exchange. Thus the farmer . . . was able to sell his pig . . . for a money-credit in the storekeeper's books, while the storekeeper charged up his account. If the former could also on occasion *assign* his credit to third persons — so that the storekeeper acted in effect as his bank — then barter became a tolerably flexible and efficient means of trading. (Baxter, 1956, pp. 273-4)

Baxter is discussing accounting in colonial America. His description fits accounting in early New South Wales equally well.

R. H. PARKER is Professor of Accountancy, University of Exeter.

The measure of value used in barter bookkeeping is, in a very literal sense, a 'current cash equivalent'. Each exchange of goods is measured at the current market price in terms of the unit of account. It is the equivalent of the cash which would have changed hands if the unit of the account were also serving as a means of payment.

Characteristics of the New South Wales Economy

The characteristics of the New South Wales economy from 1788 to the 1820s were such that bookkeeping barter played an essential role.

The characteristics may be summarized as follows:

(1) Population was small but increasing.
(2) Trade went through three phases.
(3) Barter was common.
(4) Money was scarce, varied and bad.
(5) Credit was an essential part of many transactions; delays in settlement were often long.
(6) The larger merchants perforce also engaged in banking activities.

Population

Although in principle covering two thirds of a continent, in practice New South Wales had for a quarter of a century a settled area around Sydney of less than 1500 square miles (3900 hectares) bounded by the Nepean and Hawkesbury rivers and the Pacific Ocean. In 1813, the year in which a crossing was found through the Blue Mountains to the west, the non-aboriginal population on the mainland was still only about 12 000. The non-aboriginal population of Van Diemen's Land (Tasmania), first settled in 1803, was less than 2000 in 1813. By 1821 these figures had grown to 30 000 and 7000 respectively (Shaw, 1969, p. 114; Rimmer, 1969, p. 349).

Trade

Although established as a penal settlement, New South Wales developed into a free-market capitalist economy. There were three phases (Hainsworth, 1969, pp. 282-3). In the first phase, which ended around 1800, trade was dominated by the officers of the New South Wales Corps. Trading was a part-time occupation, easily combined with other activities: 'There was no steady stream of activity, no habitual round of business' (Steven, 1969, p. 126). Trade was very much a series of disconnected ventures, was very varied in its nature, and highly speculative. During the second phase, the first decade of the nineteenth century, trading became more of a full time occupation. The officers were superseded by free settlers such as Robert Campbell, the colony's first permanent merchant (from 1800) (Steven, 1965) and emancipist traders such as Simeon Lord and Samuel Terry. The third phase, ushered in by the commercial depression of the early Macquarie years, saw the decline and demise of the amateur and the triumph of the skilled merchant. By the end of Macquarie's governorship (1821) there had emerged 'the humdrum routine of continuous calculation on an even volume of trading and profits — often underwritten by permanent partnerships' (Steven, 1969, p. 184). Business had ceased to be a part-time occupation. In the words of Hannibal Macarthur, nephew and agent of John Macarthur, 'a man could be a merchant or a farmer but not both' (Hainsworth, 1969, p. 281).

Barter

Where money, however loosely defined, is scarce, barter helps to fill the gap. Items of barter included most notably rum, wheat, cattle, pork, beer and salt. As late as 1824, the Australian Brewery in Sydney offered beer in exchange for:

> lard and salt, kangaroo skins, houses and eggs, grain and hemp, cattle and sealskins, sheep and fish oil, horses and sawn timber, cedar logs and pigs, pork and shingles, flax and poultry, tobacco and wattle-bark, cheese and wood, candles and laths, fuel and soap, shoes and coals, hides and Span sh dollars, etc., etc., etc. (*Sydney Gazette*, 21 October 1824)

Money

Early New South Wales had 'a currency system more appropriate to Bedlam than a burgeoning economy' (Hainsworth, 1972, p. 221). There was no government treasury issuing money and until 1817 no private bank with a note issue. Almost anything served as a means of payment.[1]

The most important forms of 'money' were store receipts, coins and promissory notes. Store receipts were those given in exchange for sales to the government store or Commissariat. They passed from hand to hand as internal currency to be finally 'consolidated', i.e. exchanged for a bill on London. Coins used included not only English guineas, shillings and copper but also, among others, Spanish dollars, Dutch guilders and Indian rupees.

Spanish dollars were especially important. In this period they were the nearest approach to an international money and the currency of most British colonies. Governor Macquarie produced a 'holey' dollar by stamping out of the centre of each dollar a 'dump' equal to about one-quarter of the coin, leaving a 'ring' comprising the remaining three-quarters. For a period in the 1820s, the colony was on a dollar standard and the accounts of the Bank of New South Wales, for example, were drawn up in dollars from 1823 to 1826. The balance sheet of 31 December 1825 (reproduced in Goddard, 1938, p. 693) was in dollars. The first balance sheet, that of 31 December 1817, was in sterling (Goddard, 1938, p. 694; Holder, 1970, illustration opposite p. 46). Both are reproduced in Appendix B.

Promissory notes were issued by almost everybody including convicts. Some were printed and for round amounts; others were simply scrawls and for small and broken amounts. By about 1800 some notes were issued not in payment of debts but as a business in itself.

Not all forms of money were equally acceptable. It was common for sellers to specify what they were willing to receive in payment.[2] Prices might vary according to the form of payment. A distinction grew up between 'sterling' and 'currency', the latter referring

[1] The paragraphs which follow are based on Butlin (1953). See also Mira (1981) which has excellent illustrations.

[2] There are numerous examples in Mira's (1981) index of currency references in *The Sydney Gazette*, 1803-1811.

to media of exchange having a purely local circulation and often of a very limited acceptability. 'Sterling' was applied to bills of exchange, store receipts and coins other than copper. To cope with the problem of sterling and currency, ledger accounts were often double columned and separately balanced (Butlin, 1953, pp. 97-8).

Credit

If money is scarce, credit tends to be long. Both the Commissariat and Robert Campbell were generous in the credit they granted (Steven, 1965, p. 60; Hainsworth, 1969, p. 274). It became customary for settlers to obtain goods on credit (often unspecified in length) from merchants and to transfer their crops at harvest time to their creditors (Butlin, 1953, p. 127; Steven, 1965, p. 260). Debt-collecting and litigation connected with it was a time-consuming but necessary exercise (Steven, 1965, pp. 200-1).

Merchants as Bankers

In a colony with no banks and a disorganized currency, merchants inevitably performed some banking activities. Steven (1965, p. 26) writes that:

> For many years, as was usual for a merchant, Campbell had acted as an unofficial banker, discounting bills, accepting deposits and allowing interest, collecting balances paid as salaries in England, and even administering legacies on estates in England and India.

Many settlers maintained what were in effect current accounts with merchants which were 'overdrawn' between harvests. The balance of the governments' Orphan Fund was deposited at 8 per cent interest by the Rev. Samuel Marsden, its Treasurer, with the firm of James & Riley. It was transferred to the newly formed Bank of New South Wales in 1818 (Butlin, 1953, p. 124).

The Waterloo Company (Cooper & Levey), whose ledger (not in double entry) for 1823-5 is described in McCredie (1960) was the last important example of a merchant's establishment in which banking was a department (Butlin, 1953, p. 194). The company, like many others, issued its own notes. This 'petty banking', according to Macquarie, threw open 'a door to frauds and impositions of a most grievous nature to the country at large' (Butlin, 1953, pp. 89-90) and partly explains his support for the establishment of the Bank of New South Wales.

The Role of Accounting

The most important role of accounting in such an economy was, as Baxter has expressed it, to lubricate barter:

> Ledgers contained practically nothing save accounts for persons; apparently colonial merchants for the most part saw no point in keeping any other records. Further, these accounts cannot readily be divided between those of debtors and creditors. (Baxter, 1956, p. 275)

It should not be surprising, even to twentieth century business historians and accounting historians, that in the surviving accounting records of early New South Wales 'specific estimates of profit and loss rarely occur' (Steven, 1969, p. 133) and there is little or no evidence of double entry (Goldberg, 1956, p. 331). Formal accounting as an aid to decision-making was difficult when traders carried on simultaneously a wide range of business activities which they may not always have found easy to separate from their private lives. The business records which have survived are fragmented and interwoven with personal family papers (Steven, 1969, p. 178).

Examples of Bookkeeping Barter

Bookkeeping barter requires a unit of account. For a brief period during the interregnum between Bligh's overthrow and the arrival of Macquarie even the accounts of the Commissariat were kept in wheat but this was exceptional. Usually 'the reckoning scale was money, and almost always pounds, shillings and pence' (Butlin, 1953, pp. 46, 26).

An excellent example of bookkeeping barter is the account (reproduced in Appendix A) of Captain W. Sladden with the Van Diemen's Land Commissariat, covering the period 22 November 1804 to 8 July 1806.[3] Sladden was credited with pork and kangaroo meat valued at £507 19*s.*, two 'orders' on a Lt. Lord for £25 9*s.* 6*d.* and 'cash' for £208 15*s.* 6*d.* He was debited with £415 17*s.* 'cash' in a form not stated but probably store receipts or bills, with rum and wine to the value of £176 1*s.* 8*d.* and with soap, tape, blue, cloth, shoes, thread, pins, sugar, flour, buttons and cows worth £150 5*s.* 4*d.* (*Historical Records of Australia,* III, i, 498-9; Butlin, 1953, p. 49; Rimmer, 1969, p. 330).

The ledger of Cooper & Levey for the years 1823-5 contains several similar accounts. For example, the leading trader Simeon Lord is debited with purchases of tea, pork, handkerchiefs, spades, sugar, tobacco, linseed oil, corn, butter, iron, pepper, whitning, beef, rum, lamp oil, salt, paint and wheat and credited with 'payments' in his own promissory notes, soap, an auctioneer's note and house rent (McCredie, 1960).

The Commissariat in Sydney developed a wide range of transactions in barter. In 1805, for example, John Macarthur, received 'One Hundred of the finest wooled Ewes from Government Stock' for which he was 'to pay Grain into the Stores at the rate of two pounds Sterling for each Ewe' (*Historical Records of Australia,* I, v, 511; Butlin, 1953, pp. 60-61). This appears to be an example of an exchange of present sheep for future wheat. The current cash equivalent of the sheep is explicitly stated; presumably that of the wheat was determined at the date of delivery.

Robert Campbell sold his cargoes of imported goods to settlers on the Hawkesbury by granting extensive credit and accepting bills drawn on the Government Store for grain and animal food (Steven, 1965, pp. 44, 58, 60).

Accounting Other than Bookkeeping Barter

There are indications of more sophisticated accounting concepts. Riley, Wentworth and Blaxcell, who contracted with Macquarie to build Sydney Hospital (including the present Parliament House and the Mint) for a monopoly to import rum, refer in a letter to the Governor to 'the Interest of the Capital lying dormant' (Hainsworth, 1968, p. 161). Hainsworth instances 'a crude but effective substitute for depreciation' by the device of charging the cost of outfitting a merchant ship for a voyage to Tahiti against the return

[3] Readers may need to be reminded that there were 12 pence in a shilling and 20 shillings in a pound.

from the voyage. The cost arose from the very heavy wear and tear suffered by a wooden sailing ship on its *previous* voyage (Hainsworth, 1972, pp. 162-3).

Measures of financial position were not entirely lacking. Appendix B reproduces the balance sheets of the Bank of New South Wales at 31 December 1817 and 31 December 1825. The former is more a trial balance than a balance sheet. It will be noticed that the most liquid asset is described as 'Bills in Treasury, Store Receipts and specie on hand'; the least liquid, 'Office Goods and Furniture' is shown at 'cost'.

The balance sheet at 31 December 1825 is notable for being drawn up in Spanish dollars. The most liquid assets are 'Dollars in Chest', 'Govt. Store Receipts' and 'Bills'.

Textbooks and Teachers

Where did the bookkeepers learn their craft? British text books were, of course, available to them. Which ones they used is a matter of conjecture. Robert Campbell and his colleagues are likely to have used Scottish texts, especially as several Scottish texts on bookkeeping were best sellers in Britain during the 18th century. Campbell was born in 1769 in Greenock in the west of Scotland. It is probable that he attended the Grammar School there and received instruction in bookkeeping amongst other subjects (Steven, 1965, p. 11). Also born in Greenock was the Reverend J. D. Lang whose surviving ledger, with entries dated between 1837 and 1843, contains worked bookkeeping exercises based on Robert Hamilton's *An Introduction to Merchandise* (Goldberg, 1956, p. 328). Hamilton's book was first published in 1777 (Pryce-Jones and Parker, 1976, pp. 12-14).

Private schools were advertised in *The Sydney Gazette,* first published in 1803, and it is in these advertisements that we find the first references to the teaching of bookkeeping. The texts of the first five such advertisements (dating from the years 1804-06) are given in Appendix C.

The teachers mentioned are William Pascoe Crook, John Mitchell and James MacConnell, John and James Kenny, Thomas Taber, and Mr and Mrs H. Perfact. Crook and Taber refer to 'bookkeeping', Mitchell and MacConnell to 'Book-keeping according to the Italian mode' (i.e. double entry bookkeeping), the Kennys to 'Book-keeping after the Italian mode', and the Perfacts to 'merchants accompts'.

Apart from the six persons named above, a number of others are known to have been teachers in New South Wales in the early days of the colony. All of them are likely to have taught arithmetic; whether they also taught bookkeeping is not known. They include Isabella Rosson and William Richardson, who married Isabella (both were convicts transported on the First Fleet), Mary Johnson, Thomas McQueen, Susannah Hunt, William Webster, Isaac Nelson, Jeremy Cavanaugh, Matthew Hughes, D. Parnell and George Howe (the editor of *The Sydney Gazette*) (McGuanne, 1906-7; Goodin, 1950; Shellard, 1968-9; Cleverley, 1971).

Many of the bookkeeping teachers were ex-convicts. In spite of his name Crook was not; in the Paciolian tradition he was a missionary, a teacher and a businessman. Taber and Crook are in fact sufficiently important in the history of Australia to merit entries in the *Australian Dictionary of Biography* (Pike, 1966, 1967).

Thomas Taber (Pike, 1967, p. 502), 'tall, bony, clean faced, with rather long sharp features and lank straight hair' according to McGuanne (1906-7, p. 74), was born in

London in 1763. Sentenced to life imprisonment in 1796 (Cleverley, 1971, p. 30), he arrived in New South Wales in 1797 with his wife and three children. Although a watch finisher by trade, he was, along with William Richardson and Isaac Nelson employed by the Reverend Richard Johnson, the first chaplain to the colony, in the wattle and daub church which Johnson had constructed on his own initiative. The Church was burned down, probably deliberately, in 1798 but the school carried on. Taber became parish clerk of St Phillip in 1800. In 1802 he was transferred to Parramatta but he was back in Sydney in 1805. In June 1806 he received a full pardon for his teaching services and opened his private academy which was advertised in *The Sydney Gazette*. He and his sons received grants of lands and successfully pioneered the Menangle district. He retired in 1824, was granted a government pension for 'unremitting attention to . . . duty as Schoolmaster in this colony upwards of twenty-five years' and died in 1842.

William Pascoe Crook (Pike, 1967), 'a little swaddling chap' according to McGuanne (1906-7, p. 74), was born on 29 April 1775 at Dartmouth in Devon. He received a rudimentary education in Plymouth and then entered domestic service. He was accepted by the London Missionary Society as an artisan missionary and given instruction in tin-plate working. After missionary work in the Pacific and England he arrived in Sydney in 1803 where he was engaged by the Rev. Samuel Marsden, who had succeeded Johnson as chaplain, to open a school at Parramatta (see text of advertisement in Appendix) which at the end of 1804 became possibly the first boarding school in Australia (Jervis, 1961, p. 87). He was later active as an itinerant Congregational minister and in various business enterprises. He died in Melbourne in 1846. A portrait of Crook in the Dixson Gallery, Sydney, is reproduced in Shellard (1968). There is a memorial plaque in the Uniting (formerly Congregational) Church in Pitt Street, Sydney.

Less is known of the other bookkeeping teachers. Mitchell, having received a conditional emancipation in 1803 (*The Sydney Gazette*, 19 June 1803), advertised his school a second time in *The Sydney Gazette* of 28 December 1806 with no mention of James MacConnell. On 7 June 1807, the newspaper reported that Mitchell's pupils had presented an address to Governor King. On 30 August, however, it was announced in the *Gazette* that John Mitchell and Elizabeth Thompson were 'about to leave this Colony in the Sydney Cove, (under His Excellency's permission)'.

James Kenny was an Irish convict who arrived in 1793. His brother John was apparently a free settler for no evidence of conviction has been found (Whittaker, 1980, p. 16). They advertised their school in October 1805. John also ran a bakery but in January 1807 was tried and executed for the murder of a Mary Smith at Parramatta. Two and a half columns of *The Sydney Gazette* of 25 January 1807 were devoted to an account of his trial at which Samuel Terry the merchant and Surgeon Wentworth (father of W. C. Wentworth) were witnesses. James moved his school from Sydney to Wilberforce (on the Hawkesbury river) where he had a small farm (Goodin, 1950, p. 102). The Kennys' school in the Rocks area of Sydney has been reconstructed at Old Sydney Town in Somersby, N.S.W. (Whittaker, 1980, pp. 16-17).

Mr and Mrs H. Perfact's (or Perfect) first advertisement appeared in June 1806. They also served as managers of the colony's orphanage from 1807 to 1809. On 26 March 1809 an advertisement in *The Sydney Gazette* announced that Mrs S. Perfect would open on 3 April a school 'to instruct young Ladies only, in Needle-work, Reading,

Writing, and Accounts at the house late Mrs Bennett's Spring Row [now George Street] Sydney'. It seems clear that bookkeeping in early New South Wales was by no means an exclusively male accomplishment.

There is no direct evidence as to the textbooks used by these early teachers. It is possible that book-keeping was taught as part of arithmetic. The most popular British texts on arithmetic in this period included those by Cocker and Fisher (Karpinski, 1965, p. 78). Cocker's *Arithmetick,* first published in 1678, went through about one hundred editions in the British Isles (Karpinski, 1965, p. 75). His book is said to have been used by Mitchell, McConnell and Parnell (McGuanne, 1906-7, p. 74). George Fisher brought out editions of Cocker and was the author of *The Instructor: or, young man's best companion,* which included material on spelling, reading, writing, arithmetic and 'merchants accompts' (Quester, 1940). The use of a copy of this book to administer an illegal oath led to the transportation to New South Wales in 1816/17 of the attorney William Adams Broadribb (or Brodribb) (Peacock, 1965, p. 53; the case is reported in *R. v. Brodribb,* 6 Car. & P. 571). His son of the same name became a successful pastoralist and politician, being mayor of Woollahra in 1878 and a member of the N.S.W. Legislative Council from 1881 to his death in 1886 (Nairn, Serle and Ward, 1969, pp. 237-9).

The teaching of accounting at university level in New South Wales began in 1907 at the University of Sydney, but another 45 years were to pass before the first full time appointment (R. J. Chambers as senior lecturer) in 1952 (Brown, 1962). Chambers' teaching and writings have helped to give Australia an international reputation in academic accounting.

Summary

Accounting in the guise of bookkeeping barter played an essential role in the early Australian economy, enabling traders to overcome at least in part the problems posed by a disorganized currency. Many transactions were recorded at what were literally current cash equivalents. The teaching of bookkeeping can be traced back to the earliest days of Australian history.

APPENDIX A

STORE ACCOUNT PAID BY CAPTAIN SLADDEN FOR MATERIALS FOR ERECTING A HOUSE

Capt'n W. Sladden
To Mr. Fosbrook, D'y Comm'y.

Dr.

1804.					£	s.	d.
Novr.	22	To	56 lbs. Yellow Soap	@ 12½d.	2	18	6
Oct.	30	"	19½ Gallons Port Wine	@ 12s. 1d.	11	15	7
Jany.	14	"	12 do.	"	7	5	0
Feby.	20	"	14 do.	"	8	9	2
Apl.	19	"	9 do.	"	5	8	9
July	18	"	8 do. American Rum	11s.	4	8	0

APPENDIX A — *continued*

STORE ACCOUNT PAID BY CAPTAIN SLADDEN FOR MATERIALS FOR ERECTING A HOUSE

Capt'n W. Sladden
To Mr. Fosbrook, D'y Comm'y.

Dr.

					£	s.	d.
1804.							
"	23	"	4 do. Port Wine	12s. 1d.	2	8	4
Aug'st	26	"	10 do. East I. Rum	13s.	6	10	0
"	"	"	Cash		100	0	0
Sep.	28	"	10 Gallons E. I. Rum	13s.	6	10	0
"	"	"	9 " Port Wine	12s. 1d.	5	8	9
Oct.	15	"	10 " E. I. Rum	13s.	6	10	0
Novr.	3	"	10 " do.	"	6	10	0
"	13	"	4 Pieces narrow Tape	2s. 2½d.	0	8	10
"	"	"	1 Piece Russia Duck 37 yds.	2s. 2d.	4	0	2
"	"	"	1 do. White Callico 28 do.	19½d.	2	5	6
"	"	"	3 do. Ferret	5s. 6d.	0	16	6
"	"	"	1 lb. Pins		0	3	10
"	19	"	16 Gallons E. I. Rum	13s.	10	8	0
Decr.	4	"	6 do. do.		3	18	0
"	"	"	9 do. Port Wine	12s. 1d.	5	8	9
"	22	"	3 do. E. I. Rum	13s.	1	19	0
"	"	"	15 lbs. Yellow Soap	12½d.	0	15	7½
1805.							
Jany.	4	"	1 Gallon E. I. Rum	13s.	0	13	0
"	15	"	1 lb Stone Blue	2s. 6d.	0	2	6
"	22	"	10 Gallons E. I. Rum	12s.	6	0	0
Feb.	5	"	44 do. do.		26	8	0
Mar.	1	"	6 yards Russian Duck	2s. 2d.	0	13	0
"	"	"	1 pr. Women's Shoes		0	4	6
"	"	"	½ lb. White Thread	7s. 0½d.	0	3	6½
"	"	"	1 lb. Pins		0	3	10½
"	4	"	28 Gallons E. I. Rum	12s.	16	16	0
"	15	"	8 yards Russia Duck	2s. 2d.	0	17	4
"	"	"	56 lbs. Yellow Soap	12½d.	2	18	0
"	"	"	8 Gallons E. I. Rum	12s.	4	16	0
May	14	"	10 do. do.		6	0	0
"	"	"	2 lbs. Worsted	4s. 10½d.	0	9	9
June	9	"	10½ Gallons E. I. Rum	12s	6	6	0
"	25	"	1½ yards Common Blue Cloth	8s. 6d	0	12	9
July	12	"	1 lb Stone Blue		0	2	6
Aug.	2	"	12 yards Russia Duck	2s. 2d	1	6	0
"	3	"	212 lbs. Sugar	10d	8	16	8
"	23	"	14 yards Calico Check	1s. 9d	1	4	6
"	"	"	336 lbs. Flour	6d	8	8	0
Sep.	12	"	56 lbs. Mottled Soap	1s. 1d	3	0	8
"	"	"	Cash		10	0	0
"	23	"	do.		20	0	0
Oct.	21	"	do.		35	0	0
Nov.	16	"	100 lbs. Flour	6d.	2	10	0
"	17	"	Cash		20	0	0
Decr.	6	"	50 lbs. Mottled Soap	1s. 1d.	2	14	2
"	"	"	Cash		38	0	0
"	31	"	25 lbs. Mottled Soap	1s. 1d.	1	7	1
"	"	"	2 Dozen Shirt Buttons	3¾d.	0	0	7½
1806							
Jany.	16	"	56 lbs. Flour	6d.	1	8	0

APPENDIX A — *continued*

Store Account Paid by Captain Sladden for Materials for Erecting a House

Capt'n W. Sladden
To Mr. Fosbrook, D'y Comm'y.

April	19	"	Cash		20	0	0
May	14	"	do.		102	17	0
"	"	"	35 Gallons Port Wine	10s. 4½d.	18	15	4
"	"	"	12 dozen do.	33s. 7d.	20	3	0
"	"	"	3 Cows	£25	75	0	0
"	"	"	8 Gallons Rum at Port Phillip		4	0	0
July	8	"	Cash		70	0	0
					£742	4	0

Cr.

1804.					£	s.	d.
Feby.	23	By	112 lbs. Fresh Pork	1s. 6d.	9	6	0
Aug.	21	"	554 lbs. Kangaroo	1s.	27	4	0
Sep.	30	"	1,339 " do.		66	19	0
Oct.	31	"	392 do.		19	12	0
1806 From Feby. to May		"	2,495 do.	8d. }			
		"	318 do.	1s. }	122	17	0
		"	478 do.				
		"	1,781 do.		89	1	0
June		"	951 do.		47	11	0
July		"	1,560 do.		78	0	0
"		"	132 Fresh Pork	1s. 6d.	9	18	0
Aug'st		"	554 Kangaroo	1s.	27	14	0
"		"	197 do.		9	17	0
Septr.		By	Order on Lt. Lord		21	9	6
"		"	Cash		208	15	6
"		By	Order on Lt. Lord		4	0	0
					£742	4	0

Leonard Fosbrook, D'y Commissary.

Source: Historical Records of Australia, Vol. III, No. i, pp. 498-9.

APPENDIX B

BALANCE SHEETS OF THE BANK OF NEW SOUTH WALES

Abstract Balances
(as at 31 December 1817)

Dr.	£	s.	d.	£	s.	d.	Cr.	£	s.	d
Notes in Circulation	5,635	8	0				Bills in Treasury, Store Receipts and specie on hand	£3,613	2	10
Personal Balances	1,859	4	8				Bills of Exchange falling due	5,693	5	1
				£7,494	12	8	Mortgages	1,381	0	0
Bank Subscriptions —							Office Goods and Furniture — cost	340	10	4
1st Instalments	1,500	0	0				Salaries, Wages, Stationery, etc.	373	1	10
2nd "	1,350	0	0							
3rd "	775	0	0							
				3,625	0	0				
Discount	250	13	0							
Premiums	30	14	5							
				281	7	5				
				£11,401	0	1		£11,401	0	1

R. Campbell, Jnr., Accountant.
Certified correct. E. S. Hall, Cashier.
Compared correct 13 January 1818. J. T. Campbell, President, W. D. Wentworth, Wm. Redfern, Thos. Wylde, R. Jenkins.

BARTER AND CURRENT CASH EQUIVALENTS

Balance Sheet
(as at 31 December 1825)

LIABILITIES.	Dollars.	ASSETS.	Dollars.
Capital paid up	43,200.00	Dollars in Chest	127,479.50
Notes in circulation	115,940.00	Govt. Store Receipts	26,691.24
Deposits	297,158.98	Bills	291,208.28
Dividends unclaimed	460.00	Mortgages	20,295.67
Profit and Loss, June 30 to Dec. 31, 1825	11,195.21	Furniture	1,505.50
	468,180.19*		468,180.19

Source: R. H. Goddard, 'An Historical Survey', *Chartered Accountant in Australia*, Vol. 7, 1938
* Error in additions as in Goddard

APPENDIX C

ADVERTISEMENTS FROM THE SYDNEY GAZETTE 1804-6

19 August 1804

Mr Crook has resumed the charge of the Public School kept in Parramatta Church; and wishing to have a few Young Gentlemen to Board and Lodge with him, he has taken a House where he can accommodate them.

The branches of Instruction will be adapted to the situation for which the Pupil may be designed, who will be taught to read, speak and write the English Tongue with accuracy and propriety, Book-keeping, Geometry, Trigonometry, and Mensuration practically applied in Navigation, Surveying, Gauging, etc. He will endeavour to store their minds with a general knowlede of Geography, History and Astronomy, making every part of Education as pleasing as possible.

Application may be made to Mr Crook personally or by Letter.

23 December 1804

The Public are respectfully informed, that an ACADEMY will be opened for the Instruction of Youth (to commence the first Week in January), at the House of Mr JOHN MITCHELL, Sydney.

Parents who are desirous of entering into terms for the Education of their Children, are requested to apply to John Mitchell and James MacConnell, who will teach, viz. English grammatically, Writing, Book-keeping after the Italian mode, French grammatically, and Mathematics. As every pain will be taken with the Pupils, the Terms consequently must be liberal. It is also a well-known fact to many respectable Gentlemen in this Colony, that John Mitchell has rendered ample satisfaction to the Parents of the different Youths he has already had under his tuition.

6 October 1805

John and James Kenny respectfully acquaint their Friends and the Public in general, that they will open SCHOOL at Sydney on Monday the 30th instant, at No. 8, on the Rocks, at the back of the residence of Mr Henry Kable. Parents and Guardians who may please to place their Children under their tuition may rely on the strictest attention to their speedy improvement in Reading, Writing, Vulgar and Decimal Arithmetic, Mensuration and Book-keeping according to the Italian mode.

10 November 1805

Thomas Taber, Vestry Clerk of the Parish of St Philip, Sydney, respectfully acquaints his friends and the Public in general that he will open School on Monday 18th Inst., at No. 1, Back Row East, at the back of the residence of Serjeant Richardson, Parents and Guardians who may please to place their children under his tuition may rely on the strictest attention to speedy improvement in Reading, Writing, Arithmetic, Book-keeping etc. on the most reasonable terms.

6 June 1806

An Academy will be opened on Monday next the 2nd of June, by H. and Mrs Perfact, for the instruction of children in reading, writing, merchants accompts, and needle work at Mr Edward's, No. 6, Spring Row, Sydney; where every attention will be paid to the morals of the pupils.

H. Perfact will attend persons of either sex who may wish for private instruction at their own houses.

REFERENCES

Baxter, W. T., 'Accounting in Colonial America' in A. C. Littleton and B. S. Yamey, *Studies in the History of Accounting,* Sweet & Maxwell, London 1956.

Brown, R. S. 'Accountancy Teaching in the University of Sydney', *AAUTA News Bulletin,* October 1962.

Butlin, S. J., *Foundations of the Australian Monetary System 1788-1851,* Melbourne University Press, 1953.

Cleverley, John F., *The First Generation. School and Society in Early Australia,* Sydney University Press, 1971.

Goddard, R. H., 'An Historical Survey', *Chartered Accountant in Australia,* Vol. 7, 1938.

Goldberg, L., 'Some Early Australian Accounting Records', *Australian Accountant*, 1952, reprinted in revised form in A. C. Littleton and B. S. Yamey, *Studies in the History of Accounting*, Sweet & Maxwell, London. 1956.

Goodin, V. 'Public Education in New South Wales before 1848', *Journal of the Royal Australian Historical Society*, Vol. xxxvi (4 parts), 1950.

Hainsworth, D. R., *Builders and Adventurers*, Cassell Australia, North Melbourne, 1968.

———, 'Trade within the Colony' in G. J. Abbott and N. B. Nairn, *Economic Growth of Australia 1788-1821*, Melbourne University Press, 1969.

Hainsworth, D. R., *The Sydney Traders*, Cassell Australia, Melbourne, 1972.

Holder, R. F., *Bank of New South Wales: A History*, Vol. I: 1817-1893, Angus and Robertson, 1970.

Jevons, W. S., *Money and the Mechanism of Exchange*, Kegan Paul, Trench & Co., 1883.

Jervis, J., *The Cradle City of Australia. A History of Parramatta 1788-1961*, The Council of the City of Parramatta, 1961.

Karpinski, L. C., *The History of Arithmetic*, Russell & Russell, 1965.

McCredie, H., 'An Early Ledger of the Firm Messrs Cooper & Levey, 1823-5', *Bulletin of the Business Archives Council of Australia*, I vii, 1960.

McGuanne, J., 'Early Schools of New South Wales', *Journal of the Royal Australian Historical Society*, Vol. 11, Part iv, 1906-7.

Mira, W. J. D., *Coinage and Currency in New South Wales 1788-1829 and An Index of Currency References in The Sydney Gazette 1803-1811*, The Metropolitan Coin Club of Sydney, Strathfield, 1981.

Nairn, N. B., A. G. Serle and R. B. Ward, *Australian Dictionary of Biography*, Vol. 3: 1851-1890, A-C, Melbourne University Press, 1969.

Peacock, A. J., *Bread or Blood*, Victor Gollancz, 1965.

Pike, D. (ed.), *Australian Dictionary of Biography 1788-1850*, Melbourne University Press, 2 vols, 1966 and 1967.

Pryce-Jones, J. and R. H. Parker, *Accounting in Scotland. A Historical Bibliography*, 2nd ed., Institute of Chartered Accountants of Scotland, 1976.

Quester, K., '"Young Man's Best Companion"', *Accountant*, Vol. 103, 7 December 1940, p. 430.

Rimmer, W. G., 'The Economic Growth of Van Diemen's Land 1803-1821' in G. J. Abbott and N. B. Nairn, *Economic Growth of Australia 1788-1821*, Melbourne University Press, 1969.

Shaw, A. G. L., 'Labour' in G. J. Abbott and N. B. Nairn, *Economic Growth of Australia 1788-1821*, Melbourne University Press, 1969.

Shellard, J., 'Public Education in Early New South Wales', *The Education Gazette* (N.S.W.), Vol.lxii, Nos. 2-12, 1968-69.

Steven, M., *Merchant Campbell 1769-1846*, Oxford University Press, Melbourne, 1965.

Steven, M. J. E., 'Enterprise' and 'The Changing Pattern of Commerce' in G. J. Abbott and N. B. Nairn, *Economic Growth of Australia 1788-1821*, Melbourne University Press, 1969.

Whittaker, J., *Old Sydney Town Heritage Park Somersby Guide*, Somersby, N.S.W., 1980.

Accounting People

R. H. PARKER

British Men of Account

> I hold every man a debtor to his profession.
>
> Francis Bacon

Introduction

Accountancy as we know it today is very much a product of the nineteenth century. Before we start to look at the origins of the modern profession, however, let me remind you that the accountants have always been with us: sometimes in rather unexpected places. Accountants have to be literate as well as numerate so it is appropriate that the beginnings of accounting are also the beginnings of writing. The earliest clay tablets discovered in Sumeria (*c.* 3500 BC) are mainly records kept by priests of temple incomes (Hooke [12], pp. 745-6). The earliest writings in Greek — the Minoan Linear B tablets of Crete and Mycenae — have recently been described by a leading authority as 'the account books of anonymous clerks' (Chadwick [4], p. ix). The palace archives of Pylos and Knossos represent 'the records of a comprehensive and pervasive bureaucracy . . . There is endless counting and classifying, measuring and weighing, assessing and collecting and distributing' (Page [15], p. 180). In England accounting begins with the Domesday Book (1086) and the Pipe Rolls, an almost unbroken series of which extends from the twelfth to the nineteenth century. The *Dialogus de Scaccario* (Dialogue of the Exchequer) of Richard, Son of Nigel, Treasurer of England and Bishop of London, written in the late twelfth century, is a detailed and severely practical treatise on the accounting methods of the English Exchequer.

The Pipe Roll was a narrative of revenues and expenditures. Notched sticks known as 'tallies' were used as receipts and continued to be used in English governmental accounting until 1826. In 1834 they were thrown into the heating stoves of the House of Commons where they caused such a blaze that the Parliament buildings were burned to the ground. Such are the problems of change in accounting.

Meanwhile the rather more sophisticated double entry system of recording business transactions had been developed about the year 1300 in the city states of Northern Italy and it was in Venice in 1494 that the earliest printed treatise on accounting was published as part of a book on mathematics. The author was Luca Pacioli, a Franciscan friar. According to the science historian George Sarton, the 'book was so comprehensive and clear and contained so many useful novelties . . . and it was

---

R. H. PARKER is Professor of Accountancy, University of Exeter. This is taken from his Inaugural Lecture, delivered in that University on 22 April 1977.

distributed so well (in the best market, Venice) that it exerted a great influence on the textbook writers throughout Latin Europe. In that respect we may consider it one of the outstanding books in mathematical history' (Sarton [19], p. 28).

Pacioli is a fascinating character. He was born in the same Tuscan town, Borgo San Sepulcro, as Piero della Francesca and appears in two of the latter's paintings (in one as St Peter the Martyr). He was also a friend and colleague of Leonardo da Vinci, who illustrated Pacioli's book on proportion (Taylor [5]).

Growth of the Accountancy Profession

My main concern, however, is with the modern professional accountant. Modern times for accounting began in Scotland in the 1850s. The first secretary of the first professional body, the Society of Accountants in Edinburgh, was a Mr Alexander Weir Robertson (1819-79), the founder of a 'dynasty' of Scottish chartered accountants: one member of each of the next four generations of the family became a Scottish CA.

The English were slower: the Institute of Chartered Accountants in England and Wales was formed only in 1880, less than a century ago. The Institute of Chartered Accountants in Ireland was established in 1888. Not all accountants are or have been chartered. The most important non-chartered body, the Society of Incorporated Accountants and Auditors was amalgamated with the U.K. chartered institutes in 1957. The first secretary of the Society was James Martin who commented caustically in 1897 that Scottish chartered accountants put the initials CA 'upon their intimations of birth, their marriages and deaths, nay, even on their tombstones' (Martin [14], pp. 33-4).

Some relevant figures are given in Table 1. Fifty years after the formation of the first Scottish chartered body (i.e. in 1904) there were just over 4000 chartered accountants in the British Isles and over 2000 incorporated accountants. At the time of the 1957 amalgamation there were over 27,000 chartered accountants and over 11,000 incorporated accountants. In 1976 there were about 76,000 chartered accountants, the number having doubled during the previous twenty years. There are also about 37,000 qualified but non-chartered accountants. Not all these 113,000 qualified accountants are resident in the British Isles.

The growth of academic accounting in Britain is much more recent. In 1904 there

TABLE 1

GROWTH OF THE ACCOUNTANCY PROFESSION

	1904	1957	1976
Scottish chartered accountants	906	6,187	9,268
English chartered accountants	3,177	20,124	63,370
Irish chartered accountants	62	1,044	3,004 (1975)
Incorporated accountants	2,068	11,335	—
	6,213	38,690	75,642
Professors of accounting (full-time)	None	3	30

Sources: R. Brown (ed.), *History of Accounting and Accountants*, Edinburgh, 1905; A. A. Garrett, *History of The Society of Incorporated Accountants 1885-1957*, Oxford, 1961; Registers of Members.

was one part-time chair of accounting, established two years before at the University of Birmingham and occupied by Lawrence R. Dicksee, a pioneer author of many best-selling textbooks on accounting and auditing. By 1957 there were three full-time chairs in England (Birmingham, the London School of Economics and Bristol) and two part-time chairs in Scotland. In 1976 there were 30 full-time chairs of accountancy in Britain.

What is the explanation of the remarkable growth in the number of qualified accountants? My thesis will be that it is the response to the needs of a complex and ever-changing commercial and industrial society. More specifically, I want to look at the needs of the creditor, the shareholder, the manager and the taxpayer and the way in which accountants have met those needs.

'It might be said', an accounting historian wrote in 1964, 'that the accountancy profession was born through bankruptcies, fed on failures and frauds, grew on liquidations and graduated through audits' (Robinson [17], p. 30). There has also, one might add, been postgraduate work in taxation and management accounting.

Creditors

The accountancy profession was born of the need to deal with the plight of the creditor. Limited liability (i.e. the right of shareholders not to pay the debts of their companies in full) was generally available from 1856 onwards. Many limited liability companies were, as Table 2 shows, dissolved almost as fast as they were formed. About one-quarter were dissolved within three years of registration, about one-half within ten years and getting on for three-quarters within twenty years. Much of the work involved was handled by accountants.

James McClelland, first president of the Glasgow chartered accountants and founder of a firm which now forms part of one of the largest U.K. accounting firms,

TABLE 2

COMPANY REGISTRATIONS AND DISSOLUTIONS IN ENGLAND AND WALES, 1856-83

	'Effective'* companies registered	Percentage of effective companies dissolved within 3 years of registration %	Percentage of effective companies dissolved within 10 years of registration %	Percentage of effective companies dissolved within 20 years of registration %
1856-65	3,104	21	49	61
1866-74	4,233	24	57	70
1875-83	6,240	28	57	72
	13,577	25	55	69

* Excluding: unlimited companies; companies limited by guarantee; companies registered as formed before July 1856; companies registered in Scotland, Ireland or the Stannaries; companies making no returns after filing the initial documents; and companies whose paid-up share capital was never more than £500.

Sources: Calculated from Table C of H. A. Shannon, 'The First Five Thousand Limited Companies and their Duration', *Economic History*, Vol. 2, 1930-3, and Tables A and B of H. A. Shannon, 'The Limited Companies of 1866-1883', *Economic History Review*, Vol. 4, 1933.

told an audience of accountancy students in 1869 that they would be 'in the position of enquiring into, and administering, sometimes to the fortunes, and at other times to the necessities of [their] fellow-men . . . devoting [their] talents to the relief of families in misfortune' and 'sometimes called upon to be the advisers and comforters of the widow and the fatherless' (McCelland [13], pp. 23-4).

The reputations and fortunes of many of the profession's founding fathers were made in liquidation work. One instance among many is Thomson McLintock who one hundred years ago founded in Glasgow at the age of 26 the firm which still bears his name. He became both an English and a Scottish chartered accountant (in that order) and 'formed his primary reputation as an accountant in Glasgow as the result of his handling of catastrophes relating to the City of Glasgow Bank crash in 1878' (Winsbury [24], p. 15).

The early preoccupation with catastrophe and disaster does much to explain the accountant's traditional conservatism later summed up as follows by a leading American academic accountant:

> The accountant transcends the conservatism of the proverb, "Do not count your chickens before they are hatched", saying "Here are a lot of chickens already safely hatched, but for the love of Mike, use discretion and don't count them all, for perhaps some will die." (Hatfield [10], p. 256, n. 13)

Stressing the needs of creditors rather than shareholders or managers led to an emphasis on balance sheets — statements showing the state of affairs at a particular point in time — rather than the more dynamic profit and loss account which shows the profit or loss for a period and how it has been earned. The purpose of a balance sheet, in the often quoted words of Buckley, J. in 1906, was 'primarily to shew that the financial position of the company is at least as good as there stated, not to show that it is not, or may not, be better'.[1]

The rationale for disclosure in company accounts was simple. Creditors were lending money to a business entity the owners of which had been granted the privilege of limiting their liability to pay the entity's debts. In return the entity should be required to disclose its financial position and above all should not *overstate* its financial strength.

Shareholders

The needs of creditors are not, however, necessarily coincident with those of *shareholders*. Since World War I it is their needs which have come to dominate the thinking of accountants.

Table 3 suggests why. The number of companies has greatly increased, the vast majority of them now being relatively small private companies. At the same time the large companies have become much larger. Whereas before World War I about 2000 enterprises were responsible for approximately half of the country's total manufacturing output, by 1970 the figure was 140 and by 1975 it was 100. The importance of this to the accountant is emphasized by the recent findings of Dr Prais, in his study of the evolution of giant firms, that financial factors have been far more

[1] Newton *v.* B.S.A. Co. (1906) 2 Ch. 378 at p. 387.

important than developments in technology or the desire for greater market power [16].

The divorce of ownership from control — whether real as in large public companies or more of a legal fiction as in small private companies — produced a need for audits by independent third parties. Such audits were required of all limited liability companies from 1900 onwards and auditing quickly overtook bankruptcy and liquidation work as the main occupation of accountants in public practice. Relatively few accountants are now concerned with bankruptcies and liquidations although recent economic conditions have led to some revival.

TABLE 3

SELECTED COMPANY STATISTICS 1911-75

	No. of companies (nearest 1000)	No. of public companies (nearest 1000)	Estimated no. of enterprises accounting for approximately half of total manufacturing output
1911	54,000	25,000	2000
1970	519,000	15,000	140
1975	592,000	16,000	100

Sources: A. A. Garrett, ***History of The Society of Incorporated Accountants 1885-1957***, Oxford 1961, App. VIII; S. J. Prais, ***The Evolution of Giant Firms in Britain***, Cambridge 1976, p. 7; Department of Trade, ***Companies in 1975***, London 1976.

The emphasis on shareholders rather than creditors led to three important changes.

First, the practice of creating secret reserves — once regarded as the height of financial wisdom and making some sense from the creditors' point of view — fell out of favour. The turning point was the Royal Mail case of 1931. Before 1920 the Royal Mail Steam Packet Co. had made considerable profits and built up substantial secret reserves. During the 1920s it ceased to make profits but concealed this fact by drawing on its reserves and without disclosing to its shareholders that it was doing so. Such a procedure was no longer thought of as being in the interests of the shareholders and the managing director went to jail. 'Shareholders', said Mr Justice Wright, 'should not be regarded as sheep who will look up if they are not fed' ([1], p. 237). It is interesting to note that while, as we have seen, Thomson McLintock had made his reputation in the City of Glasgow Bank liquidation, his son Sir William McLintock made his as an expert witness during the Royal Mail trial (Winsbury [24], p. 39).

Second, there has been a shift away from the balance sheet and an increased stress on the profit and loss account. Coupled with this was a rather delayed shift in the rationale for disclosure in company accounts:

> In the past the paramount purpose of accountability, at least in the eyes of the law, has usually been identified with the prevention of fraudulent and other abuses of financial stewardship . . . The wider economic interest of society demands disclosure because a free economy operates through the spontaneous attraction of resources to points of highest productivity, using the mechanism of markets and prices; and to this process the provision of finance is crucial . . . the needs of society by way of disclosure in company accounts can be broadly identified with those of shareholders looking for the maximum rate of return from their investments. (Rose [18], pp. 7, 10, 11)

Third, accountants have found themselves in the sometimes uncomfortable position of determining to quite a large extent the contents and significance of the reports companies make to their shareholders.

The philosophy of the British Companies Acts is based on disclosure and the showing of what has been known since 1948 as a true and fair view. Legislation has lagged behind the best accounting practice. It was not until 1908 that public companies were compelled by law to publish a balance sheet, not until 1929 that they were compelled to publish a profit and loss account, not until 1948 that they were compelled to publish group accounts, and not until 1967 that they were compelled to publish a sales figure. Companies are still not required by law to publish a source and application of funds statement.

Furthermore, the Companies Acts do not lay down the format of published financial statements nor do they attempt to state how profit should be measured or how the assets and liabilities in the balance sheet should be valued. All these very important matters have been left to the accountancy profession. Since 1971 an Accounting Standards Committee, composed entirely of members of the accountancy profession but strongly backed by the Stock Exchange, has issued a series of accounting standards which although having no legal standing are much more than simple recommendations. The Committee is generally thought to have been reasonably successful. A distinguished American practitioner, however, thinks that the British 'have been operating their institutional arrangements with a combination of naïveté and smugness'! (Defliese [7], p. 36).

The problems of accounting for inflation are severely testing the system. The original proposed solution of the Accounting Standards Committee was abandoned in favour of one worked out by a government-appointed committee, which in turn has been watered down by a proposal to make just three adjustments. Inflation accounting has also shown that accountants have relied too much on practical experience and too little on original thought.

Different approaches have been followed in other countries. In the United States, for example, a federal regulatory body, the Securities and Exchange Commission (SEC), was given statutory authority in 1934 to lay down accounting principles. It has delegated some of this authority to the accountancy profession. How much is a matter of dispute. Three well-informed and authoritative opinions voiced in the early 1970s were that

(a) the SEC has surrendered most of its power to the accountancy profession — and that this is a good thing;
(b) the SEC has surrendered most of its powers to the accountancy profession — and that this is a bad thing; and
(c) the SEC has cleverly delegated all the hard work to the accountancy profession but retained for itself the real power.[2]

In West Germany, legislation on company accounts goes well beyond that in Britain. The Companies Act prescribes both standard forms of balance sheet and

[2] The views of, respectively, Sidney Davidson (an accountant), Homer Kripke (a lawyer) and Charles Horngren (an accountant). See Burns [7] pp. 170-1.

profit and loss account and the rules of valuation to be used. The accountancy profession is active mainly as an interpreter and implementor of company legislation.

Both the American and German models have had their advocates in Britain. It now seems unlikely that a British version of the SEC will be established. Our membership of the EEC, however, means that a move towards the German system is likely although the situation is still rather confused and uncertain.

Managers

The growth of large-scale companies generated a need not only for audits but also for more and better internal accounting for management. Cost and management accounting is less a product of the industrial revolution than of the second half of the nineteenth century when companies became more capital intensive, thus making overheads more important, and when increasing competition made price-fixing much less easy. The first important work on the subject was published in 1887. Cost accounting techniques spread rapidly during World War I and in 1919 an Institute of Cost and Works Accountants (ICWA)[3] was formed. The Councils of the English Institute and the Society of Incorporated Accountants successfully opposed the granting of a royal charter to the new body. Cost and works accountants were, they claimed, with remarkable snobbery, 'not engaged in professional work, but . . . employed in the service of traders' (Stacey [21], p. 99).

But there were many chartered accountants who were prepared to enter the service of traders. In the 1970s less than half of chartered accountants are partners in or employed by practising firms. Many have succeeded well in their new occupation. In a survey of the directors of the 445 largest public companies in the early 1950s it was found that 16 per cent of directors had accounting experience compared with 17 per cent with engineering experience and 6 per cent with legal experience. Two-thirds of the engineers, however, were directors of engineering firms (Copeman [6], pp. 92-3).

A notable example of an accountant in management was Francis D'Arcy Cooper, a member of the family firm of chartered accountants, Cooper Brothers & Co. (now part of the international firm of Coopers & Lybrand). By the early 1920s the firm of Lever Bros had become, in the words of the historian of Unilever, 'a vast business with worldwide ramifications' but it was also 'still a personal autocracy just as it has been over thirty years before when it consisted of small factory at Warrington' (Wilson [23], Vol. 1, p. 269). It was Cooper who saved Lever Bros from a critical financial situation and who was, in 1929, one of the two principal architects of Unilever.

Like Unilever many British companies have expanded overseas and from quite early in the history of the profession firms of accountants have followed them. The big international firms are in effect multinational companies. Most of them are of mixed British and American origin.

The American profession in fact owes much to early immigrants from Britain. One of the earliest and perhaps the most distinguished was George O. May who was born,

[3] The ICWA changed its name to The Institute of Cost and Management Accountants in 1972 and obtained a royal charter in 1975.

the son of a Teignmouth grocer, in 1875 at a time when, as he pointed out in his Memoirs, income tax was two (old) pence in the pound. May was articled in Exeter 1892-7, spending his time, incidentally, almost entirely on bankruptcy work. He then joined Price Waterhouse & Co. first in London and then in New York where he became the senior American partner in 1911. In the 1930s he was one of the principal architects of the relationship already referred to between the American accountancy profession and the Securities and Exchange Commission (Grady [9]).

Taxpayers

We turn next, after this digression, to the needs of the *taxpayer*. In the popular mind accountants are closely linked with taxation. It was, however, not until World War I that taxation became an important aspect of professional accountancy work. It has remained so ever since.

Table 4 suggests why. The standard rate of income tax, perhaps the most visible part of the system, increased fourfold during World War I and has remained high. Taxes on income, as the second column shows, take up a larger and larger percentage of the gross national product.

The income tax system would not provide so much work for accountants, however, if, in spite of everything, it were relatively simple to understand. We all know that it is not. A crude quantitative measure of the increasing complexity of the system can be gained by counting the number of pages devoted to direct taxation in the statue book. When the law was consolidated in 1918, 180 pages were required; when it was next consolidated in 1952, 510 pages were needed; in 1977 an estimated 2000 pages would be necessary.[4]

If it is true that taxation work has kept many accountants prosperous, it is also true that our modern system of taxation could not operate without the accountancy profession.

TABLE 4

SELECTED TAXATION STATISTICS 1900-73

	Standard Rate of Income Tax (year ended 5 April)	Taxes on Income as % of Gross National Product at Factor Cost %
1900	8d.	1
1914	1s.2d.	2
1918	5s.0d.	10
1939	5s.6d.	8
1957	8s.6s.	13
1973	38.75% (7s.9d.)	14

Source: C. H. Feinstein, *National Income, Expenditure and Output of the United Kingdom 1855-1965* (1972), Tables 2 and 12; *National Income and Expenditure 1965-1975* (1976).

[4] *British Tax Review*, 1976, no. 2, p. 69.

New Users of Accounting Information

Creditors, shareholders, managers and taxpayers, then, are the traditional users of accounting information. In recent years the list of user groups has been expanded. *The Corporate Report*, a discussion paper issued by the Accounting Standards Committee in 1974, also mentions employees, analysts/advisers, business contacts, the government and the public in general. The extension of industrial democracy and worker participation — whether or not on the lines suggested by the Bullock Report — will bring an important new client for the accountant. A 'workers' handbook' on accounting has already been published (Hird [11]).

The Corporate Report also draws attention to the need for more 'social accounting'. This it defines as the reporting of those costs and benefits, which may or may not be quantifiable in money terms, arising from economic activities and substantially borne or received by the community at large or particular groups not holding a direct relationship with the reporting entity. It recognizes this as an area of growing concern to the accounting profession and one in which it has an opportunity to help develop practical reporting techniques (ASSC [2], pp. 57-8).

The recognition of new groups of users may mean a downgrading of the importance of the profit and loss account and increasing attention being given to statements showing how the wealth created by an entity is distributed to all interested parties, not just to shareholders. Such statements are already the norm in Yugoslavia (Connock [5]).

The rationale for disclosure is changing again. It is no longer just limited liability or even the rational allocation of resources. In the view of the authors of *The Corporate Report* there is an implicit responsibility to report publicly (whether or not required by law or regulation) incumbent on every economic entity whose size or format renders it significant.

Women of Account

In what position is the profession to tackle these new challenges? Can it be certain that it is getting a reasonable share of the available talent? Here there are, in my opinion, two areas of concern although in both there have been great improvements in the last ten years or so. I am thinking first of the lack of women accountants and second of the lack of academic accountants.

The title of this lecture was chosen with some care: almost all accountants are *men* of account. You may remember that Mrs Malaprop thought that young ladies needed only a 'supercilious' knowledge of accounts and for a long time they had little chance of anything more. In the early days of the profession no women were admitted. It was not until 1920 that a woman had a chance of becoming an English chartered accountant (the first was Miss Mary Harris Smith). Twenty years later there were still well under 100 of them and even in 1970 there were less than 1000. In 1976 there were just over 1600 — less than 3 per cent of the total membership. For the Scottish and Irish Institutes the figures are 3 per cent and 1 per cent. The percentages for the non-chartered accountants are much the same. There are as yet no women on the Councils of the English and Scottish Institutes and — let it be admitted — no women professors of accounting. More women are now coming into accountancy (9 per cent of the admissions to the English Institute in 1976) but there is clearly still a long way to go.[5]

Academic Accountants

Although the position has improved in recent years, academic accountants are still very thin on the ground in Britain. Let me recall the figures for 1976: well over 100,000 qualified accountants but only 30 full-time professors of accounting, and very few of them indeed at the head of departments or sub-departments of any size.

The point can be illustrated further. The report of the long range enquiry into education and training for the accounting profession published in 1974 points out that 'One has only to compare the number of accounting teachers in almost any British university with the number of teachers of law and engineering, say, to see how undernourished accounting is as an academic discipline by comparison with these two professions' (Solomons [20], p. 40). In twelve leading universities in 1972, for example, according to the report, there were 124 professors of engineering, 35 professors of law and 13 professors of accountancy. In the whole of the University of London in 1977 there are only three professors of accountancy (two at the London Business School, one at the London School of Economics); there is none at Oxford or Cambridge. The Institute of Chartered Accountants in England and Wales and the University of Manchester received their charters in the same year (1880) but there was no chair of accountancy in Manchester until 1969. At the beginning of the twentieth century in what was still the world's leading commercial and industrial nation only Birmingham and London universities provided courses in accounting.

At the end of World War II there was not one professor of accounting in the whole of England and Wales (part-time chairs in Birmingham and London having lapsed). In the next eleven years there were three appointments to chairs. Since 1962 and especially since 1969 growth has been relatively vigorous and from October 1977 there will be 35 professors of accounting in Britain (there are none in Northern Ireland) all but two of whom were appointed in the last ten years. In about half the universities the existing professor is the first to be appointed in his university in his subject.

Why has the growth of academic accounting in Britain been so recent? Unlike the United States and Germany, Britain achieved its industrial revolution with little or no help from its universities which, in England if not in Scotland, became increasingly in the nineteenth century non-vocational institutions intent on producing 'gentlemen'. The universities were attended by a very small proportion of the population. Increasing social democracy and rising standards of secondary education have led, however, to a greatly increased number of graduates. The inadequacies of British industrial performance led in the 1960s to a boom in management education with a consequent growth in the teaching of accounting to undergraduates or postgraduates seeking careers in business rather than in the profession. In the 1970s it has been realized that, at a time when jobs are scarce, accountants are needed in bad times as

[5] The English figures are based on data kindly provided by the Institute of Chartered Accountants in England and Wales. See also [8].

well as good to cope with, as James McClelland put it you will remember, both the fortunes and the necessities of their clients.

At the same time the concepts and techniques of accounting are becoming more sophisticated and complex. The old professional habit of solving practical problems as they arise works less and less well. (Inflation accounting is a good example of this.) As a result the leaders of the profession are realizing the importance of academic teaching and research in accounting.

All these factors have favoured the university teaching of accounting. Those who in the past who would have gone into the profession straight from school now go to university first. Table 5 shows how the intake of graduates into the English and Scottish Institutes has increased in recent years. The intake is increasing very rapidly but at the same time there is still plenty of scope for more graduates to enter the profession. In 1976 only 45 per cent of both the English and Scottish intake was graduate.

TABLE 5

GRADUATE RECRUITMENT INTO THE ACCOUNTANCY PROFESSION 1971-6

	Institute of Chartered Accountants in England and Wales		Institute of Chartered Accountants of Scotland	
	Total Admissions	Graduate %	Total Admissions	Graduate %
1971	2473	17	206	14
1972	2739	23	241	36
1973	3013	25	297	30
1974	3141	33	235	44
1975	3342	33	328	54
1976	2240	45	291	45

Source: Statistics supplied by the Institute of Chartered Accountants in England and Wales and the Institute of Chartered Accountants of Scotland.

Not all graduate entrants read accountancy at university and there are still practising members of the profession who would prefer that they do not do so. Practitioners of the law have expressed similar views as Professor Bridge pointed out in his inaugural lecture two years ago [3]. The arguments in favour of 'non-relevant' graduates, to use the accepted jargon, appear to be as follows:[6]

(i) A university is a place where one should get a 'broad general education' not a 'narrowly vocational' one. This criticism is mistaken on two counts. First, professional education has always been an important part of the universities' function, whether the profession in question was the church, the law, medicine, teaching or government. Second, there is confusion between a broad education and a non-vocational education. 'Relevant' degrees include not only accountancy but also economics, law and statistics and often another social science. Many non-relevant degrees concentrate on a single discipline.

(ii) Two disciplines are better than one. Accounting will be studied for

[6] The paragraphs which follow owe much to *Prospectus for a Profession* [20], pp. 104-9.

professional examinations so it is preferable to read something else at university. If this means that the intending accountant should obtain *two degrees* then there is obviously something to be said for it but in Britain today we equally obviously lack the necessary resources. If it means that accounting should only be taught outside the universities then it is really a third argument, namely that

(iii) A 'professional' subject such as accounting should be learned 'on the job' not at university. This argument is based on a half-truth. It has been well answered by Professor Solomons: 'Some aspects of the accountant's art are indeed best learnt on the job, just as a surgeon could not learn all he needs to know about surgery by listening to lectures about it or watching demonstrations. But it is a long time since surgeons learnt *all* of their surgery by serving an apprenticeship' ([20], p. 106).

(iv) Non-relevant graduates do better in professional examinations than relevant graduates. This has undoubtedly been true. It may of course be a reflection on the professional examinations. The most likely explanation is that it is only very recently that university accounting departments have attracted the best students. That they are now doing so — and may I remind you that in Exeter we are currently turning away over 96 per cent of those who apply to read Accountancy Studies — is a sign that academic accounting is at last coming of age in Britain.

Conclusion

The rise of the accountant — and indeed the professional in general — is an important but rather neglected part of recent British history. I have tried to show you how important accountants are to our present economic and social system. I have tried above all to show that what accountants do is not some arcane mystery but a response to the changing needs of society. Men of account and women of account will always be needed. It is in society's interest as well as their own that they should be educated for their responsibilities and not just trained as technicians.

REFERENCES

1. *The Accountant*, 8 August 1931.
2. Accounting Standards Steering Committee, *The Corporate Report*, London July 1975.
3. Bridge, J. W., *The Academic Lawyer: Mere Working Mason or Architect?* University of Exeter, Exeter 1975.
4. Chadwick, J., *The Mycenaean World*, Cambridge University Press, 1976.
5. Connock, M., 'Workers' Management in Yugoslavia', *Accountancy*, December 1974.
6. Copeman, G. H., *Leaders of British Industry*, Gee, London 1955.
7. Defliese, Philip L. in T. J. Burns (ed.), *Accounting in Transition: Oral Histories of Recent U.S. Experience*, College of Administrative Science, Ohio State University, Colombus, Ohio 1974.
8. Dunlop, Anna B. G., 'Women Accountants', *Accountant's Magazine*, April 1974, and 'Women Accountants', *Accountant's Magazine*, July 1974.
9. Grady, P. (ed.), *Memoirs and Accounting Thought of George O. May*, Ronald Press, New York 1962.

10. Hatfield, H. R., *Accounting*, Appleton-Century, New York 1927.

11. Hird, C., *Your Employers' Profits*, Workers' Handbook No. 2, Pluto Press, London 1975.

12. Hooke, S. H., 'Recording and Writing' in C. Singer, E. J. Holmyard and A. R. Hall (eds), *A History of Technology*, Vol. 1, Clarendon Press, Oxford 1954.

13. McClelland, J., *The Origin and Present Organisation of the Profession of Chartered Accountancy in Scotland*, Glasgow 1869.

14. Martin, J., *The Sanctification of the Lie, Grace, grace unto it! A Tribute to the Queen's sixty years' reign*, Carter and Pratt, Glasgow 1897.

15. Page, D. L., *History and the Homeric Iliad*, University of California Press, Berkeley and Los Angeles 1959.

16. Prais, S. J., *The Evolution of Giant Firms in Britain*, Cambridge University Press, 1976.

17. Robinson, H. W., *A History of Accountants in Ireland*, The Institute of Chartered Accountants in Ireland, Dublin.

18. Rose, H., *Disclosure in Company Accounts*, 2nd edn, Institute of Economic Affairs, London 1965.

19. Sarton, G., *Six Wings: Men of Science in the Renaissance*, The Bodley Head, London 1958.

20. Solomons, D., with T. M. Berridge, *Prospectus for a Profession*, Advisory Board of Accountancy Education, London 1974.

21. Stacey, N. A. H., *English Accountancy 1800-1954*, Gee, London 1954.

22. Taylor, R. Emmett, *No Royal Road: Luca Pacioli and his Times*, University of North Carolina Press, Chapel Hill, N.C. 1942.

23. Wilson, C., *The History of Unilever*, Cassell, London 1954.

24. Winsbury, R., *Thomson McLintock & Co — the First Hundred Years*, Thomson McLintock, London 1977.

BRITISH ACCOUNTANTS

A Biographical Sourcebook

Edited by R. H. Parker

ARNO PRESS
A New York Times Company
New York • 1980

INTRODUCTION

Britain has played a significant role in the development of modern accountancy but little research has been carried out into the lives of the men who founded and built up the British profession. The purpose of this sourcebook is to make more readily accessible some of the information which has already been published in the hope that accounting historians will be encouraged to devote more attention to biographical research. That such research is worthwhile I have no doubt. Accounting is man-made and we cannot hope to understand it properly if we are not aware of the men who made it and the environment in which they worked. The history of accountants is an essential part of the history of accounting.

The biographies of 65 accountants are included in this book. In 56 cases the source was an obituary; 43 of these are from The Accountant, the only journal which had a consistent policy of publishing obituaries of leading accountants, whatever professional body they belonged to.

In three cases - James Brown (1864), McClelland (1879) and Meston (1892)* - the biography is taken from The Accountants' Magazine's admirable "Eminent Accountants of the Past" Series; in two cases - Fletcher (1883) and Richard Brown (1918) - a biography has been taken from J. C. Stewart's equally admirable Pioneers of a Profession (Scottish Committee on Accounting History, 1977). Two biographies - Price (1887) and Deloitte (1898) - are taken from histories of firms; one - Touche (1935) - is an article written 25 years after the subject's death; and another - Pears (1972) - is an interview with the subject just before he died.

Obituaries must, of course, be used with care. They do not always give a completely "true and fair view" of their subject. De mortuis nil nisi bonum. Few obituaries are as candid as that of Robert Leef Murray in The Accountants'

* It has been thought helpful to the reader to give the date of death of all accountants referred to in this Introduction.

Magazine, vol. 20, 1961. This included the following passage:

> Comparatively few members of the [Edinburgh] Society had the pleasure of Mr. Murray's acquaintance, as he took but little interest in the affairs of the Society. Indeed, it is alleged that only on one solitary occasion did he grace a general meeting with his presence.

Sometimes they get the facts wrong: Pixley (1933) was called to the Bar in 1894 and not in 1904 as his obituary states.

Criteria for Inclusion

Although I did not hesitate to ask for advice, the choice of which accountants to include was ultimately a personal matter. I was concerned to illustrate the growth of the profession as a whole without undue stress on any one aspect of it. I have excluded accountants living in 1980 and accountants of British birth whose working life was spent mainly elsewhere: notable examples are Arthur Young (1948) and George O. May (1961).

Perhaps the best known names in the profession are those which have survived through association with one of the leading international or national firms. I have assumed that these would be of interest to most readers. It is for this reason that biographies have been included of McClelland (1879), Price (1887), John Young (1888), Arthur Cooper (1892), Turquand (1894), Deloitte (1898), Moore (1913), Frederick Whinney (1916), Waterhouse (1917), Thomson McLintock (1920), Ernest Cooper (1926), Harmood-Banner (1927), Arthur Whinney (1927), Pixley (1933), Touche (1935), Peat (1936), Marwick (1939), William McLintock (1947), Mann (1955), Judd (1961), Barton (1962), Binder (1966) and Mayhew (1966). Some of the names - that of Turquand, for example, the first president of the English Institute - have disappeared in recent mergers.

Leading practitioners do not always write the best books. The profession owes an equal debt to those who have recorded, systematized and even changed accounting practice and theory. Included under this heading are Guthrie (1904),

Murray (1906), Richard Brown (1918), Fells (1925), Dawson (1926), Millar (1929), Cropper (1930), Dicksee (1932), Garnsey (1932), Pixley (1933), Dickinson (1935), Norton (1939), Lisle (1940), Carter (1944), Leake (1949), de Paula (1954), Mann (1955), Spicer (1956), Cutforth (1958), Edwards (1976) and Bray (1979).

Not all the 19th century pioneers gave their names to firms which survived to the 1970s. Among those included in this book are James Brown (1864), (who always insisted that accountant be spelt accomptant), Ball (1879), Fletcher (1883), Quilter (1888), Meston (1892), Harding (1893), Chadwick (1895) and Trevor (1895).

For a long period it was financially impossible for many worthy recruits to become chartered accountants. The incorporated and certified accountants produced their own leaders, among them Martin (1935), Townsend (1938), Nelson (1950), Keens (1953) and Latham (1970).

In the early days of the profession it was not possible for women to become qualified accountants and they have only entered the profession in any numbers in very recent years. None could therefore be included here.

Many of the accountants in this book deserve more lengthy treatment. Accounting Thought and Education: Six English Pioneers (Institute of Chartered Accountants in England and Wales, 1980) by J. Kitchen and R. H. Parker devotes a chapter each to Guthrie (1904), Fells (1925), Dicksee (1932), Pixley (1933), de Paula (1954) and Cutforth (1958). There is a memorial to Bray (1979) in The Accounting Review, Spring 1980.

Scottish Influence

One cannot but be struck by the number of leading accountants who were Scots or of Scottish origin. They include some of the pioneer members of the English Institute as well as, obviously, the founders of the Scottish bodies. Thomson McLintock (1920) qualified as both an English chartered accountant and a Scottish chartered accountant - in that order. English accountants of

Scots birth include John Young (1888), a farmer's son from Moray, who, according to his obituary, "built the first house on Blackheath"; and Peat (1936), a farmer's son from Kincardineshire who was, as Lord Plender wrote in his appreciation of Peat, sent by his father "to London to earn a living" and there "called on Robert Fletcher & Co., and had the good fortune to be engaged as a junior clerk". Fletcher (1883) was a founder member of the Aberdeen Society who had moved to London to assist in the reorganisation of the London, Chatham and Dover Railway.

Several other Scots CAs also moved south, e.g. Thomson McLintock's son Sir William McLintock (1947), who, qualifying in Glasgow in 1896, "throughout the [First] war and for some time afterwards ... usually worked in [the firm's] London [office] for part of the week and in Glasgow for the remainder, with two nights in the train". He moved permanently to London in 1921.

Sir John Mann (1955), is another example of a Glaswegian moving to England. In 1910 on the death of his father John Mann, senior, (whose biography is given in Pioneers of a Profession) he became senior partner of the firm. From 1915 to 1918 he worked at the Ministry of Munitions in London and after the war opened a London office and settled in England permanently, retiring as senior partner of Mann, Judd & Co., in 1941. His successor as senior partner, Harold Judd (1961), was also a Glasgow chartered accountant who worked in munitions during the First World War and moved south.

A final example is Sir George Touche (1935), a member of the Edinburgh Society who, as Professor Murphy puts it in her Business History Review article, "went to London to seek his fortune in the financial capital of the world. There he embarked on a fourfold career in investment trusts, accountancy, the civil life of the City of London, and national politics".

Not all Scots moved to England, of course. James Brown (1864), the first president of the Edinburgh Society; McClelland (1879), first president of the

Glasgow Institute; and Meston (1892) of Aberdeen prospered at home. Richard Brown (1918) of Edinburgh was not only a successful practitioner but the most distinguished of early British accounting historians. Laird (1927) was the first professor of accounting (part-time) in a Scottish University.

Biographies of all who became Scottish chartered accountants 1854 to 1879 (there were, of course, no non-Scottish chartered accountants before 1880) are given in Pioneers of a Profession. Mrs.Moyra Kedslie is engaged on a collective biography of Scottish CAs 1854 to 1904.

Several leading members of the English accountancy profession were of Scottish descent though not birth. Examples are Murray (1906), a leading Manchester practitioner, and co-author with Carter (1944) of the earliest important British text on income tax (1st ed. 1895) and Knox (1926), a science graduate of University College London, a leading Sheffield practitioner and the first non-London accountant to become president of the English Institute.

Quakers

The Quaker influence on English accountancy would also repay examination. The Cooper brothers were the sons of "Mr. Emanuel Cooper, an eminent Quaker, well known in commercial circles as the chairman of the London and County Bank ... whose name was also equally familiar in connection with the abolition of slavery". Price (1887) also had Quaker connections.

Social Origins

Popular mythology suggests that success was always available in Scotland (but not in England) for the "lad o' pairts" (nobody paid much attention in this context to the lassies). To what extent, in fact, did the accountancy profession in Britain provide a chance for those of humble origin to rise in the world? Until we have firmer evidence from collective biographies we can but speculate.

Obituaries are not always helpful sources here. Only 20 of the biographies included here give details of the father's occupation. John Young (1888), Richard Brown (1918), Baird (1927) and Peat (1936) were Scots farmers' sons. James Brown (1864) was a "son of the manse". Price's (1887) father was a pottery manufacturer. Arthur and Ernest Cooper (1892, 1926) and Touche (1935) were the sons of bankers. Moore's (1913) father was a surgeon and Woodburn Kirby's (1932) a doctor. Turquand's (1894) father was an official assignee of the Court of Bankruptcy and Deloitte's (1898) secretary of a firm of provision merchants. Dicksee's (1932) father was an artist; Judd's (1961) a missionary in China. Knox's (1926) father, we are told, was an M.A. of Aberdeen University. Harmood-Banner (1927), Arthur Whinney (1927), William McLintock (1947) and Mann (1955) were the sons of accountants.

There are occasional hints in the biographies of more modest backgrounds. "While yet a lad", James Meston (1892), "turned to the City of Aberdeen, and entered the service of a mercantile house there in a comparatively humble capacity"; Binder (1966) was a junior clerk in Yorkshire and then Nottingham who at the age of 20 travelled to London and took a post as a correspondence clerk, a position for which he had qualified by teaching himself shorthand. He was later "given articles" and qualified as an English chartered accountant in 1908. Bray (1979), who qualified as an incorporated accountant first, was also "given" chartered articles.

"Given" means that a premium was not charged. The charging of premiums was intended, in the words of Pixley (1933), to limit membership of the English Institute to the same class of persons as those at Woolwich, Sandhurst and the Inns of Court (The Profession of a Chartered Accountant, London, 1897, Arno Press 1978, p.128).

Despite the suggestions above, Scotland was little different. Cairncross reported in 1937 that "almost a majority [of Glasgow CAs] are the children of a tiny fraction of business and professional people. As in other professions, wealth and influence are as important in shaping the opportunities and interests of children as the ability with which they are endowed" ("The Social Origins of Chartered Accountants", Accountant, 18 September 1937, p.374). As late as June 1942 the editorial writer of The Accountants' Magazine argued that "the premium brings a good type of young man, in the same way as the law of supply and demand brings an economic price for goods of other kinds".

It seems likely that, although their obituaries are silent, many of those who came up by other than the chartered route - men like Fells (1925), Martin (1935), Latham (1970) and Edwards (1976) - rose by ability and hard work from comparatively humble beginnings. It can also be hazarded that not all of the English "founding fathers" - those who became members in 1880 - would have got there afterwards. Guthrie (1904), for example, appears to have been very much a self-made man.

The Work of an Accountant

The changing nature of the work of accountants is well illustrated by the biographies. In the earliest, the emphasis is heavily on liquidations and trusteeships. James Brown's (1864) business mainly consisted of large sequestrations. Many large trusteeships and liquidations passed through the hands of McClelland (1879). Young's (1888) obituary states that "it would be endless to try to enumerate all the banks and large business concerns in which he had had the work and responsibility of winding up". Some obituaries, that of Harding (1893), for example, do provide such a list. Harding, who was president of the English Institute 1882-83 , actually resigned from the Institute in October 1883 in order to accept appointment as Chief Official Receiver.

Turquand (1894) was, states his obituary, "engaged in many of the most important liquidations of the last half-century". In conjunction with Harding he was one of the liquidators of Overend Gurney & Co., which failed in 1866. Kemp (1907) "enjoyed a splendid reputation as an able expert accountant in the

City ... and during the course of his long career he was entrusted with the winding up of many well-known concerns ..." Ernest Cooper (1926) recalled that "an accountant was regarded as associated with and dependent upon insolvency ... to be seen talking to or having your office entered by an accountant was to be avoided, particularly in the stressful times of 1866". However, company promotions were important for some practitioners - Chadwick (1895), for example.

Although taxation work did not become of general importance until the First World War, some accountants were active in this field quite early. Murray (1906) began his career by "gaining experience in the Inland Revenue offices of various northern districts". In conjunction with Carter (1944), one of his articled pupils, he wrote the earliest (1895) standard work on income tax. It was Chadwick (1895), a Liberal M.P. from 1868 to 1880, who moved on 19 May 1871 for the appointment of "a Select Committee to enquire into the mode of assessing Income and Property Tax ...".

Auditing now provides the bread and butter of most accountants in public practice. The earliest standard works were written as late as the 1880s and 1890s by Pixley (1933) and Dicksee (1932).

The growth of the railways also provided work for accountants. From about 1880 onward, railway securities were the largest group by value on the London Stock Exchange, forming 37% of the total in 1913 (W. J. Reader, A House in the City, London, 1979, p.67). According to his obituary, Ball (1879) and his firm Quilter Ball & Co. "were mainly instrumental in forming the bases upon which railway accounts have since become thoroughly settled", creating order "out of the utmost diversity and confusion". Ball's firm was eventually absorbed by Deloitte's, and The Accountant wrote in Deloitte's obituary (1898) that "the present system of keeping English Railway Accounts is due very largely to Mr. Deloitte's initiative in the eighteen-sixties when he acted as professional accountant to the Great Western Railway".

Railway rates became a bone of contention between railway companies and "traders". Fells (1925) was a leading expert witness before the Railway and Canal Commission Court on the side of the traders.

The Textbook Writers

Long-lived textbooks are typical of most professions. Pixley (1933), Dicksee (1932), de Paula (1954) and Cutforth (1958) all wrote best-selling texts on auditing. Dicksee, Cropper (1930) (whose obituary notice in The Accountant was contributed by his publisher), Norton (1939), Carter (1944), Leake (1949) and Spicer (1956) contributed extensively to the professional and student literature on bookkeeping and accounting. Lisle (1940) edited an ambitious and successful Encyclopaedia of Accounting.

Accounting and the Universities

Academic accounting did not begin to flourish in Britain until very recently. There are thus no equivalents of the Americans Hatfield or Littleton in this book. Edwards (1976) is the only full-time academic included. Although he was a professor of economics, several of his 1930s articles have become accounting classics. Dicksee (1932) was the first professor (part-time) of accounting at both Birmingham University and the London School of Economics. Dawson (1926) was one of his successors at Birmingham; de Paula (1954) succeeded him at the L.S.E. Laird (1927) is the only Scottish part-time professor in the list; Bray (1979) briefly held a chair attached to the Society of Incorporated Accountants.

Many British accountants have had no connection with universities, either as undergraduates or as teachers. The degrees of Knox (1926) (B.Sc., London), Dickinson (1935) (M.A., Cantab.) and Mann (1955) (M.A., Glasgow) were exceptional, although many of the Scots - e.g., James Brown (1864) and Moore (1913) - attended university lectures in law.

Knights, Baronets and Peers

Twenty-four of the accountants in this book received a knighthood, baronetcy or peerage. Such official and social recognition of accountants was seldom granted before the First World War. Exceptions were Harding (1893) who was knighted on his retirement as Chief Official Receiver; Peat (1936) knighted in 1912 for public services; Harmood-Banner (1927), who was knighted in 1913, the year he was elected Lord Mayor of Liverpool; and Plender (1946) (see below).

The War brought many accountants into government work. Several were knighted for their services including Arthur Whinney (1927) who became Assistant-Accountant-General of the Navy. Garnsey, who died aged 49 in 1932 at the height of a brilliant career, Dickinson (1935), who had returned to England from the United States in 1913, Jenkinson (1935) and Mann (1955), were all closely connected with the Ministry of Munitions during the War and received knighthoods. Townsend (1938), another knight, was Controller of Government Factories between the Wars.

Plender (1946), who was extensively involved in government work of all kinds,was knighted in 1911, created a baronet in 1923 and a peer in 1931. Latham (1970), the only other peer in this book (accountancy still lags well behind the law in this respect!) had a very different career: a pioneer member of the Labour Party, he was Leader of the London County Council from 1940 to 1948. He was President of the National Union of Clerks in 1916 and of the Association of Certified Accountants from 1951 to 1954.

It was often the second generation which received the honours: Arthur Whinney (1927) rather than Frederick (1916); Francis D'Arcy Cooper (1941) rather than Arthur (1892) or Ernest (1926); William McLintock (1947) rather than Thomson (1920); John Mann, junior (1955) rather than John Mann, senior (1910); Nicholas Waterhouse (1964) rather than Edwin (1905).

In Conclusion

The British accountancy profession has come a long way in a comparatively short period. It owes many of its characteristics, both good and bad, to the men whose biographies are set out in this book. Their lives deserve the attention of accounting historians.

BIOGRAPHIES INCLUDED IN CHRONOLOGICAL ORDER OF DATE OF DEATH

(ACC = The Accountant, TAM = The Accountant's Magazine)

Date	Name	Source of Biography
1864	James Brown	TAM, 4, 1900, 85-90
1879	John Ball	ACC, 23.8.1879, 5-6
1879	James McClelland	TAM, 1, 1897, 294-300
1883	Robert Fletcher	J. C. Stewart, Pioneers of a Profession, 80
1887	Samuel Lowell Price	G. E. Richards, History of the Firm /Price Waterhouse & Co./
1888	William Quilter	ACC, 14, 1888, 754
1888	John Young	ACC, 14, 1888, 813-4
1892	James Meston	TAM, 7, 1903, 196-200
1892	Arthur Cooper	ACC, 18, 1892, 657
1893	Sir Robert Palmer Harding	ACC, 19, 1893, 1093
1894	William Turquand	ACC, 20, 1894, 290-1
1895	David Chadwick	ACC, 21, 1895, 771-2
1895	Charles Robinson Trevor	ACC, 21, 1895, 917-8
1898	William Welch Deloitte	/Sir Russell Kettle/, Deloitte & Co. 1845-1956, 5-11
1904	Edwin Guthrie	ACC, 31, 1904, 236-7
1906	Adam Murray	ACC, 35, 1906, 353-4
1907	Charles Fitch Kemp	ACC, 37, 1907, 580-1
1913	Alexander Moore	TAM, 17, 1913, 6-7
1916	Frederick Whinney	ACC, 54, 1916, 582-3
1917	Edwin Waterhouse	ACC, 57, 1917, 242
1918	Richard Brown	J. C. Stewart, Pioneers of a Profession, 55-6
1920	Thomson McLintock	TAM, 24, 1920, 159-161
1925	John Manger Fells	ACC, 74, 1926, 11

1926	Ernest Cooper	ACC, 74, 1926, 56-7
1926	Sidney S. Dawson	ACC, 74, 1926, 758
1926	George Walter Knox	ACC, 75, 1926, 743
1927	T. P. Laird	TAM, 31, 1927, 527-530
1927	Sir John Harmood-Banner, Bt.	ACC, 76, 1927, 341
1927	Sir Arthur Whinney	ACC, 76, 1927, 840
1929	Robert Cockburn Millar	TAM, 33, 1929, 290-4
1930	Lionel Cuthbert Cropper	ACC, 83, 1930, 332-3
1932	Lawrence R. Dicksee	ACC, 86, 1932, 236, 283-4
1932	Sir Gilbert Garnsey	ACC, 87, 1932, 9-10
1932	Sir Woodburn Kirby	ACC, 87, 1932, 679-680
1933	Francis W. Pixley	ACC, 88, 1933, 595-6
1935	Sir Arthur Lowes Dickinson	ACC, 92, 1935, 345
1935	Sir George Touche, Bt.	Mary E. Murphy, Business History Review, 34, 1960, 467-477
1935	Sir James Martin	ACC, 93, 1935, 292-3
1935	Sir Mark Webster Jenkinson	ACC, 93, 1935, 638
1936	Sir William Barclay Peat	ACC, 94, 1936, 157
1938	Sir Reginald Townsend	Cost Accountant, 1938, 183-4
1939	James Marwick	ACC, 101, 1939, 108
1939	George Pepler Norton	ACC, 101, 1939, 230
1940	George Lisle	TAM, 44, 1940, 83-4
1941	Sir Francis D'Arcy Cooper, Bt.	ACC, 105, 1941, 360
1944	Roger Neale Carter	ACC, 112, 1945, 5, 14
1946	Lord Plender	ACC, 114, 1946, 43-4
1947	Sir William McLintock, Bt.	ACC, 116, 1947, 297
1949	Percy Dewe Leake	ACC, 121, 1949, 610
1950	Charles Hewetson Nelson	Accountancy, 61, 1950, 121-2
1953	Sir Thomas Keens	Accountancy, 65, 1954, 15-16

1954	Frederic Rudolf Mackley de Paula	ACC, 131, 1954, 669-670, 705-6; 132, 1955, 105-6
1955	Sir John Mann	TAM, 59, 1955, 182-3
1956	Ernest Evan Spicer	Accountancy, 67, 1956, 83
1958	Sir Arthur Cutforth	ACC, 138, 1958, 469
1961	Harold Godfrey Judd	TAM, 65, 1961, 148-9
1962	Sir Harold Barton	ACC, 147, 1962, 557
1966	Sir Bernhard Binder	ACC, 155, 1966, 91-2
1966	Sir Basil Mayhew	ACC, 155, 1966, 643-4
1968	Sir Russell Kettle	ACC, 158, 1968, 914-5
1969	Sir Harold Howitt	ACC, 161, 1969, 783
1970	Lord Latham	Certified Accountants Journal, 62, 1970, 313-4
1972	Sidney John Pears	Accountancy, 83, July 1972, 17-21
1976	Sir Ronald Edwards	ACC, 174, 1976, 91
1979	Frank Sewell Bray	Accountancy, 90, March 1979, 37

Those first councillors . . .

Several of today's firms can trace descent from the first Council of the Institute

Busy professional men and women seldom have time to look back along the road they and their predecessors have travelled. The centenary of the Institute of Chartered Accountants in England and Wales (ICAEW) is a useful time at which to remember the great changes which have taken place in accounting during the past 100 years. The profession was, of course, much smaller in the early days. The first ICAEW List of Members (1881) contains 1,025 members. In contrast, the 1979/80 List discloses a membership of 68,010.

The strengths of any profession are continuity and change. We should not lightly throw away our inheritance, but we must equally beware of repeating the mistakes along with the successes of our founding fathers. One way to look at this process of continuity and change is to trace the fate of the firms of the leading practitioners of 1880. A quick glance at the 1881 List of Members reveals a number of familiar names. (Throughout this article, except in the accompanying tables, the names of members of the first Council of the ICAEW are given in italics.)

At 14 George Street (now Mansion House Place), *Arthur Cooper*, Ernest Cooper, Francis Cooper and Edward Hewitt Fletcher were in partnership as Cooper Brothers & Co. At 4 Lothbury, *William Welch Deloitte*, Henry Dever and *John George Griffiths* were practising as Deloitte, Dever, Griffiths & Co.

The firm of Harding, Whinney & Co, at 8 Old Jewry had as partners *Robert Palmer Harding*, William Hurlblatt, John Smith and *Frederick Whinney*. *Samuel Lowell Price*, Edwin Waterhouse and George Sneath were in practice at 44 Gresham Street as Price, Waterhouse & Co. There was no firm with the name of Peat in it, but William Barclay Peat was the Middlesbrough partner of the London firm of R. Mackay & Co at 3 Lothbury. The London partners were *Roderick Mackay*, Christopher Thomas Moore and Alexander Thomson.

That we have not mentioned the founders of the other leading firms of 1980 is a reminder that Arthur Young was a Scot who emigrated to the US, and that James McClelland, the Moores, Sir George Touche and Thomson McLintock were all Scottish chartered accountants (McLintock, in fact, was both an English and a Scots CA: he was admitted to the ICAEW in 1880 and to the Glasgow Institute in 1891).

The first Council. A more systematic approach is to look at all the 45 members of the first Council. That many of the names are no longer remembered is as important as the fact that some of them have survived.

The names of the first councillors are listed in clause 2 of the Royal Charter. Figure 1 reproduces this list with the addition of the name and location of the firm. (At this time and for long afterwards all members of the council had to be in public practice). In some cases members practised under their own names.

It will be noted that only five firms had

Professor R. H. Parker BSc(ECON) FCA, professor of accounting, University of Exeter

a golden heritage

Figure 1
First Council of the ICAEW

Alfred Allot	Sheffield
Jarvis William Barber (Barber Brothers & Wortley)	Sheffield
John Bath (John Bath & Sons)	London
Josiah Beddow (Josiah Beddow & Son)	London
John Blackburn (H. W. & J. Blackburn)	Bradford & Leeds
Henry Bolland (Gibson, Bolland & Jackson)	Liverpool
James Charles Bolton (J. C. Bolton & Son)	London
Thomas Browning	Manchester
George Augustus Cape (Cape & Harris)	London
Edward Carter (Carter & Carter)	Birmingham
William Cash (Cash & Stone)	London
David Chadwick (Chadwicks, Collier & Co)	London & Manchester
Arthur Wigham Chalmers (Chalmers & Wade)	Liverpool
Arthur Cooper (Cooper Brothers & Co)	London
Joseph Davies (Davies, Voisey & Davies)	Warrington
William Welch Deloitte (Deloitte, Dever, Griffiths & Co)	London
Walter Newton Fisher	Birmingham
John George Griffiths (Deloitte, Dever, Griffiths & Co)	London
Edwin Guthrie (Thomas, Wade, Guthrie & Co)	Manchester
Robert Palmer Harding (Harding, Whinney & Co)	London
Alfred Cotton Harper (E. Norton Harper & Sons)	London
Edward Norton Harper (E. Norton Harper & Sons)	London
Edward Hart (Hart Brothers, Tibbetts & Co)	London
Charles Fitch Kemp (C. F. Kemp, Ford & Co)	London
George Walter Knox (Knox & Burbidge; Knox, Craig & Co)	Sheffield & London
George Herbert Ladbury (Ladbury, Collison & Viney)	London
Roderick Mackay (R. Mackay & Co)	London & Middlesbrough
Henry Grosvenor Nicholson (H. G. Nicholson & Co)	Manchester
Edward Thomas Peirson	Coventry
Samuel Lowell Price (Price, Waterhouse & Co)	London
Thomas William Read	Liverpool
Joseph John Saffery (J. J. Saffery & Co)	London
Thomas George Shuttleworth (Tasker & Shuttleworth)	Sheffield
George Edwin Swithinbank (G. E. Swithinbank & Co; G. E. Swithinbank, Briggs & Co)	London & Bristol
Frederick Tendron	London
John Henry Tilly (Tilly & Co)	London
William Turquand (Turquand, Youngs & Co)	London
James Waddell (J. Waddell & Co)	London
Charles Henry Wade (Thomas, Wade, Guthrie & Co)	Manchester
William Henry Watson (John Watson & Sons)	Sheffield
Thomas Abercrombie Welton (Quilter, Ball & Co)	London
Frederick Whinney (Harding, Whinney & Co)	London
John Unwin Wing (Wing, Wing, Lilley & Co)	Sheffield
John Young (Turquand, Youngs & Co)	London

William Welch Deloitte, president 1888-89

George Walter Knox, president 1896-97

offices in more than one city. Five firms—Deloitte, Dever, Griffiths & Co; Thomas, Wade, Guthrie & Co; Harding, Whinney & Co; E Norton Harper & Sons; and Turquand, Youngs & Co—had two of their partners on the Council.

Figure 2 lists the presidents and vice-presidents of the ICAEW from 1880 to 1902. Throughout the 19th century the presidency of the ICAEW was dominated by the London firms (*George Walter Knox*, president 1896-97 was only half an exception—he practised in both Sheffield and London) and by members of the first Council (the two exceptions, Edwin Waterhouse 1892-94 and Ernest Cooper 1899-

Figure 2
Presidents and vice-presidents 1880-1904

	President	*Vice-president*
1880-82	William Turquand	Robert Palmer Harding
1882-83	Robert Palmer Harding	Arthur Cooper
1883-84	Arthur Cooper	Frederick Whinney
1884-88	Frederick Whinney	William Welch Deloitte
1888-89	William Welch Deloitte	Joseph John Saffery
1889-90	Joseph John Saffery	Adam Murray*†
1890-91	Joseph John Saffery	Thomas Abercrombie Welton
1891-92	Thomas Abercrombie Welton	Edward Carter†
1892-94	Edwin Waterhouse*	John George Griffiths
1894-96	Charles Fitch Kemp	George Walter Knox†
1896-97	George Walter Knox†	Walter Newton Fisher†
1897-98	John George Griffiths	Walter Newton Fisher†
1898-99	John George Griffiths	Ernest Cooper*
1899-1900	Ernest Cooper*	John Sutherland Harmood-Banner*
1900-01	Ernest Cooper*	Alfred Augustus James*
1901-02	Walter Newton Fisher†	Alfred Augustus James*
1902-03	Alfred Augustus James*	Francis William Pixley*
1903-04	Francis William Pixley*	Thomas George Shuttleworth†

**Not a member of the First Council †Not a London practitioner*

1901, were partners of such members).

Jarvis William Barber, whose name is not in Figure 2, was vice-president 1910-11 and president 1912-13. *Alfred Cotton Harper* was vice-president 1921-22.

Only two of the firms represented in Figure 1 have retained their original names: Josiah Beddow & Son and (allowing for the loss of a comma) Price Waterhouse & Co. Figure 3 lists these two firms and all those firms whose name has survived in an altered but still recognisable form.

What happened to the firms of the other councillors? In six cases (Bath, Bolland, Browning Nicholson, Tendron and Waddell) there appears to be no successor firm. (I would be delighted to hear from any descendants I have failed to locate—Waddell apparently died in New York in 1892). In many other cases their firms have been taken over or absorbed. These are listed in Figure 4.

A striking difference between the English accountancy profession 100 years ago and today is the present dominance of a few very large firms. As Richard Briston has shown 'The UK Accountancy Profession in the Move Towards Monopoly Power' (*The Accountants' Magazine*, November 1979, pp458-460), this tendency has become even more marked during the past decade. The names of these firms are prominent in Figures 3 and 4.

Several strands, for example, lead to Ernst & Whinney. *Frederick Whinney* was apprenticed to *Robert Palmer Harding*, first vice-president and second president of the Institute, and taken into partnership in 1857. Harding resigned his membership of the Institute in 1883 on his appointment as Chief Official Receiver. *John Young* and *William Turquand* (first president) were in practice together as Turquands, Youngs & Co from at least 1857. The merger with Barton, Mayhew & Co was followed by merger with what is now Ernst & Whinney in 1979. Ernst & Whinney can thus claim descent from three out of the first four presidents of the Institute.

The third president was *Arthur Cooper*. His fellow councillor *Edward Carter's* Birmingham firm was amalgamated with Cooper Brothers & Co (later Coopers & Lybrand) in 1960. Coopers & Lybrand can also claim descent from *Walter Newton Fisher's* Birmingham firm and from the Manchester office of *David Chadwick's* firm (the London office was taken over by Mellors, Basden & Co).

The fifth and 11th presidents of the Institute were *William Welch Deloitte* and *John George Griffiths*, partners in the firm known in 1880 as Deloitte, Dever, Griffiths & Co. The other links of Deloitte's

William Turquand, president 1880-82

with the first councillors are *William Cash*, whose firm Cash Stone & Co became in 1964 part of Harmood-Banner, Cash, Stone & Mounsey, which merged with Deloittes in 1974, and *Thomas Abercrombie Welton*, whose firm of Quilter Ball & Co, after several changes of name, merged with Deloitte's as early as 1918.

Another member of the first Council was *Roderick Mackay*. He was the partner of Robert Fletcher who had come down to London from Aberdeen in 1867 to establish the firm which on Mackay's death in 1891 was renamed W. B. Peat & Co, and in 1911 Peat, Marwick, Mitchell & Co. *Edwin Guthrie's* firm in Manchester became the Manchester office of Peat, Marwick, Mitchell & Co in 1955.

Touche Ross and Co is a firm of Scottish and North American descent which has absorbed the English firms descended from *Thomas William Read* of Liverpool and from *Charles Fitch Kemp* of London. Kemp's firm, originally C. F. Kemp, Ford & Co, became Kemp Chatteris. When Read died in 1895, his firm was continued by his son, Theodore William Read; when the latter died in 1899 the firm was carried on by Edmund D. White. Both Kemp Chatteris and Edmund D. White & Sons were eventually absorbed by Touche Ross and Co.

Price Waterhouse & Co is represented by *Samuel Lowell Price*. There is also a rather tenuous link with *George Edwin Swithinbank*, who was a partner in firms in London, Bristol, Rotherham and Sheffield. I have been unable to trace successors of the London and Yorkshire firms; but G. E. Swithinbank, Briggs & Co, of Bristol merged in 1888 with Hudson,

Figure 3
Firms of first councillors which have survived with an unchanged or altered, but still recognisable name

1880	*1980*
Barber Brothers & Wortley	Barber, Harrison & Platt
Beddow (Josiah) & Son	Beddow (Josiah) & Son
Cape & Harris	Cape & Dalgleish
Chalmers & Wade	Chalmers, Impey & Co
Cooper Brothers & Co	Coopers & Lybrand
Deloitte, Dever, Griffiths & Co	Deloitte Haskins & Sells
Harding, Whinney & Co	Ernst & Whinney
Hart Brothers, Tibbetts & Co	Hart Brothers, Reddall & Co
Knox & Burbidge	Knox, Franklin & Co
Knox, Craig & Co	Knox Cropper
Ladbury, Collison & Viney	Viney Merretts
Edward Thomas Peirson	Peirson (Edward Thomas) & Sons
Price, Waterhouse & Co	Price Waterhouse & Co
J. J. Saffery & Co	Safferys
Tilly & Co	Brown, Peet & Tilley Howard, Tilly & Co
Watson (John) & Sons	Watson (John), Sons & Wheatcroft

Smith, Williams & Co to form Hudson, Smith, Briggs & Co, which is now the Bristol office of Price Waterhouse & Co.

Successor firms. Figure 5 lists the 26 successor firms of the first Council, the figure in brackets showing the number of 'descents'. The first three firms on the list have already been discussed. Many of the others are also well worth a mention. Chalmers, Impey & Co can claim descents from *Anthony Wigham Chalmers*, of Liverpool, whose firm at the date of the charter was known as Chalmers and Wade, and from *Joseph Davies*, of Warrington. Davies was in practice with a Lewis Voisey, whose firm eventually became Chalmers, Wade, Voisey and Co, and is now the Warrington office of Chalmers, Impey & Co.

Sheffield is one of the few District Societies to have published a centenary history [Alan M. Hoe, *The Sheffield & District Society of Chartered Accountants. The First Hundred Years. Centenary 1877-1977 (1977)*] and from this we learn that W. G. Hawson & Co have absorbed the firms descending from *Alfred Allot* and *John Unwin Wing*. The vicissitudes of the careers of Allot and Wing are discussed by Bruce Anderson and Alan Hoe in their article, 'Company promotion and the accountancy profession in nineteenth century Sheffield' published in the winter 1979

Figure 4
Firms of first councillors taken over or absorbed

Taken over or absorbed by	*Name of councillor*
Ball Baker Carnaby Deed	Bolton
Chalmers, Impey & Co	Davies
Coopers & Lybrand	Carter
Coopers & Lybrand	Fisher
Coopers & Lybrand	Chadwick (Manchester office)
Cork (W.H.), Gully & Co	Nicholls
Deloitte Haskins & Sells	Cash
Deloitte Haskins & Sells	Welton
Ernst & Whinney	Turquand
Ernst & Whinney	Young
Hawson (W.G.) & Co	Allot
Hawson (W.G.) & Co	Wing
Hays Allan	Harper (father and son)
Mellors, Basden & Co	Chadwick (London office)
Peat, Marwick, Mitchell & Co	Guthrie
Peat, Marwick, Mitchell & Co	Mackay
Price Waterhouse & Co	Swithinbank (Bristol office)
Robson Rhodes	Blackburn
Spicer & Pegler	Wade
Thornton Baker	Shuttleworth
Touche Ross & Co	Kemp
Touche Ross & Co	Read

Figure 5
Successor firms to the first councillors

(Number of councillors shown in brackets)

Cooper & Lybrand (4)
Deloitte Haskins & Sells (4)
Ernst & Whinney (4)
Chalmers, Impey & Co (2)
Hawson (W.G.) & Co (2)
Hays Allan (2)
Peat, Marwick, Mitchell & Co (2)
Price Waterhouse & Co (2)
Touche Ross & Co (2)
Ball Baker Carnaby Deed (1)
Barber, Harrison & Platt (1)
Beddow (Josiah) & Son (1)
Brown, Peet & Tilly (1)
Cape & Dalgleish (1)
Cork (W.H.), Gully & Co (1)
Hart Brothers, Reddall & Co (1)
Howard, Tilly & Co (1)
Knox Cropper (1)
Knox, Franklin & Co (1)
Mellors, Basden & Co (1)
Peirson (Edward Thomas) & Sons (1)
Robson Rhodes (1)
Safferys (1)
Spicer & Pegler (1)
Thornton Baker (1)
Viney Merretts (1)
Watson (John), Sons & Wheatcroft (1)

issue of *Accounting and Business Research*.

Hays Allan is the successor of the firm of *Edward Norton Harper* and *Alfred Cotton Harper*, a firm practising until quite recently as Harper, Feather & Paterson. Ball Baker Deed & Co (later Ball Baker Carnaby Deed) absorbed in 1972 the firm of Bolton, Pitt & Breden, which had been formed in 1898 by *James Charles Bolton*, George Stanhope Pitt (an incorporated accountant who was president of the Incorporated Society of Accountants and Auditors 1923-1926) and Thomas Henry Breden.

George Augustus Cape's firm of Cape & Harris became in 1885 Cape & Dalgleish, a name which has been retained ever since. Cape died in 1889, leaving John Dalgleish to carry on as the sole partner. The firm gave its name to a leading auditing case: *Wilde & Others v Cape & Dalgleish* [1897] Acct L.R. 81, where fraud was not discovered owing to the auditors omitting to examine the passbook. The defence was that an audit of the cash transactions was not part of the original arrangements, but this could not be substantiated and a settlement was arrived at.

A number of the firms of 1880 have more than one descendant. An example is the firm of Thomas, Wade, Guthrie & Co. *Charles Henry Wade* and *Edwin Guthrie* separated in 1895. As already stated, Guthrie's firm was eventually absorbed by Peat, Marwick, Mitchell & Co; Wade's firm now forms part of the Manchester office of Spicer & Pegler.

John Henry Tilly's firm of Tilly & Co became, in 1904, Tilly, Brown & Peet, and has two successor firms: Howard, Tilly & Co, of London, and Brown, Peet & Tilly, of Croydon. The two firms of Walter Knox (Knox & Burbidge, of Sheffield, and Knox Craig & Co, of London) have survived as Knox Franklin & Co, of Sheffield (associated with Pannell Fitzpatrick & Co and Pannell Kerr Forster & Company) and Knox Cropper, of London.

Francis Nicholl's firm went through a number of changes of name and partners: in 1881 it was called Nicholls & Leatherdale, in 1885 Francis Nicholls & Co, and from 1888 onwards Francis Nicholls, White & Co. It is now merged with W. H. Cork Gully & Co. *Edward Hart's* firm is still readily recognisable as Hart Brothers, Reddall & Co. *Edward Thomas Peirson's* Coventry firm is now Edward Thomas Peirson & Sons, of Market Harborough. *Joseph John Saffery's* firm of J. J. Saffery & Co is now Safferys.

John Blackburn's Bradford and Leeds firm of H. W. & J. Blackburn eventually became Blackburns Coates & Co and later Blackburns, Robson, Coates & Co. It is now part of Robson Rhodes. Blackburn was a member of the Council for a record 51 years (1880-1931).

Thomas George Shuttleworth's Sheffield firm of Tasker & Shuttleworth had become T. G. Shuttleworth & Son by 1891, and is now part of Thornton Baker. The latter firm also has a tenuous link with *Jarvis William Barber*. Joshua Wortley & Sons separated from Barber Brothers & Wortley in 1903, and joined Thornton Baker in 1962. Another Sheffield firm, John Watson, Sons & Wheatcroft, is the successor of *John Watson's* firm.

In 1881 *George Herbert Ladbury* was a partner in Ladbury, Collison & Viney. Both Ladbury and Collison soon retired, and by 1893 the firm was known as Viney, Price & Goodyear, one of the predecessor firms of Viney Merretts.

How does the Council of 1980 compare with that of 1880? It is now much larger (74 as compared with 45). It is no longer composed solely of practitioners; 49 of the councillors are in practice, 25 in commerce, industry, Government service, or academic life. Figure 6 lists those firms which can claim both a descent from a Councillor of 1880 and a member of Council in 1980.

Seven founding fathers. The continuing names of importance from 1880 are clearly *Cooper, Deloitte, Price* and *Whinney*. That their names have survived is a tribute both to them and to their successors. The absorption of Welton's firm by Deloitte's in 1918 was an early instance of a firm which failed to cope with the problem of succession. Apart from the four just mentioned, the most interesting members of the first Council are *Guthrie, Knox* and *Turquand*.

For further details of Guthrie see J. Kitchen and R. H. Parker, *Accounting Thought and Education: Six English Pioneers*, ICAEW, 1980.

Arthur Cooper was the second son of Emanuel Cooper, a Quaker who became chairman of the London and County Bank and who was active in the abolition of slavery. Both Arthur and his elder brother, William, gained their experience of accountancy in the office of Quilter, Ball & Co, the firm of which Welton was senior partner in 1880. William set up business on his own account in 1854, and was joined in 1856 by Arthur. The firm occupied offices in George Street (now Mansion House Place) for over 100 years—from 1854 to 1959. The Bank of China now stands on the site.

William and Arthur were later joined by their brother Ernest, who in a talk given in 1927 recalled that in the 1860s: 'We could hardly, south of the Tweed, claim to be a profession . . . An accountant was regarded as associated with and dependent upon insolvency, and I well remember that to be seen talking to or having your office entered by an accountant was to be avoided, particularly in the stressful times of 1866 [the year of the Overend Gurney crash].

Arthur Cooper's obituary in THE ACCOUNTANT (August 27, 1892) refers to his work as liquidator, receiver, auditor and trustee. He was a Fellow of the Institute of Accountants (the most prestigious of the predecessor bodies of the ICAEW). He became vice-president of the ICEAW in 1882-83, and president in 1883-84. He was chairman of the Institute's Building Committee but did not live to see Chartered Accountants' Hall completed. He died in 1892, aged 59.

William Welch Deloitte was the grandson of a Count de Loitte, who left France during the Revolution in 1793 and later became a teacher of French at a college in Hull. Deloitte's father was secretary to a firm of provision merchants; he married the daughter of a West Indies planter named Welch. Deloitte spent 12 years on the staff of the Official Assignee in Bankruptcy of the City of London. In 1845 at the age of 27 he started practice on his own account at 11 Basinghall Street, later moving to 4 Lothbury where the firm, under various names, remained until 1905.

According to his obituary in THE ACCOUNTANT the double account system of keeping English railway accounts was very largely due to Deloitte's initiative in the 1860s, when he acted as professional accountant to the Great Western Railway. He was also the originator of a system of hotel account keeping, and investigated frauds perpetuated on the Great Northern Railway in 1857 and on the Great Eastern Steamship Company in 1870. His firm audited nearly all the large cable companies. Deloitte was vice-president of the ICAEW 1884-88, and president 1888-89. He retired in 1897 and died in 1898.

Edwin Guthrie was born in Bermondsey in 1841. A few years later, the family moved to Liverpool. In 1861, he was working as a bookkeeper to a general merchant. When he married in 1869, his occupation was given as estate agent. In the early 1870s he left Liverpool and went into practice in Manchester with John Thomas and *Charles Henry Wade*. Neither Guthrie nor Wade, both of whom were to become members of the first Council of the ICAEW, joined the Manchester Institute of Accountants when it was formed on 6 February 1871. In 1878, however, they set up the Accountants' Incorporation Association to protect the interests of those not members of any existing accountancy body. Both were signatories of the petition for a royal charter.

Guthrie also became involved in the institutional beginnings of the American profession. In 1883, he formed the first English accounting firm in New York, Barrow, Wade, Guthrie & Co (merged with Peat, Marwick, Mitchell & Co in 1950). The American Association of Public Accountants (one of the predecessor bo-

Frederick Whinney, president 1884-88

Arthur Cooper, president 1883-84

Figure 6
Firms (including successor firms) with Council members in both 1880 and 1980

	Number of councillors	
	1880	*1980*
Barber, Harrison & Platt	1	1
Chalmers, Impey & Co	2	1
Coopers & Lybrand	4	4
Deloitte Haskins & Sells	4	3
Ernst & Whinney	4	2
Mellors, Basden & Co	1	1
Peat, Marwick, Mitchell & Co	2	3
Price Waterhouse & Co	2	4
Spicer & Pegler	1	2
Thornton Baker	1	2
Touche Ross & Co	2	3
	24	26

dies of the American Institute of Certified Public Accountants) was formed at a meeting held in 1886 at Guthrie's New York office.

Guthrie was an active speaker and writer. His articles in THE ACCOUNTANT on such matters as the want of uniformity in accounts, depreciation, local authority accounts, and the payment of interest out of capital were both authoritative and provoking. He sought principles, but was not lacking in practical experience. He was, for example, chairman of the Finance Committee of the Lancashire County Council from 1889 until his death in 1904.

George Walter Knox was born in London in 1842, the only son of George Knox, MA, of Aberdeen. He was educated at University College School, Mill Hill School and University College, London, where he graduated in science in 1863, having gained the Birkbeck Gold Medal for analytical chemistry and a silver medal for botany. He is an early exception to the rule that chartered accountancy in England and Wales did not attract graduates.

Knox began to practise as a public accountant in Sheffield about 1870. He was a prominent member of the Sheffield Institute of Accountants, one of the predecessor bodies of the ICAEW. He was vice-president of the ICAEW 1894-96, and president 1896-97. He opened an office in London in 1884, and both Knox Franklin & Co, of Sheffield, and Knox Cropper, of London, descend from the firms he founded.

Knox was for 18 years chairman of the ICAEW's Examination Committee. His firm acted as auditors to the Salvation Army, whose system of accounting he instituted. He married in 1866 a daughter of H. O. Wills, of Bristol. He died in 1926 at the age of 84, one of the last survivors of the first Council. His portrait by Sir William Llewelyn hangs in Chartered Accountants' Hall.

Samuel Lowell Price, son of Charles Price, a pottery manufacturer of Bristol, was born on 12 January, 1821. He began to practice accountancy in London in 1848. In 1865 he was joined in partnership by W. H. Hoyland and Edwin Waterhouse. Hoyland retired from the partnership in 1874, and the firm's name became Price, Waterhouse & Co. It has remained unchanged since, apart from the elimination of the comma in 1940.

Samuel Lowell Price married in 1848 Emma Nutter Price, who was related to him by marriage. The marriage took place in Wansbeck, Denmark, as the laws of England at the time did not provide for such a marriage.

Price was one of the founders in London in 1870 of the Institute of Accountants. He died in 1887.

William Turquand was the first president of the ICAEW. He was born about 1819, the son of an official assignee in the Court of Bankruptcy. THE ACCOUNTANT in its obituary (31 March, 1894) states that he was engaged in many of the most important liquidations of the second half of the 19th century, including several banks and insurance companies. He was liquidator of Overand, Gurney & Co with *Robert Palmer Harding*. Before becoming first president of the ICAEW, he was vice-president of the Institute of Accountants 1870-77, and president 1877-80.

Frederick Whinney was apprenticed to *Robert Palmer Harding*, and taken into partnership in 1857. 'Joining the profession at a very favourable time', wrote THE ACCOUNTANT in his obituary notice (May 20, 1916), 'Mr Whinney soon made a great reputation, both as a liquidator and as an auditor'. He was appointed to complete the liquidation of Overand, Gurney & Co. which proved to be a very intricate and protracted business.

He was president of the ICAEW for four consecutive years, from 1884 to 1888, and gave evidence before the Davey Committee on company law in 1895. He retired from practice in 1905, and died in 1916 at the age of 87, the firm at this date bearing the name of Whinney, Smith & Whinney.

Memorial

FRANK SEWELL BRAY

1906–1979

Frank Sewell Bray was born in London on October 12, 1906, joined the firm of Tansley Witt & Co., chartered accountants, of which he later became senior partner, in the early 1920s, and qualified as an incorporated accountant in 1932 and as a chartered accountant in 1937. Author of numerous books and articles, he became a part-time Senior Nuffield Research Fellow in Cambridge University in 1947, co-editor of *Accounting Research* in 1948, Stamp-Martin Professor in 1952, and Knight Commander of the Order of St. Gregory (a papal distinction) in 1960. He retired in 1977 and died on January 29, 1979.

Such are the bare bones of a career. Unlike most memorialists, I did not have the pleasure and privilege of knowing my subject personally. I write, therefore, as a contemporary accounting historian and as the editor since 1975 of the successor journal to *Accounting Research* (which, through no fault of Bray's, ceased publication in 1958).

That such an excellent and necessary journal as *Accounting Research* should have lasted no more than a decade requires a word of explanation, but one must first go back to the beginning, for Bray's career as accounting practitioner and accounting academic can only be understood in the context of the time and place in which he grew up, both of which may appear strange to many readers of THE ACCOUNTING REVIEW.

LIFE AND TIMES

In the year that Bray was born, the Institute of Chartered Accountants in England and Wales was 26 years old and the Society of Incorporated Accountants and Auditors was celebrating its twenty-first birthday. To become a member of the former, it was necessary to serve articles for five years with a practicing firm at a zero or very small salary and to pay a premium. The financial demands of becoming an incorporated accountant were less and this was the route perforce taken by the young Bray, born into a relatively humble family in southeast London. He would have preferred to become an academic but there the possibilities were even less.

By 1932 Bray was an incorporated accountant and had succeeded so well that Tansley Witt granted him chartered articles at no cost. Gaining honors in both the intermediate and final examinations, he qualified as a chartered accountant in 1937. He was already active within the Incorporated Accountants Research Committee, established in 1935 as the first Research Committee in the British accountancy profession. Bray believed, not without justification, that the incorporated accountants were the intellectual leaders of the profession.

During the 1940s he published his first books (I shall look a little later in more detail at his writings) and worked his way up within his firm, becoming senior partner in 1948.

The late 1940s and the 1950s were a period of intense activity for him. In 1946, he became a member of a sub-committee of the Joint Exploratory Committee set up by the Institute of Chartered Accountants in England and Wales and the National Institute of Economic and Social Research. The Committee eventually produced a rather disappointing and now almost forgotten report entitled *Some Accounting Terms and Concepts* [1951]. More importantly Bray was brought into close contact with the economist J. R. N. Stone (now Professor Sir Richard Stone) who had just become the first director of the newly established Department of Applied Economics at Cambridge University and was at that time and for many years thereafter devoting a good deal of effort to developing the principles of national economic accounting.

Stone has written:

> Frank Sewell Bray was a man passionately interested in accounting ideas which he approached in a scientific spirit. He firmly believed that accounting practice could only be improved within a framework of correct theory based on exact principles. This may conjure up for those who did not know him a formidable image of cold precision. The truth was quite the reverse. He was laughing and open, understanding and generous and took life's disappointments and reverses with philosophical good humour. But behind this easy-going exterior the drive and energy were there to realize many of his hopes for accounting research [1979].

In October 1946 Bray was, while remaining in practice in London, appointed to one of the first two Senior Nuffield Research Fellows in Stone's Department. He remained a Fellow until 1955 when Stone was appointed P. D. Leake Professor of Finance and Accounting and ceased to be director.

In 1946, THE ACCOUNTING REVIEW was 20 years old and the world's only academic accounting journal. There was clearly room for another one. Bray was one of those in 1948 responsible for the establishment of *Accounting Research* and he became its co-editor with Leo Little of the University College of the South West of England (now more briefly known as the University of Exeter and by a happy coincidence the present editorial home of *Accounting and Business Research*). Bray described the new journal, which was sponsored by the Society's Research Committee, in an article he wrote for THE ACCOUNTING REVIEW in 1949:

> And this seems the place to comment upon the need which for some time past has been felt in some circles for a periodical given up to articles on advanced prospects of accounting and those subjects which are intimately associated with it. It is therefore hoped to fill the gap by the publication in Great Britain of a new periodical of standing to be called *Accounting Research*. This journal will be sponsored by the Research Committee of the Society of Incorporated Accountants, and its editorial policy will be directed to keeping close contacts with all branches of the profession and with the universities in all countries. It will be published by the Cambridge University Press twice yearly and the first issue should be ready towards the end of October, 1948.
>
> It will be the policy of *Accounting Research* to publish articles which make a real contribution to the theoretical and practical development of the accounting art, so that the intention is to provide a scholarly medium for making known advanced work undertaken by accountants whether they are engaged in professional practice, as executive officers in industry, or as teachers in universities. Moreover, it is also intended that special regard shall be had to the publication of postgraduate research studies. Thus, those subjects which because of the length at which they need to be treated, or because of the advanced standard of the work they demand cannot be included in the weekly and monthly professional journals will find their natural place in *Accounting Research*.

> If accounting is to reveal itself as having an honourable part in the play of learning and knowledge, then it must allow and expect changing points of view. So too it must encourage the publication of clear and well meditated accounts of new ideas, in order that everyone concerned with the advancement of the profession may understand what those ideas are about, as a precursor to tests of their merits. Just now the accountancy profession is meeting several new points of view—a healthy sign which bodes well for the development of its art—and in Great Britain, at least, the need has been felt for a medium in which there can be adequate publication of new ideas and methods at a deeper level than is ordinarily possible in the usual periodicals circulating within the profession. It is contemplated that *Accounting Research* will meet this need.
>
> And lastly we should wish to make a particular point of the declared intention of the editors of *Accounting Research* to draw from outside, as well as from inside, the United Kingdom for its contributors, and it is hoped that not only accountants, but economists and statisticians will evince an interest in this new publication. Thus we may hope that it will serve a purpose in the same scheme of things as that expected from the introduction of the universities into the field of professional education and research [1949c, pp. 275–276].

In 1949, Bray was invited by the Commonwealth Institute of Accountants on a lecture tour of seven Australian Universities where, well ahead of developments in Britain, an academic accounting profession was beginning to blossom. A similar tour in Britain at that time would have been unthinkable. As Solomons has recently reminded us [1974, p. 39], from 1932 to 1947 there were *no* full professors of accounting in England and Wales, full time or part time. In 1947 William T. Baxter was appointed to a chair at the London School of Economics (just around the corner from both Incorporated Accountants' Hall and Tansley Witt's office) and in 1955 Solomons himself was appointed to a chair at Bristol University [1974, p. 37].

In 1952, Bray succeeded Bertram Nelson as chairman of the Incorporated Accountants' Research Committee and was appointed Stamp-Martin Professor at Incorporated Accountants' Hall. (The chair was named after Lord Stamp, a distinguished applied economist, and Sir James Martin, a former president of the Society.) Solomons has described this as "a well-intentioned, probably ill-advised and certainly short-lived attempt to promote academic research in accounting outside an educational institution" [1974, p. 29].

It was short-lived because of the integration of the Society in 1957 with the Chartered Institutes. In the long run this was clearly for the good of the British profession, removing as it did elements of unnecessary divisiveness and snobbishness. In the short run it was harmful. The "new climate" in the English Institute [Zeff, 1972, pp. 27–32] was still almost a decade away. The Council of the Institute had scant regard for professors and academic journals. The *Report of the Committee on Education and Training* [ICAEW, 1961], an astonishing document to reread in 1980, preferred correspondence courses to university tuition. For Bray, the merger meant the discontinuance of both his chair and his editorship. The work of the Research Committee also came to an end. His disappointment must have been bitter.

Reasons given for the decision to discontinue *Accounting Research* are varied, ranging from the fact that it had been incurring a loss to the belief by many members of the Institute's Council that its articles, most of which were written by academics, were abstruse and of no practical value [Zeff, 1972, p. 27].

It was, in fact, an excellent journal with a roll call of contributors that any editor would envy. It was typical of *Accounting Research* and of Bray that they were drawn from throughout the English-speaking world and included economists as well as accountants. The contributors to Volume 1, for example, included Bray himself, F. R. M. de Paula of the U.K., G. O. May of the U.S.A., and A. A. Fitzgerald of Australia, and economists such as J. R. N. Stone, G. L. S. Shackle and A. R. Prest. Later volumes included articles from the academic accountants W. T. Baxter, R. J. Chambers (his first article published outside Australia), S. Davidson, H. C. Edey, L. Goldberg, R. L. Mathews, R. Mattessich and D. Solomons and from the economists G. C. Harcourt (his first article), A. T. Peacock, W. B. Reddaway, R. C. Tress and B. S. Yamey.

Even accounting practitioners were well represented (editors of academic accounting journals know how difficult such articles are to get) by E. L. Kohler, W. W. Werntz and Sir Richard Yeabsley.

Louis Goldberg of the University of Melbourne expressed a widely held opinion when he wrote to *The Accountant* in December 1958, expressing grief at the obituary notice of *Accounting Research:*

> Among my personal acquaintances, many accountants—practising as well as academic—looked on *Accounting Research* as one of the very few learned journals in the world in its field. It had established for itself a unique place in accounting as a journal which was open to any kind of article, from whatever source, which gave evidence of original thought or research. It was not subject to the views or outlook of any professional body and its pages embodied the spirit of the open mind [1958].

Bray wrote little on accounting matters in the 1960s, his last important work in the field being a chapter on "Accounting Postulates and Principles" [1966].

He devoted himself increasingly to the business of his firm but remained active in other spheres. He acted, for example, as chairman for the Centre for Interfirm Comparison which had been established in 1959 by the British Institute of Management in association with the British Productivity Council.

A sincerely religious man, he had been for many years financial adviser to a number of Roman Catholic Dioceses and Religious Orders. He was a member of the independent committee of inquiry set up by the National Council of Social Service, under the chairmanship of Lord Goodman, to examine the effect of charity law and practice on voluntary organizations. The committee made a number of important recommendations on, *inter alia*, charity taxation, accounts and audit [NCSS, 1976] an area which is beginning to generate a surprising amount of interest in Britain.

In his retirement, Bray hoped to write a study of Fénelon, for whose work, especially the *Discourse on Prayer* and the *Treatise on the Existence of God*, he felt a deep regard. He did not live to fulfill this task. After a short illness he died on January 29, 1979, in his 73rd year. He is survived by his wife and son.

Writings

It is time now to look in more detail at Bray's writings. He wrote eight books between 1944 and 1957: *Design of Accounts* (with H. B. Sheasby) [1944]; *Precision and Design in Accountancy* [1947], a collection of his early writings; *Farm Accounts* (with C. V. Dawe) [1948]; *Social Accounts and the Business Enterprise Sector of the National Economy* [1949a]; *The Measurement of Profit*

[1949b]; *The Accounting Mission* [1951], based on lectures given during his Australian tour; *Four Essays in Accounting Theory* [1953]; and *The Interpretation of Accounts* [1957], based on lectures he gave as Stamp-Martin Professor. *The Accounting Mission* is currently available in the "Accounting Classics Series" series edited by Robert Sterling. The others are out of print.

Bray had a writing style all his own, which occasionally baffles the reader. He was, for example, capable of writing such an extraordinary sentence as:

> Throughout this discussion we have sought to emphasise the importance of identifying the generic distinction between capital and current with those *actual* transactions, measurable in terms of units of money, which are promoted by the economic traversal of an enterprise along the paths of temporal periods intentionally limited for the purpose of recurrent survey, and in so doing we have commended a substitution of the adjectival use of the word capital by the term resting [1949b, p. 14].

Four themes recur throughout his writings:

(1) an emphasis on an academic and philosophical approach, on theory and on the importance of research;
(2) an emphasis on design, form, and standardization;
(3) an emphasis on the links of accounting with economics, especially in the field of national income accounting; and
(4) problems of profit measurement and accounting for inflation.

Philosophy, Theory and Research

Bray began his writing career with letters to the *Incorporated Accountants' Journal* (renamed *Accountancy* in 1938). As early as May 1932, he was writing to the editor that "I, in common with many other students, have spent the last nine years of my life in receiving instruction in technical accountancy, added to which my office duties and responsibilities have been in a similar direction; as I grow older [he was then 25], I desire to develop a philosophic outlook" [1947, p. 108]. In the January 1934 issue, he was arguing, in another letter, that "Many distinguished accountants have contributed to our professional knowledge, but so far there does not appear to have been any attempt at organised research, a development of fundamental importance in the field of scientific inquiry" [1947, p. 112].

Bray's mature ideas on research are set out in the lecture he gave at the University of Sydney on October 20, 1949. He argued that the least practical thought of today is often the most practical in execution tomorrow and that a hankering after short-term results depresses rather than gives birth to ideas. He stressed the need for fundamental and long-term research as especially necessary for a subject which "has moulded itself upon the solution of expedient issues." "I look for the day," he concluded, "when . . . accounting research schools are securely established in all our Universities. And to my professional brethren I would say: see to it, and press for it, that such research schools, if they should ever chance to come into being here, are made secure upon the foundation of Chairs of Accounting" [1951, pp. 59, 66].

In one of his Stamp-Martin lectures, he argued that "in the history of the professions it has often transpired that new ideas, even when they seem to lie at some distance from main interests, eventually become matters of vital concern with great utilitarian significance" [1957, pp. 86–87].

Bray was one of a small number of British academics expressing such ideas in the 1950s. Few practitioners were listening, alas! Bray's friend W. Bertram Nelson was one of the exceptions, pointing out with some penetration that "An estrangement between the practice and theory of any profession is always a waste of time" [ICAEW, 1961, p. 84].

Design, Form and Standardization

Bray believed strongly in order, precision, design, uniformity, and standardization. The elements of uniformity were information, classification, choice and use of terms, and conventions of measurement [1947, pp. 87–88].

Design of Accounts [Bray and Sheasby, 1944], described by de Paula [1948, p. 119] in a review as "an invaluable contribution to our professional knowledge and technique," is almost entirely devoted to specimen forms of accounts, drawn up on the principles of clarity, arrangement in groups under headings, unambiguity, ease of comparison, and compliance with statutory requirements. *Farm Accounts* [Bray and Dawe, 1948] also lays great stress on specimen forms. By far the greater part of *Social Accounts and the Business Enterprise Sector of the National Economy* [Bray, 1949a] is taken up with accounts and statements.

Standardization of, or uniformity in, the main forms of account he regarded as essential. It was necessary to think out "a few really fundamental forms" which would be capable of adoption to all problems as they arose, whether of management or stewardship [Bray, 1953, p. 72]. These forms he found, as we shall see later, in the economic relationships set out by Keynes and transposed into accounting terms by Stone and others.

Bray's regard for form is unusual for a British accountant but not for a continental European. He was obviously influenced by H. W. Singer's analysis of *Standardised Accountancy in Germany* in a book of that name published for the National Institute of Economic and Social Research by the Cambridge University Press [1943]. Curiously enough, however, Bray apparently never discussed the example of the French national accounting plan, the first and second editions of which were published in 1947 and 1957 [CNC, 1965].

Bray clearly believed that a set of formal accounts could be derived which would apply to every entity:

> [T]he Keynesian identities . . . give birth to a series of fundamental accounts which are just as relevant for firms or companies as for the nation as a whole. . . . they are not only fundamental but universal as well, and . . . they contribute the key to all accounting designs [Bray, 1953, p. 25].

He believed in a "pure theory of accounting which seeks to apply universal concepts of structure, form and measurement to any and every economic activity which requires to be viewed by means of accounts. In short, an invariant pattern exemplifying such a view of economic activity as points to an effective use of resources" [Bray, 1954, p. 138]. These he set out as follows [Bray, 1957, p. 34]:

I. Current

(a) Operating activity Real

(b) Income — Real
± Financial items
± Transfers
± Disposable income

(c) Outlay — Disposable income
= Consumption
+ Saving

II. Source and Use of Funds (Capital Changes)

(a) Saving and internal operating provisions
(b) Real asset formation
(c) Valuation changes
(d) Financial incomings and outgoings, and changes in monetary claims.
(The ultimate resolution of the accounting identity: Saving = Investment)

III. Capital

Real wealth and net monetary claims.

The accounts illustrating these are, for a company, the profit and loss account; "sources, earmarkings and utilization of funds" *i.e.*, a funds statement (Bray often called this a "resting account"); and a balance sheet.

Although he recognized that consumption was not relevant in company accounting, Bray never really considered whether forms which derive from Keynesian economic identities (form I represents the *ex post* relationship between income, consumption, and investment, II the equality of *ex post* savings and investment for a period and III the equality of *ex post* savings and investment at a point in time) are relevant for any other purpose than preparing the accounts of the nation as a whole. Why should the accountant not draw up a profit and loss account simply to serve the needs of shareholders?

But for Bray national accounting was dominant:

> A mature system of national accounting must ultimately call for some aggregation of private accounting results, and there must be no impediments occasioned by lack of uniformity in private accounting practices. Thus, as national accounting develops, private accounting will need to devise some conforming uniformity not only in relation to the *design* of private accounts, but also to the principles of income measurement and asset valuation [1946, p. 483].

In some ways, on the other hand, Bray never shook off the effects of his long practical training in double entry bookkeeping. His essay on "Accounting Principles" begins with the acute and well-expressed observation in paragraph 1 that:

> The rules of an acquired skill, when brought to the settled tendency of habit and committed to textbooks, are very apt to be mistaken for fundamental doctrines when they are still little more than the discrete boundaries of an empirically constructed technique [1953, p. 2].

But in paragraph 13 we are told that the familiar idea of double-entry is quite fundamental to all accounting theory [1953, p. 4].

Economics and National Economic Accounting

Bray saw many reasons why accountants should study economics:

(a) in order to determine the accountant's position in the scheme of things (as he put it in the letter of May 1932 already quoted and in a letter to *The Accountant* of October 9, 1933). This was his "cultural" reason [1947, pp. 108, 111];
(b) because in his view financial accounting statements were "statistical documents in the field of applied economics" [1949a, p. 27] and "chronicles of economic dealings" [1951, p. 3]; and
(c) because a study of the use of accounting forms for national economic purposes should force accountants to re-examine and call into question the adequacy of conventions which were subconsciously set to the service of traditional ends [1949b, p. 55].

He also saw a good reason why economists should take an interest in accounting:

> the accounting approach to the presentation of information on economic transactions is the best means so far employed in explanation of national income statistics and . . . it is by far the best method of affirming those economic identities which lie at the heart of the new economics [1951, p. 21].

Bray's concern for national economic accounting and economic thinking led him to propose, well ahead of his time, not only that economists should make more use of the accountant's traditional financial statements but that accountants should adopt new forms themselves, *viz.* what are now known in the UK as source and application of funds statements and statements of added value.

Bray called for a redesigned profit and loss account "to give a reasonably clear idea of the output value added by a company as achieved through its input allocations of labour and capital" and also stated that "Information on the source and use of industrial finance would be greatly facilitated if companies could be induced to publish a summary account of their capital incomings and outgoings, much as the best companies do in America" [1953, pp. 41, 43].

Bray collaborated on a number of occasions in his writings with economists; for example, in his book *Farm Accounts* [Bray and Dawe 1948], which he wrote with C. V. Dawe of the University of Bristol, and in an article with Richard Stone [1948].

Profit Measurement and Accounting for Inflation

Bray began, for all his interest in economics, as a supporter of the traditional accounting conventions of profit measurement. In a letter to *The Economist* of May 17, 1944, in reply to letters from the economist Singer, he concluded that if Singer could suggest a better basis for drawing accounts than that which relied on the accounting principle of historical cost, he for one would be very glad to know it [1947, p. 113]. In July, 1945, in correspondence with Singer he expressed himself strongly:

> . . . I am not inclined to favour the view that replacement values, or values resulting from the application of index numbers should be substituted for recorded costs in the keeping or main statement of accounts.
>
> I feel that historical costs are in point of fact the only real objective dependable data available for the construction of accounting records [1947, p. 121].

He did envisage, however, a second section of the profit and loss account in which adjustments could be made [1947, p. 122].

Not very convincingly, he argued that the historical cost principle was fairly implicit in company legislation and that therefore accountants were obliged to retain the principle in the legal accounting documents they are called upon to formulate [1947, p. 124]. Early in 1945, he expressed the view that the prime basis for the preparation of accounting documents could not be anything other than monetary cost and that economists would have to take out of accounts prepared on this basis that evidence which they required and readjust it in line with their conception of economic theory [1947, p. 37]. He expressed the differing approaches well when he wrote that economists regard a fixed asset as a production good while accountants tend to regard it as a delayed consumption good [1947, p. 59]. In 1946, he thought it might be possible to give economists something of what they wanted by a supplementary valuation of a fixed asset by adjusting the original cost by a general price index.

It was Bray's appointment as a part-time Senior Nuffield Research Fellow in the Department of Applied Economics at Cambridge which appears to have changed his views. The changeover can be seen in his Cambridge monograph *Social Accounts and the Business Enterprise Sector of the National Economy* [1949a] where the main text favors the conventional accounting valuations of cost or lower market value for inventories while the appendix recommends that both opening and closing inventories should be shown in the operating account at "last cost" prices.

His book on *The Measurement of Profit* [1949] is disappointing. As A. R. Prest pointed out in a review [1950], Bray does not add much to our fundamental knowledge of the nature of income and capital, being content to summarize the views of Pigou and Hicks, without attempting to push their analyses further. Bray did, however, clearly recognize, while so many of his fellow accountants failed and continued to fail so long to recognize, that the existing accounting conventions conceived in an era of relative monetary stability had lost their force [1949, p. 55]. Bray made no substantive contribution to inflation accounting, but he was well aware of the problems and of the urgency of tackling them.

In Conclusion

Bray moved in the three worlds of economics, accounting practice, and academic accounting. What were his contributions to each of them? Stone has written that Bray confirmed economists in their belief that:

> there was nothing wrong in what they were doing from an accounting point of view. On details, accountants might be able to point to situations that the economists had not really thought about and suggest solutions, but the accounts they would incorporate into a social accounting system would not differ materially from those proposed by economists [1979].

Bray was clearly a success as a practitioner (under his leadership, Tansley Witt became one of the top 20 firms in the U.K., but his immediate impact on practice was small. It is only recently that the British accounting profession has tackled inflation accounting, funds statements, and value added statements. To what extent Bray helped to create a climate in which such practices would eventually be accepted is hard to gauge.

Finally, Bray was not in the mainstream of British academic accounting either personally or in the ideas he espoused. The London School of Economics, not Cambridge, has been the breeding ground of British academic accounting. Cambridge University has confined its teaching and research to macroaccounting and has virtually ignored microaccounting.

Nor have British accounting academics accepted the primacy of national accounts. For most of Bray's life they stressed the needs of shareholders. Today, they are emphasizing the differing needs of the various user groups.

Bray's influence, then, was indirect rather than direct. He helped to make academic accounting possible rather than creating it himself. His most important contribution, I suggest, and I acknowledge my own bias, was his editorship of *Acvounting Research.*

R. H. Parker

REFERENCES

Bray, F. Sewell, Review of H. W. Singer, *Standardised Accountancy in Germany*, in *Economic Journal* (September 1946), pp. 482–484.

———, *Precision and Design in Accountancy* (Gee & Co., 1947).

———, *Social Accounts and the Business Enterprise Sector of the National Economy* (Cambridge University Press, 1949a).

———, *The Measurement of Profit* (Oxford University Press, 1949b).

———, "The English Universities and the Accounting Profession," THE ACCOUNTING REVIEW (July 1949c), pp. 273–276.

———, *The Accounting Mission* (Melbourne University Press and Cambridge University Press, 1951; Scholars Book Co., 1973).

———, *Four Essays in Accounting Theory* (Oxford University Press, 1953).

———, "Accounting Dynamics," *Accounting Research* (April 1954) pp. 133–153.

———, *The Interpretation of Accounts* (Oxford University Press, 1957).

———, "Accounting Theory and Company Law," *Journal of Business Law* (1959), pp. 18–25, 154–162.

———, "Accounting Postulates and Principles," in Morton Backer, (ed.), *Modern Accounting Theory* (Prentice-Hall, 1966), pp. 28–47.

———, and C. V. Dawe, *Farm Accounts* (Oxford University Press, 1948).

———, and H. Basil Sheasby, *Design of Accounts* (Oxford University Press 1st ed. 1944, 2nd ed. 1947, 3rd ed. 1949, 3rd ed. rev. 1956).

———, and Richard Stone, "The Presentation of the Central Government Accounts," *Accounting Research* (November 1948).

Conseil National de la Compatabilité (CNC), *Plan Comptable Général* (Paris, 1965).

de Paula, F. R. M., "Design of Accounts," in his *Developments in Accounting* (Pitman, 1948, repr. Arno Press, 1978), pp. 119–122.

Goldberg, L., "The Demise of *Accounting Research*," Letter to *The Accountant* (13 December, 1958).

Institute of Chartered Accountants in England and Wales (ICAEW), *Report of the Committee on Education and Training* (1961).

Joint Exploratory Committee, *Some Accounting Terms and Concepts* (Cambridge University Press, 1951).

National Council of Social Service (NCSS), *Charity Law and Voluntary Organisations* (Report of the Goodman Committee) (1976).

Prest, A. R., Review of F. S. Bray, *The Measurement of Profit* in *Accounting Research* (July 1950), pp. 458–459.

Singer, H. W., *Standardised Accountancy in Germany* (Cambridge University Press, 1943).

Solomons, David (with T. M. Berridge), *Prospectus for a Profession. The Report of the Long Range Enquiry into Education and Training for the Accounting Profession* (Advisory Board of Accountancy Education, 1974).

Stone, Richard, Letter to R. H. Parker, 25 June 1979.

Zeff, Stephen A., *Forging Accounting Principles in Five Countries* (Stipes Publishing Company, 1972).

Australia's First Accountancy Body —The Adelaide Society of Accountants

—by R. H. Parker, Lecturer in Accounting, University of Adelaide.

Origin of Professional Accountancy

Professional accountancy in the form familiar to us today is a product of the 19th century. In Britain by the 1850's "the pursuit of commerce, trade and industry, particularly in the larger towns, engendered the need for competent persons with knowledge and ability to practice accountancy"[1]. The Society of Accountants in Edinburgh and the Institute of Accountants and Actuaries in Glasgow were established in 1853; the Society of Accountants in Aberdeen was formed in 1867. Royal Charters were granted to these bodies in 1854, 1855 and 1867 respectively. The Incorporated Society of Liverpool Accountants and the Institute of Accountants (London) were formed in 1870. Further institutes of accountants were established in Manchester and Sheffield in 1873 and 1877. In 1880 a Royal Charter was granted to the Institute of Chartered Accountants in England and Wales into which were amalgamated the Society of Accountants in England and the four bodies referred to above. The Society of Accountants and Auditors (later known as the Society of Incorporated Accountants and Auditors) was established in 1885.

Formation of the Adelaide Society of Accountants

It is therefore not surprising that similar organisations of accountants were formed in the Australian Colonies from the 1880's onwards. The first such society was founded in Adelaide in November, 1885. What *is* surprising is that the first society was formed in Adelaide, a relatively small and commercially unimportant city compared to Melbourne and Sydney.

Three possible explanations may be suggested, although it must be admitted that there is no particular evidence for any of them. First, that as the accountants in Adelaide probably formed a smaller and more compact group than in Melbourne or Sydney it was easier for them to join together in a society. Secondly, that South Australians were—some would say still are—more prone to copy English institutions and habits than were the inhabitants of Victoria or New South Wales. Thirdly, that it was due to the enthusiasm of a few individuals.

In any case the accountants of Melbourne were not long in forming their own society. The Incorporated Institute of Accountants in Victoria (later the Commonwealth Institute of Accountants) was established in that city in 1886.

The newly-formed Adelaide Society of Accountants was greeted by one local newspaper with a bitter-sweet editorial which is worth quoting in full.

Early Newspaper Comments

SOCIETY OF ACCOUNTANTS— We have been shown a copy of the rules of a society to be called the Adelaide Society of Accountants. They are exceedingly lengthy, and on one or two points not quite so clear or so skilfully arranged as they might be. The society consists at starting of 19 fellows, whose special privilege it is to enter without election and without the payment of an admission-fee. Subsequent candidates for admission as fellows will have to pay an entrance fee of £5/5/- and the annual subscription of £2/2/-, and to undergo an examination. If these preliminaries are satisfactorily settled, and the candidates are elected by the council, they will be entitled to all the privileges of the society, one of them being that they may write F.A.S.A. after their names. It should be mentioned that all the members are to be fellows. The general objects of the society are worthy of all praise, especially the desire.

> to foster in commercial circles a higher sense of the importance of systematic and correct book-keeping, and to encourage a greater degree of efficiency in those engaged in accounting and auditing.

The proof of the pudding is in the eating, and if the society is successful in accomplishing these desirable reforms it will not exist in vain. No doubt the question will arise whether the 19 gentlemen who have founded the institution possess the needful qualifications to entitle them to set up as authorities. On that point it is not for us to speak. The society may develop in to one of two things. It may become an authority on matters connected with the duties of an accountant, and its imprimatur may be accepted as a sort of hall mark, or it may degenerate into a mere Trade Union organisation determined to boycott all who refuse to acknowledge its authority. Whether it achieves the former position will depend entirely upon the skill and knowledge of those constituting it and especially of the governing body. If it degenerates into the latter it will soon become a laughing-stock. Many persons have a decided objection to putting initials after their names except those which are the badge of definite scholarship, and we can readily believe that some competent accountants may not care to use the mystic initials which this society proposes to authorise its members to place after their names. The business of an accountant is a very useful one, but it is not one that requires exceptional skill or learning, and it will be a mistake to try and surround it with an air of profound mystery. In so far, however, as the society aims at raising the standard of general and technical knowledge among accountants it has a wide, field before it, and we trust it will be eminently successful[2].

Objects of the Adelaide Society of Accountants

The objects of the new society were:

(i) to incorporate the society under Act of Parliament and obtain a charter;

(ii) to watch over and protect the interests of its members;

(iii) to provide facilities for the reading of papers, etc., and generally to do all such things as from time to time may be considered desirable towards elevating the status and best interests of the profession;

(iv) to foster in commercial circles a higher sense of the importance of systematic and correct book-keeping, and to encourage a greater degree of efficiency in those engaged in accountancy and auditing[3].

It is interesting to compare these original objects with those set out in the amended Constitution and Rules adopted just over 10 years later on January 31, 1896[4].

The Society was incorporated in 1886 but a charter had not been obtained so the first object was altered to read

Objects Amended

"(a) To obtain a charter if and when it shall be deemed advisable so to do."

The second object of 1885 was repeated as sub-clause (e) except that "the interests of its members" now became "the interests of the profession".

The third object of 1885 was expanded to read

"(b) To provide facilities for the dissemination of professional knowledge, the inculcation of the principles of sound practice, and generally to take such action as from time to time may be considered desirable with the object of elevating the status and promoting the advancement and best interests of the profession."

The fourth object of 1885 talked of fostering in commercial circles a higher sense of systematic and correct bookkeeping. In 1896 the word "accountancy" replaces the humbler "bookkeeping". Sub-clause (c) of 1896 reads:

"To increase the confidence of the banking, mercantile and general community in certified Accountants and Auditors by admitting to the Society such persons only as shall (save as hereinafter provided) pass satisfactory examinations in the theory and practice of Accountancy."

The words in brackets need amplification. Those exempted from the society's examinations were, in effect:

(1) Fellows of approved kindred bodies in Great Britain, the other Australian Colonies, etc., and

(2) "gentlemen of distinction or acknowledged ability in the profession" whose applications were approved by three-quarters of the members present at any duly constituted meeting of the society[5].

There was no mention of professional ethics or etiquette in the objects of 1885. In 1896 a new sub-clause was inserted stating that one of the objects of the society was

"(d) To afford means of reference for the amicable settlement of professional differences, and to decide upon questions of professional usage and etiquette."

The constitutions of both years provided for forfeiture of membership by any member found guilty of "dishonourable conduct, or, in the exercise of his profession of gross carelessness or culpable negligence"[6].

Foundation Members

The Society had 19 founder members[7] —A. Abrahams, W. J. Brook, W. S. Douglas, J. H. Fry, H. James, D. Kekwick, V. Lawrence, G. T. Lane, W. J. Oldham, J. B. Spence (the first president), H. Stodart, J. S. Scott, J. T. Turnbull, H. Turner, J. E. Thomas, F. D. Woodforde (the first secretary), F. Wright (the first vice-president), W. L. Ware and J. F. Yuill. Some of them appear to have practised as estate agents and sharebrokers as well as accountants and auditors.

Change of Name and Absorption

In 1899 the society changed its name to that of The Institute of Accountants in South Australia, Incorporated. In 1925 this Institute was absorbed by the Australasian Corporation of Public Accountants, a body with membership throughout Australia which had been established in 1907. In 1928 this body was granted a Royal Charter and became the Institute of Chartered Accountants in Australia. The Adelaide Society of 1885 thus finally achieved a charter[8].

If the *Register's* leader-writer were alive today he would no doubt agree that the Adelaide Society of Accountants did, through its successor, come to be "an authority on matters connected with the duties of an accountant", that its *imprimatur* has become accepted as "a sort of hall mark", and that it did not "degenerate into a mere Trade Union organisation". But would he still hold to his view that the *business* (not, be it noted, profession) of an accountant although very useful does not require exceptional skill or learning? Accountancy has certainly been generally accepted as a profession but it is doubtful whether all would regard it as a *learned* profession. It is pleasing to note the General Council of the Institute considers it certain that the Institute will be moving closer to the universities in the near future[9].

1 Nicholas A. H. Stacey, **English Accountancy — A Study in Social and Economic History.** (Gee, London, 1954), page 19.

2 **The South Australian Register,** November 28, 1885, page 5. The first meeting of the Society was also briefly reported in **The Adelaide Observer** of the same date.

3 The Adelaide Society of Accountants **List of Members.** Constitution and Rules (1885) (copy in Public Library, Adelaide). Clause 2 of Constitution.

4 The Adelaide Society of Accountants: **List of Members. Constitution and Rules** (1896) (copy in Public Library, Adelaide).

5 In fact only two persons, apart from the foundation members, were admitted without examination. See R. M Steel: **An Accountant Takes Stock of the Past and Glances into the Future,** The Chartered Accountant in Australia, Volume 2[illegible], 1950, at pages 169 and 231.

[6] 1885 Constitution, Section 39; 1896 Constitution, Section 56.

[7] The Adelaide Society of Accountants. **List of Members. Constitution and Rules** (1885). Membership figures for later years are as follows: 1893—41; 1898—70; 1920—over 135.

(R.M.Steele, op. cit., at pages 165, 166, 168.)

[8] R. M. Steele; op. cit. Mr. Steele was Registrar of the Institute of Accountants in South Australia Inc. from 1920 to 1925; State Registrar of the Australasian Corporation of Public Accountants from 1920 to 1928; and State Registrar of the Institute of Chartered Accountants in Australia from 1928 to 1951. I am indebted to the present Registrar, Mr. G. L. Duffield, for drawing my attention to Mr. Steele's article.

[9] As reported in **The Chartered Accountant in Australia**, July, 1961, page 53.

To round off Mr. Parker's excellent historical record of the progressive stages of organised accounting bodies in South Australia it should be recorded that, in 1949, the remaining funds of The Institute of Accountants in South Australia (Incorporated) (approximating £600) were taken over by the Council of The Institute of Chartered Accountants in Australia by mutual arrangement.

In doing so, the Institute assumed a moral obligation to utilise the funds and any income therefrom to improve the existing library facilities of the South Australian Branch of the Institute—such library to be available at all times to the few remaining members of the old South Australian Institute. The fund is still in existence and as recently as May, 1961, the General Council of The Institute of Chartered Accountants in Australia placed a minute on record that access to the S.A. Branch library is to be given to any surviving member of The Institute of Accountants of South Australia (Incorporated) and to any descendant of such a member.

Editor—Chartered Accountant in Australia.

Accounting Literature

The First Scottish Book on Accounting:

Robert Colinson's *Idea Rationaria* (1683)*

R. H. PARKER, B.SC.(ECON.), F.C.A.

It was near the end of the 17th century, and the initiative in publishing books on accounting was beginning to pass from the Netherlands (where it had gone from Italy) to Scotland. As the writer of a poem in praise of the author of this book put it in the contemporary style of poetic diction:—

"Let Florence, Venice, Holland no more boast;
The Flag of Traffique's in our Northern Coast:"

The following century brought many Scottish books on accounting, but Robert Colinson blazed the trail. There is a copy of his book in the Antiquarian Collection of The Institute of Chartered Accountants of Scotland.

The 1680s were an important decade in Scottish history. Scots law was presented as a complete and coherent system for the first time in Stair's *Institutes*, published in 1681. The deposition of James VII and II in 1688 marked the effective end of a dynasty which had ruled Scotland since 1371. In the religious settlement which followed presbyterianism was firmly established.

It was during this same decade, in 1683, that the first Scottish book on accounting was published, nearly two centuries after Pacioli's *Summa* of 1494 † and 140 years after the first book on the subject in the English language, Hugh Oldcastle's *A briefe instruction and maner how to keepe bookes of Accompts* . . . of 1543. The long delay reflects the relatively underdeveloped state of the Scottish economy and the ready availability of textbooks from south of the Border.

By 1683 there was, as J. Row Fogo observed, "no particular merit . . . in producing a good work on book-keeping".[1] Robert Colinson's *Idea Rationaria* is, however, "sensible and reasonably straightforward"[2] and for this reason, as well as for its chronological importance in the history of accounting in Scotland, it is worth a short article. The practices recommended in it are typical of their time and show interesting variations from those of the present.

The Book

The title page is reproduced opposite. Note the reference to the "Italian Methode", as double-entry bookkeeping was still commonly called; the method of teaching by "Queries and Answers" which is characteristic of the period; and the names of the recommended books of account.

The arrangement of Colinson's book is as follows:—

(*a*) Title page (see reproduction).

(*b*) Dedication to the Honourable Mr James Kennedy, "Lord Conservator of the Priviledges of the Scots Nation in the 17. Provinces of the Netherlands, and his Majesties Resident there, for all affaires of his Majesties ancient Kingdom of Scotland, &c".

(*c*) Two laudatory poems by Mr Ninian Paterson and Mr J. Kniblo. These are of no great literary merit, but Professor Yamey regards them as one of the attractions of the book to present-day readers.[3] Elsewhere[4] he has considered at length the strength of Paterson's claim for double entry, that:—

> This was the fam'd, and quick invention, which
> Made Venice, Genoa, and Florence rich:

(*d*) Table of Contents.

(*e*) A letter to the "Merchants in Edinburgh, And all other Lovers of this Profitable Science".

* This article is taken from the Appendix to "Accounting in Scotland: a historical bibliography", compiled by Janet E. Pryce-Jones; annotated by R. H. Parker; 96 pages; 11 illustrations; author index; title index; £2·50.

The bibliography is the first publication of the Scottish Committee on Accounting History of The Institute of Chartered Accountants of Scotland. It has just been published.

An order form for it appears at page i.

† Summa de Arithmetica etc., Venice, which contains the first printed exposition of double-entry bookkeeping and of which there are two copies in the Antiquarian Collection of The Institute of Chartered Accountants of Scotland.

[1] R. Brown (ed.): A History of Accounting and Accountants; (Edinburgh: *Jack*, 1905), page 155.

[2] B. S. Yamey, H. C. Edey and H. W. Thomson: Accounting in England and Scotland; (London: *Sweet & Maxwell*, 1963), page 171.

[3] *ibid.*

[4] B. S. Yamey: "Scientific Bookkeeping and the Rise of Capitalism", Economic History Review, June 1949, reprinted in W. T. Baxter: Studies in Accounting (London: *Sweet & Maxwell*, 1950).

R. H. Parker was appointed to the Chair of Accountancy in Dundee University in 1970. He has written a number of articles on accounting history and also the book, "Management Accounting: an Historical Perspective" (1969), which contains a valuable bibliography of material on this subject.

Professor Parker's recent published work includes a Penguin book on "Understanding Company Financial Statements" (1972).

He is Convener of the Scottish Committee on Accounting History, a committee of The Institute of Chartered Accountants of Scotland.

With regard to this article, Professor Parker says: "I am indebted to Professor B. S. Yamey, of the London School of Economics, and Professor T. A. Lee, of Liverpool University, for their comments on a previous draft."

IDEA RATIONARIA,

OR

THE PERFECT ACCOMPTANT,

Necessary for all Merchants and Trafficquers;

CONTAINING

THE TRUE FORME OF *BOOK-KEEPING*,

According to the *Italian* Methode:

Wherein is First,

The Introduction to the Forme,

244. *Queries* and *Answers*, with Instructions how to Ballance the *Leger*, two *Waste-Books* transported in two *Journals*, out of which are transported 2. *Legers* both Ballanced.

After which followes

A MONETH-BOOK,
INVOYS-BOOK,
FACTOR-BOOK,
SPECIE or CASH-BOOK;
Instructions how to keep a Book of Petty-Charges *or* Pocket-Book.

By ROBERT COLINSON.

EDINBURGH,

Printed by DAVID LINDSAY, Mr. JAMES KNIBLO, JOSUA van SOLINGEN and JOHN COLMAR, in the Year 1683.

(*f*) Thirty-one pages describing the "Convenience" of bookkeeping; the various books of account Colinson deems it necessary to keep: Waste Book, Journal, Ledger, Factor Book ("to place down what is sent you by others, to dispose of the charges and sales"), Invoice Book, Month Book ("which tells you what summes you are to pay every moneth in the year, and day when, and who is to pay you"), Book of Petty Charges, Specie or Cash Book (necessary where more than one currency is dealt in: Row Fogo points out that, in addition to the national coinage, which was very bad, there were large quantities of foreign money in circulation particularly English and Dutch), Copy Book of Letters; and 244 questions and answers to "find out the right Debitor and Creditor upon all the Posts[5] of the Wast-Book, when you transport them to the Journal, and first of placing down the Inventar of the Stock". The questions and answers are interrupted between nos. 138 and 139 for a brief instruction (not in question and answer form) on balancing accounts, transferring them to a new book and on "companies-accompts" (*i.e.* partnership accounts).

(*g*) Two specimen sets of books (waste-book, journal and ledger).

The Author

Who was Colinson? Both Paterson and Kniblo refer to him as "Captain". He tells us that he has been "both a Student and Practitioner [of commerce] now these 25 years". It is clear from several references that, like many Scottish merchants of his time, he had lived and traded in the Low Countries. The title of his book is in Latin; his only quotation in a foreign language is in Dutch.

The Rules

The usual method of expounding the rules of double entry in English language textbooks on bookkeeping up to the 18th century was "to present a great mass of rules applicable to the particular cases of a large variety of transactions",[6] to do so by means of a series of questions and to follow this by a specimen set of books. Some, but not all, authors also included a general rule. Occasionally this was in verse. Dafforne, for example, the only English author on bookkeeping to whom Colinson refers, wrote as follows in "The Merchant's Mirrour"[7]:—

> The Ower, or the Owing thing,
> Or what-so-ever comes to thee:
> Upon the Left-hand see thou bring;
> For there the same must placed bee.
>
> But they unto whom thou doest owe,
> Upon the Right let them bee set;
> Or what-so-ere doth from thee goe,
> To place them there doe not forget.

Colinson fortunately does not break into verse, but neither does he, regrettably, include a general rule. Instead, he immediately plunges into detail. Here are the first three questions and answers:—

(1) Q. What make you Debitor for the first branch of your Stock [i.e. Capital], which is ready money?
A. Cash Debitor to my Stock, for so much as I have in it at the beginning. This word Cash is used now generally for money Accompts, it comes from the Italian word Cassa, which is a money Chest, or the like, which keeps it; therefore you Charge it Debitor for what is in't.

(2) Q. What is Debitor for the several Marchandize that you have lying by you unsold?
A. Such goods, naming them in your Journal, or as many of them as you will keep a particular Accompt of, Charging every one by itself Debitor, to Stock for the whole value it cost, with the Charges it hath cost since bought.

(3) Q. What is Debitor for your houses?
A. Such a house called so and so, every one of them what they stand me Debitor to Stock for all Charges, and Reparations to this day.

Specimen Accounts

In connection with this last entry some contemporary writers recommended the inclusion of both private and business assets in the accounts. Colinson is quite clear about the necessity to separate business and private assets:—

> Now I say, a man may have a private stock which he will conceal, and a stock in trade [i.e. business assets] also; but then he must bring none of his private stock into his trading stocks Books, lest he confuse himself. Wherein can this private stock consist? it must be in Lands, Houses, Rents, Jewels, and House-furnishing, &c. for

[5] *i.e.* items; the modern French word is "poste".

[6] J. G. C. JACKSON: "The History of Methods of Exposition of Double-entry Book-keeping in England"; in A. C. LITTLETON and B. S. YAMEY: "Studies in the History of Accounting" (London: *Sweet & Maxwell*, 1956), at page 288.

[7] RICHARD DAFFORNE: "The Merchant's Mirrour" (London, 1636); introductory pages to specimen ledger. There is a copy of this book in the Antiquarian Collection of The Institute of Chartered Accountants of Scotland.

F. 15 *Edinburgh, Anno* 1682.

PROFITE and LOSS, Debet.

Febr.	14	To *Thomas Trader*	4	4	—	—
	—	To Cash for rebate to *James Trusty*	1	4	—	—
Mar.	29	To *Thomas Factor* my accompt Currant for rebate	18	8	14	2
June	9	To Cash for rebate	23	3	—	—
	29	To Cash payed for House-hold expence and servants wages	23	130	—	—
	30	To several accompts lost on them as *per* Journal	. .	253	5	4
	—	To Stock for the neat gain	1	103	11	—
		Summa	L	506	10	6

which private stock let him keep a Book, which he may easily do apart. [page 5]

In the specimen sets of books, however, Colinson includes household expense and servants' wages, and wagers (see below). Perhaps he regarded the last as a business transaction!

The accounts in the two specimen ledgers show a number of interesting variations from 20th-century practice. The Profit and Loss Account in the first ledger is reproduced below.

The first thing to notice is the absence of any reference to sales, purchases and opening and closing stocks of goods. Instead we have, *via* two entries in the journal, two items of £386.16.0[8] and £253.5.4 summarising the gains and losses on various accounts. £35.5.0, for example, is lost upon " Wines of France ", that account being debited for the cost of wine bought, £430.0.0, and charges, £6.15.0, and credited with various sales amounting in all to £472.0.0. A separate column is used to record volume in " Tuns " with a loss of half a tun " in lackage ". There are similar accounts for Seck of Zeres (*i.e.* sherry), Iron, Mader, Indigo Lauro, Clothe, Sarges, Salmond, Herrings, Stockines, Hides, Wheat, Mum-Beer and, in the second Ledger, Tallow. None of the goods accounts illustrated by Colinson has a closing balance, nor does he anywhere in his book discuss the valuation problems involved.[9] He contents himself with stating (page 20) that:—

" Debet side of goods Accompt is what they cost me with charges, Credit is what is sold or sent away, or otherwayes disposed of."

The gains and losses in the summarising journal entries also include:—

(*a*) References to a number of voyage accounts. £71.13.4, for example, is gained from a Voyage to Rotterdam in the Ship Bonaventure, goods being bought from David Mills in Aberdeen for £970 and sold by William Cornelisen in Rotterdam for £1,041.13.4.

(*b*) £30 " gained by wagering ".

(*c*) Commissions received, £47.13.8.

(*d*) £158 " lost by insuring other mens goods ".

(*e*) £30 " lost upon Sea hazard by Skippers ".

The first four items on the debit side of the Profit and Loss Account reproduced all refer to rebates allowed; the first two items on the credit side are rebates received. The remaining items are £130 " payed for House-hold expence and servants wages "; £100 for a " Prentice-fee " (the apprenticeship was presumably for a period of years but no part of the fee is carried forward); and £15.4.6 commission received from Gilbert Callant.

The fixed asset[10] accounts, *e.g.* House called Black-Hall which is debited with the original cost plus reparations and rents payable and credited with rents receivable, follow what Yamey calls the arithmetical balance basis of valuation. No attempt is made to transfer revenue expense items to the Profit and Loss Account or to revalue the asset. The balances on such accounts are obviously rather meaningless.

The last account in each ledger is the " Balance " account, to which are transferred all account balances still open after transfers to the Profit and Loss Account and transfer of the " neat gain " therefrom to Stock [*i.e.* Capital]. It is in effect an unclassified Balance Sheet contained within the books of account.

Bibliographical Note

There are copies of Colinson's book in the libraries of The Institute of Chartered Accountants of Scotland and The Institute of Chartered Accountants in England and Wales, and also in Edinburgh University Library, the National Library of Scotland and the British Museum. It is referred to in:—

(*a*) B. S. Yamey, H. C. Edey and H. W. Thomson: Accounting in England and Scotland: 1543-1800; (London: *Sweet & Maxwell*, 1963), which includes three extracts from *Idea Rationaria*.

(*b*) R. Brown (Ed.): A History of Accounting and Accountants (Edinburgh: *Jack*, 1905; reprinted by *Frank Cass*, London, 1966).

(*c*) D. Murray: Chapters in the History of Bookkeeping, Accountancy and Commercial Arithmetic (Glasgow: *Jackson, Wylie*, 1930).

The above three references are all available in the Scottish Institute's Edinburgh and Glasgow Libraries.

[8] The figure in the journal entry heading is actually £393.16.0, but the items in it add up to £386.16.0.

[9] For a historical survey of the valuation of stock-in-trade see R. H. Parker: " Lower of Cost and Market in Britain and the United States: An Historical Survey "; Abacus, vol. 1, No. 2, 1965, reprinted in R. H. Parker and G. C. Harcourt (eds.); " Readings in the Concept and Measurement of Income " (*Cambridge University Press*, 1969).

[10] Colinson does not classify assets into groups and does not use the term " fixed asset ".

Edinburgh, *Anno* 1682. 15

PROFITE and LOSS, Credite.

Febr.	16	*Per George Dane*	5	3	—	—
	—	*Per Alexander Norman*	5	1	10	—
June	29	*Per* Cash for Prentice-fee	23	100	—	—
	30	*Per Gilbert Callant* in *Aberdeen*	26	15	4	6
	—	*Per* several accompts for so much gained on them, as *per* Journal	—	386	16	—
		Summa	L.	506	10	6

A Note on Savary's "Le Parfait Négociant"

R. H. PARKER*

Jacques Savary's *Le Parfait Négociant* (first published in 1675) is the first book in which the problem of inventory valuation is discussed at any length. A translation of the relevant passage has long been available to accountants in A. C. Littleton's *Accounting Evolution to 1900*.[1] According to this translation Savary recommends that if merchandise has been newly purchased "and if one judges that it has not decreased in price at the factory . . . it should be put in [the inventory] at the current price."[2] In an article written in 1941, Littleton admitted himself puzzled by this advice and wished that he could "call up Savary's ghost and cross-question him."[3]

Since Littleton's translation is based on the sixth edition of 1712 and since the difference between the French *au prix courant* (at the current price) and *au prix coûtant* (at cost price) is so slight[4] it seemed worthwhile to check the phrase in such other editions of Savary's book as could be found. The results are as shown in the table opposite.

The answer which Savary's ghost would give, one suspects, is that *au prix coûrant* in the sixth edition is a misprint for *au prix coûtant*.

* Reader in Management Accounting, Manchester Business School, and P. D. Leake Research Fellow (1966), London School of Economics and Political Science.

[1] A. C. Littleton, *Accounting Evolution to 1900* (New York: American Institute Publishing Co., 1933), p. 152.

[2] *Ibid.*

[3] A. C. Littleton, "A Genealogy for 'Cost or Market'," *Accounting Review*, v. 16, 1941, pp. 164–5.

[4] I am grateful to Mr. H. P. Hain of the University of Melbourne for pointing this out to me.

Date	Edition	Place	Publisher	Page no., etc.	Library where inspected	Text
1675	1st	Paris	Jean Guignard Fils	Book 1, ch. XXXVIII, p. 325	BM	coustant
1676	1st (with German translation)	Geneva	Jean Herman Widerhold	Part 1, Book 1, ch. XXXVIII, p. 614	GL LSE ICA	coustant
1701	5th	Lyon	Jacques Lyons	Part 1, Book IV, ch. IX, p. 313	ICA GL	coûtant
1712	6th	Lyon	Jacques Lyons	Part 1, Book IV, ch. IX, p. 269	LSE	coûrant
1752	"new"	Geneva	Frères Cramer & Cl. Philibert	Vol. 1, Book IV, ch. IX, p. 348	GL	coûtant
1757	"new"	Paris	Frères Estienne	Part 1, Book IV, ch. IX, p. 348	GL	coutant

BM = British Museum
GL = Goldsmith's Library, University of London
LSE = British Library of Economic and Political Science, London School of Economics
ICA = Library of the Institute of Chartered Accountants in England and Wales

RECKONING, MERCHANTS' ACCOUNTS, BOOK-KEEPING, ACCOUNTING OR ACCOUNTANCY? THE EVIDENCE OF THE LONG TITLES OF BOOKS ON ACCOUNTING IN ENGLISH, 1543-1914

R. H. PARKER *

What's in a name? that which we call a rose
By any other name would smell as sweet.

Romeo and Juliet, II, ii, 43/44

Twentieth century accounting authors tend to choose relatively sober and short titles for their books such as *Introduction to Accounting* (Edey, 1978) and *Business Budgets and Accounts* (Edey, 1966). Even a title such as *Debits, Credits, Finance and Profits* (Edey and Yamey, 1974) has a slightly flighty air about it.

The earliest writers in English on the subject had no such inhibitions. The first works to be published in England (Oldcastle, 1543), Scotland (Colinson, 1683) and North America (Mitchell, 1796) provide examples from the 16th, 17th and 18th centuries respectively:

> Here ensueth a profitable treatyce called the instrument or boke to learne to knowe the good order of the kepyng of the famouse reconyng, called in latyn, dare and habere, and in englyshe, debitor and creditor.
>
> Idea rationaria, or the perfect accomptant, necessary for all merchants and trafficquers; containing the true forme of book-keeping, according to the Italian methode: wherein is first, the introduction to the forme, 244 queries and answers, with instructions how to ballance the leger, two waste-books transported in two journals, out of which are transported 2 legers both ballanced. After which follows a moneth-book, invois-book, factor-book, specie or cash-book; instructions how to keep a book of petty charges or pocket-book.[1]

* I am much indebted to M. F. Bywater, Anna B. G. Dunlop, G. A. Lee and B. S. Yamey for their helpful comments on a previous draft.

> A new and complete system of book-keeping, by an improved method of double entry, adapted to retail, domestic and foreign trade: exhibiting a variety of transactions which usually occur in business. The whole comprised in three sets of books; the last set, being a copy of the second according to those systems most generally in use, is given in order to exhibit by a comparative view, the advantages of the system now laid down. To which is added, a table of the duties payable on goods, wares and merchandise, imported into the United States of America. The whole in dollars and cents.

A title-page may be defined as "a separate page setting forth in a conspicuous manner the title of the book which follows it, and not containing any part of the text of the book which follows it." The origin of the title-page is a little obscure but it was in general use by the middle of the 16th century (McKerrow, 1927, pp. 88-89). It will be observed that the title of Oldcastle's book of 1543 takes more the form of an opening paragraph. The manuscripts which preceded printed books did not in general have title-pages, although many of them began with some such phrase as "Here beginneth ..." The title-page of Oldcastle appears to be of this kind. No copy of this work has survived, so a check is not possible.

Three stages may be discerned in the development of the title page (McKerrow, 1927, p.90): (i) merely the name or contents of the book is given, with or without the name of the author; (ii) the date of printing, the name or device of the printer or bookseller is added; (iii) it becomes an advertisement of the book designed to attract purchasers.

The third stage provides an explanation of why long titles were considered necessary. As 16th century customers went from stall to stall in St. Paul's Churchyard (for long the headquarters of English publishing) they "would find stuck up in conspicuous places on posts or walls the title-pages of books which set out in great detail at times the contents of the work, thus enabling the prospective reader to get some idea of what the book was about ... This practice, unfortunately, led to the wildest filling up of the title-page with overemphatic statements, calculated to catch the attention of the passer by" (Bennett, 1965, pp. 260-261).

Bennett cites as a dreadful example Angel Day's book on letter-writing, The English Secretorie ... (1592), the long title of which contains 127 words. He could well have cited instead the translation by "W.P." in 1596 of a book by Nicolaus Petri. The long title of the translation is as follows and contains 145 words:

> The pathway to knowledge. Conteyning certaine briefe tables of English waights, and measures, with the proportions, kindes, and numbers properly unto the same. How to cast accompt with counters, and with pen, both in whole, and broken numbers. With the rules of cossicke, surd, binomicall, and residuall numbers, and the rule of equation, or of algebere, with divers examples for the working of the same. Whereunto is annexed a most excellent Invention of Iulius Caesar Patavinus, for the buying and selling of all kind of marchandise. And lastly the order of keeping of a marchants booke, after the Italian manner, by debtor and creditor, with an instruction to lead you to the same. All more briefly done, then any heretofore hath been set foorth. Together with a table in the beginning of the booke, where you may finde the principall matters contained in the same.

Such extravagances did not by any means die out in the 16th century, although some became more explanatory and less of a "puff" (McKerrow, 1927, p.93). The long titles of Colinson (1683) and Mitchell (1796) already quoted contain respectively 78 words and 103 words. The record in the bookkeeping field appears to be held by an early 19th century Irish work (Comins, 1814), the long title of which, containing 339 words, is as follows:

> The science of commerce; or, a new and universal system of practical mercantile business and book-keeping combined, by double entry; in which the present practice of the counting-house, and all its books, are new modelled, shortened, simplified, and considerably improved upon; presenting a regular set of all the books, and the actual business as well of an individual, as of a company of general import and export merchants; which effectually shews and teaches how to conduct, carry on, and keep books, for the whole import and export trade of Ireland, (or any country) particularly that of the beef, pork, butter, corn, and linen business, in a more modern, concise, and improved mode than has been practised as yet in any counting-house, or written upon by any person prior to Philip Comins of Cork; being the result of upwards of thirty years practice and experience, in multiplied scenes of mercantile pursuits. To which is added a selection of new systems, plans,

> and forms of accounts, for anonymous co-partnership, manufacturers, wholesale warehouses, shop-keepers, country gentlemen, or farmers, and for dissolving a partnership, &c. not in any other work; with an elegant appropriate plan of practical mercantile tuition for the schools, perfectly assimilated to the actual practice and daily business of the counting-house, whereby this system can be taught, publicly or privately, immediately on inspection, and by which youth will effectually be completed in both. The whole designed with a view of establishing one universal standard of practical mercantile business and book-keeping combined, for the counting-house and schools: in both of which the merchants and bankers of Cork most strongly recommend its general adoption (vide their review of it in the preface). This system is exhibited in the most easy, comprehensive, and concise point of view, in ten books, or three sets in this volume, containing a select variety of domestic, commission, and foreign trade, and rendering company accounts in particular, so little understood heretofore in the schools, as simple and as easily learned as any common accounts between two individuals.

Long titles became less common in the late 19th and early 20th century, but did not die out until the First World War. The title of the well-known pioneering work on cost accounting of Garcke and Fells (1887), for example, is:

> Factory accounts their principles and practice. A handbook for accountants and manufacturers with appendices on the nomenclature of machine details; the Income Tax Acts; the rating of factories; fire and boiler insurance; the factory and workshop acts, etc. including also a glossary of terms and a large number of specimen rulings.

Another specialised work published just before the outbreak of the First World War (Johnson, 1912) is entitled:

> Foreign exchange in accounts. Dealing with the treatment in accounts of the Foreign Exchange in general, and showing how the foreign accounts are amalgamated with the home accounts; organisation; banking and other arrangements, systems of returns and other practical information.

A typographical explanation for long titles is given by De Vinne (1904, p.203), an American printer. According to De Vinne the crowded title-page was an inheritance of the 17th century. When the publishing printers claimed nearly all the space for their "huge devices", little could be allowed for the name of the book. When the device went out of fashion, the printer had to fill in the vacant space, for it was then understood that the title-page must always be full, either with an emblem or with large types. "When these were not to be had", wrote De Vinne, "the author was encouraged to write a long title which would serve as a synopsis of the contents of the book, or to use odd phraseology to provoke the curiosity of a listless reader."

De Vinne does lend some support to Bennett's explanation when he complains (1904, p.272) that when a title page is too full it has "the shoppy appearance of an advertisement or a poster."

According to Bennett, each title-page "made its appeal sometimes by the abundance of useful, pleasurable, or instructive fare that it promised was within, or sometimes by the sensational, topical or unusual material that it contained. Books were always presented in their best light ... In short, the title-page had to do its best to serve the same purpose as does the modern publisher's enthusiastic account which he places inside the flap of the dust jacket ..." (1965, pp.291-2).

In other words, the long title was often a blurb (a word not used before the early 20th century). Blurbs should not be taken too seriously (and, as such, may not always have been written by the author: cf. McKerrow, 1927, pp.91-92), but they do enable us, without in the first instance having to read in full the books they are advertising, to pose such questions as:

(a) what did the authors call the subject about which they were writing?

(b) to whom were their books addressed?

Only an answer to the first question is attempted here. The second has been briefly discussed by Chambers (1966, p.343).

In order to answer questions such as these we need a reliable list or lists of books on accounting in English since 1543. Happily, a number of such lists are available. Those which have been used in this paper are

Yamey, Edey and Thomson (1963), Historical Accounting Literature (1975), Pryce-Jones and Parker (1976), Dunlop (1976) and Bentley and Leonard (1934-5).

A study of these lists reveals four main descriptive phrases: "reckoning", "merchants' accounts", "book-keeping" and "accounting/accountancy". To these phrases are sometimes added words such as "in the Italian manner". Only "bookkeeping" (not now usually hyphenated) and "accounting/accountancy" are in use today, with "bookkeeping" clearly regarded as an inferior word.

RECKONING

The section of Pacioli's Summa (1494) of interest to accountants is entitled: Particularis de computis et scripturis. The earliest English writers on the subject translated computis as "reckoning", a word that English shares with German and Dutch. A more literal translation, with the Latin word influenced by French, is counting or accounting (accompting).

The word "reckoning" appears in the long titles of Oldcastle (1543), Ympyn (1547), Peele (1553) and Mellis (1588) but not in later authors. Ympyn uses the phrase "a boke of accomptes or reconynges" (in the Dutch and French versions Rekenboeck and livre de compte are used respectively: the English translation picks up both the Dutch and French phrases). Peele in 1553 refers to "a perfecte reconyng, after the order of the moste worthie and notable accompte" and in 1569 to "accomptes."

MERCHANTS' ACCOUNTS (ACCOMPTS)

The term "merchants' accounts" is not fully established until the 17th century but the long title of Weddington (1567) refers to "merchantes bokes, of accomptes", that of Petri (1596) to the "keeping of a marchants booke." Tap (1613) and Carpenter (1632) use the phrase "merchants' books of accounts"; Handson (1633) is the first to refer to "merchants accompts." The three books of Dafforne (1635, 1640, 1640) use the words "accounts", "accomptantly" and "accomptant." Collins (1635 and 1697), Liset (1660), Brown (1669), Chamberlain

(1679), Hatton (1695) and Jones (date uncertain) all use the phrase "merchants accounts" in various spellings. It is a phrase which continues into the 18th century when books on the subject became much more plentiful.

It was "Merchant's Accompts" that the philosopher John Locke in 1693 advised all gentlemen to learn perfectly "and not to think it is a Skill, that belongs not to them, because it has received its Name, and has been chiefly practised by Men of Traffick" (Axtell, 1968, p.320). When "a person of honour" (Roger North, of the family which produced Lord North, prime minister during the American War of Independence) wrote The gentleman accomptant ... in 1714 he also used the term "merchants accompts."

BOOK-KEEPING

The usual 18th century word in long titles, however, is not "merchants' accounts" but "book-keeping." Chamberlain's book of 1679 was called The accomptants guide or merchants book-keeper ... but "book-keeping" is first used in a long title by Colinson in 1683. The long title of his book has already been quoted in full.

The next use of the word "book-keeping" in a long title is in Dafforne's The English Merchants companion: or, an entertainment for the young merchants, their servants. Digested into three parts. Wherein the perfect method of merchants book-keeping, and other matters relating to traffick, is compleatly demonstrated ... The fourth edition, carefully corrected and augumented published in London in 1700. This is the fourth edition of a book which in previous editions was entitled The apprentices time - entertainer, accomptantly ... (1st ed. 1640, 3rd ed. 1670). (Bywater and Yamey, 1982, p.96).

Whilst not superseding "accounts" or "merchants' accounts" entirely, "book-keeping" rapidly became the preferred title for the subject. Sometimes both phrases were used. Snell published two works in 1701, one entitled Merchants accompts ..., the other Rules for book-keeping ...; Mair's successful texts were entitled Book-keeping methodiz'd: or a methodical treatise of merchant-accompts, according to the Italian form ... (1st ed. 1736) and Book-keeping moderniz'd: or, merchant-accounts by double entry, according to the Italian form ... (1st ed. 1773).

New words are likely to be used in the text of a book before they are used in the title. The earliest use I have found of "book-keeping" is in Dafforne's Merchants mirrour ... (1635). Dafforne had spent many years in the Netherlands and makes frequent references to Dutch authors. Colinson also makes it clear by several references in his book that, like many Scottish merchants of his time, he had lived and traded in the Netherlands. It is possible, therefore, that "book-keeping" is an importation into English from Dutch, although it is curious that, given the extent of Dutch influence, it took so long for the word to emerge. Perhaps Dafforne was more given than others to new words. Murray (1930, p.246) points out that others of his books might have supplied the New English Dictionary with the word "accountantly" and with an unexceptionable authority for "accountantship." Unlike "book-keeping" these words did not find their way into general use.

The Dutch word for "book-keeping" is boekhouden. It was not used by Ympyn, the Flemish/Dutch edition (1543) of whose book was the earliest on the subject to be published in that language. It was first used in a long title by Nicholaus Petri in 1576. A later book of Petri's, Practicque om te leeren rekenen cijpheren ende boeckhouwen ... was translated by W. P. as the Pathway to knowledge ... (1596), the long title of which has been given above, and re-worked and re-issued by John Tap in 1613 as The path-way to knowledge; containing ... a briefe order for the keeping of marchants bookes of accompts, by way of debitor and creditor. It is noteworthy that neither of these titles (nor the texts) translate boekhouden as book-keeping.

After Petri the word boekhouden or its equivalent appears in the long titles of numerous books including Stevin's Vorstelicke bouckhouding op de Italiaensche wyse ... (1607) which is referred to by name by Dafforne in his book of 1635.

It is possible that the Dutch in their turn acquired the word from the German Buchhalten. The first to use it in a long title was Johann Gottlieb in 1531. It was later used by Mennher von Kempten in a book published in 1560 in Antwerp in German. Mennher was born in Kempten in Bavaria c.1521 and moved to Antwerp and became a citizen in 1549. The content and wording of his exposition of bookkeeping are echoed in Petri (Bywater and Yamey, pp.54-57). His first book, published in French in Antwerp in 1550, included in its title the words tenir livres de compte (to keep books of account).

"Book-keeping" may also or alternatively be derived from "book-keeper." The earliest use of the latter word in an accounting text appears to be in a marginal sub-title in Peele (1569):

> Howe the monye may be committed to a seruãt to receave & pay the same to the lesse troblinge of the Master or thother bokekepers declared in ij manners. (Folio (recto) after sig. Diiij).

The book-keeper here is clearly someone in charge of books not just one who makes entries in them. Such books need not be books of account, as evidenced by the earliest O.E.D. citation, dated 1555.

It is interesting to note that a more literal translation from the Dutch, "book-holding", was in use in Scotland. The Scottish National Dictionary cites the following from the Scots Courant of 16 March, 1716:

> John Morison, A.M. is to begin his lessons of ... the Italian Method of Book-holding.

ACCOUNTING/ACCOUNTANCY

The words "accounting" and "accountancy", as distinct from "accounts" were seldom used in long titles until the 19th century.

The earliest English example appears to be North's The gentleman accomptant ... (1714) the long title of which refers to the subject as "merchants accompts" but later promises "A short and easy vocabulary of certain words, that in the language of accompting take a particular meaning."

Of approximately the same date are:

> Instructions for the collectors and other officers employ'd in Her majesties' Customs, etc, in the north part of Great Britain with ... the regular methods of accompting. (1707)

and two short books by Robert Lundin:

> The reasons for accompting by debitor and creditor with general rules for attaining to that way of accompting. (1718)
>
> The fundamental principles and reasons of accompting by debitor and creditor ... (1736)

All three of these works were published in Edinburgh. The 1736 book by Lundin is the second edition of his 1718 book.

The more successful Scottish authors of the 18th century, however, MacGhie, Malcolm, Mair, Gordon, and Robert Hamilton, did not use the word "accounting" in their long titles. Its next use in a long title (also from Scotland) comes much later in F. Hayne Carter's Practical bookkeeping adapted to commercial and judicial accounting ... (1861). This was the earliest book written by a chartered accountant.

Whilst "accounting" is a word of some antiquity, the earliest citation of "accountancy" in the Oxford English Dictionary is from the Illustrated London News of 22 April 1854. The reference is to a review of Sir John Bowring's The decimal system in numbers, coins and accounts: especially with reference to the decimalisation of the currency and accountancy of the United Kingdom (London: Nathaniel Cooke, 1854) in which "accountancy" is clearly synonymous with "accounting." Bowring (1792-1872), whose life and works are discussed at length in the Dictionary of National Biography, acted as Secretary to the Select Committee on Public Accounts (1831), was an M.P., an F.R.S. and Governor of Hong Kong. He secured the adoption of the florin as a first, but at that stage, abortive step to decimalisation of the currency. It is not clear why he used the word "accountancy" rather than "accounting." Perhaps it was the juxtaposition of "currency" in the long title.

There is no trace of "accountancy" in long titles thereafter until the

1880s.[2] In this decade it occurs in a number of papers printed in The Accountant, many of which were also available in pamphlet form. The earliest example appears to be Adam Murray's "On the progress of accountancy and the duties which come within the scope of an accountant's practice" (The Accountant, December 24 and 31, 1881). There was no attempt to distinguish between "accounting" and "accountancy."

Few even of late 19th and early 20th century books had either "accounting" or "accountancy" in their titles. Notable exceptions were Pixley, Dicksee and Lisle. Pixley's Accountancy was first published in 1908. The first edition of Dicksee's Advanced Accounting dates from 1903; his The Student's Guide to Accountancy was first published in 1897. Lisle was the author of Accounting in Theory and Practice (Edinburgh, 1899) and the editor of the 8 volume Encyclopaedia of Accounting (Edinburgh, 1903-1907).

IN THE ITALIAN MANNER

The earliest writers in English do not in their long titles, use the phrase "in the Italian manner" although they do make reference, as might be expected, to Italy.

Oldcastle (1543), rather curiously, refers to the Latin equivalents (dare and habere) of debit and credit. Ympyn's book (1547) claims to have been translated originally from Italian (he makes a mysterious reference to a work by a Jehan Paulo de Bianchi). Petri as translated by W.P. (1596) is the first to refer in a long title to the "keeping of a marchants booke, after the Italian manner." (Petri's Boeckhouwen op die Italiaensche maniere ..., 1576, appears to be first to do so in any language.) Carpenter (1632) states that he teaches "after the Italian manner", Dafforne (1635) "after the (so tearmed) italian manner."

The "Italian manner" became popular in titles at the same time as "book-keeping." As we have already seen, Colinson claimed that his book of 1683 contained "the true forme of book-keeping, according to the Italian method," although Dafforne does not use the phrase in 1700. In 1701 Snell's "merchants accompts" were "in the true Italian method" and his "book-keeping" was "according to the Italian manner."

Throughout the 18th century phrases such as these were very common in long titles in England, Scotland and Ireland. During the 19th century, when books on the subject became increasingly numerous, it became much less common. Where it was used it was mainly in new editions or adaptations of 18th century books. It probably appears for the last time in the 1870 edition of Dilworth's The young book-keeper's assistant: showing him the Italian way of stating debtor and creditor; ... (London: T. J. Allman, 1870), a book whose 7th ed. had been published in 1777.

WHAT'S IN A NAME?

Of the names discussed in this paper only "bookkeeping" and "accounting/accountancy" are in current use. Accountants do not claim today to practise "reckoning" or "merchants' accounts" or to prepare them in the Italian manner. Bookkeeping is regarded as a worthy but non-professional occupation. Are these changes in names, and the status of names, of any significance in the history of British accounting?

In the sciences there are examples of new words being adopted because the old have ceased to describe a recognised "science." "Astrology" (literally, the study of the stars) has given way to "astronomy" (literally, the law of the stars) and "alchemy" (literally the art of transmuting metals) has given way to "chemistry" (of the same literal meaning, but shorn of an Arabic prefix). The transition from "reckoning" to "merchants' accounts" to "bookkeeping" to "accounting/accountancy" does not, as do these examples, record the transformation of a subject from medieval magic to modern science, but it is, it may be claimed, a recognition of changes of some importance.

In the sixteenth and seventeenth centuries England and Scotland imported their accounting techniques and many of the words to go with them from continental Europe. The early writers had to decide whether to treat foreign words as English words, or anglicise them in some way, to invent new words or to use words already in existence. To a large extent they chose the second of these courses: hence, for example, "journal", "folio", "capital" (replacing "stock"), "cash" (replacing "money" - in Colinson's /1683/ words, "Cash is used now generally for money Accompts, it comes from the Italian word Cassa, which is a money Chest, or the like, which keeps it") and "bank", all of which are derived from the Italian.

Their first choice for the subject itself was "reckoning", a well-established English word, chosen perhaps in the spirit of these words of Peele (1553, Preface):

> "Neither have I had so much respecte, to please such as have perfect knowledge, in this order of accomptes (with subtle tearmes in other languages,) but rather used as plain and familier speache, in our oune language, as I could devise, whereby the learners, the soner might be instructed" (Peele, 1553, Preface).

"Reckoning" was, however, an imprecise word and this may explain its replacement by "merchants' accounts" which always appears to imply the use of double entry. It is clear from the long titles that the books were aimed mainly at merchants, their sons and their apprentices, although the composers of the long titles (blurbs) sometimes extended that audience. Ympyn's book (1547) is said to be for "all marchantes, receivers, auditors, notaries, and all other;" Peele's book of 1553 is "not onely unto suche, that trade in the facte of marchaundise, but also unto any other estate." Dafforne's books of 1640 were aimed at apprentices and young and inexperienced accountants. Liset's <u>Amphithalami</u> (1660) was the first on double entry to be aimed at estate owners rather than merchants. It was, its long title claimed without modesty, "very useful and convenient for Lords, Knights, gentlemen, commissioners, treasurers, comptrollers, auditors, farmers, merchants, factors, stewards and all degrees of men."

At this stage it may have been thought that "merchants' accounts" was too restrictive a term and this may explain why "bookkeeping", first used apparently by Dafforne in 1635, but not popular until the 18th century, gained in popularity.

Throughout this period the word "accounting" was available but it may well have been thought to be a less precise term than "bookkeeping." From perhaps the 1880s onwards, however, a need grew for words which expressed two separate but connected ideas: first, that accountants now formed a profession which needed to be distinguished from the subject, and second, that accountants performed tasks which were in some way "higher" than bookkeeping. "Accounting" and "accountancy" were the words available but they were too close in form to be clearly distinguished, although the latter could usefully have been reserved for the subject and the latter for the profession.

The writing of accounting history itself reflects these changes. Foster (1852) wrote of The origin and progress of book-keeping; Worthington (1895) of Professional Accountants; Brown (1905), A History of Accounting and Accountants; Woolf (1912), A Short History of Accountants and Accountancy. But Brown's "accounting" does not differ from Woolf's "accountancy."

There are today no professors of bookkeeping in British universities and no clear distinction has been made in their titles between accounting and accountancy. Dicksee, Britain's first professor in the subject, albeit part-time, held a chair of accounting at the University of Birmingham and a chair of accountancy and business methods at the London School of Economics. His later full-time successors at the London School of Economics have all been professors of accounting.

The two journals of the Institute of Chartered Accountants in England and Wales contain little bookkeeping and are aptly titled Accountancy (the monthly intended mainly for practitioners) and Accounting and Business Research (the research quarterly intended more for academics). Their American equivalents are The Journal of Accountancy and The Accounting Review. The English-speaking world at large, however, is not so precise.

REFERENCES

Axtell, J. L., The Educational Writings of John Locke (Cambridge University Press, 1968).

Bennett, H. S., English Books and Readers 1558 to 1603 (Cambridge University Press, 1965).

Bentley, H. C. and Leonard, R. S., Bibliography of Works on Accounting by American Authors (Boston: Harry C. Bentley, 2 vols. 1934-35).

Bowring, J., The decimal system in numbers, coins and accounts ... (London: Nathaniel Cooke, 1854).

Brown, R., A History of Accounting and Accountants (Edinburgh: T. C. and E. C. Jack, 1905).

Brown, Thomas, The accurate - accomptant ... (London: Will. Godbid, 1669).

Bywater, M. and Yamey, B. S., Historic Accounting Literature: A Companion Guide (London: Scolar Press, 1982).

Carpenter, John, A most excellent instruction ... (London: James Boler, 1632).

Carter, F. Hayne, Practical bookkeeping adapted to commercial and judicial accounting (Edinburgh: Edmonston and Douglas, 1861).

Chamberlain, Robert, The accomptants guide or merchants book-keeper ... (London: John Clark, 1679).

Chambers, R. J., Accounting, Evaluation and Economic Behavior (Englewood Cliffs, N. J.: Prentice-Hall, 1966).

Colinson, Robert, Idea rationaria ... (Edinburgh: David Lindsay et al, 1683).

Collins, John, An introduction to merchants accounts ... (London: Nicholas Bourn, 1653).

Collins, John, The perfect method of merchants - accompts demonstrated ... (London: Thomas Horne, 1697).

Comins, Philip, The science of commerce ... (Dublin: J. J. Nolan, 1814).

Dafforne, Richard, The apprentices time-entertainer, accomptantly ... (London: Nicholas Bourne, 1640).

Dafforne, Richard, The English merchants companion ... (London: Tho. Horne, 4th ed. 1700).

Dafforne, Richard, The merchants mirrour ... (London: Nicolas Bourne, 1635).

Dafforne, Richard, The young accomptants compasse ... (London: Nicolas Bourne, 1640).

De Vinne, T. L., A Treatise on Title-Pages ... (New York: The Century Co., 1904).

Dicksee, L. R., Advanced Accounting ... (London: Gee & Co., 1903)

Dicksee, L. R., The Student's Guide to Accountancy (London: Gee & Co., 1897).

Dilworth, T., The young book-keeper's assistant ... (London: T. J. Allman, 1870).

Dunlop, Anna B. G., An Accountant's Book Collection 1494-1930 (Edinburgh: Institute of Chartered Accountants of Scotland, 1976).

Edey, H. C., Business Budgets and Accounts (London: Hutchinson, 1966).

Edey, H. C., Introduction to Accounting (London: Hutchinson, 4th ed. 1978).

Edey, H. C. and Yamey, B. S. (eds.), Debits, Credits, Finance and Profits (London: Sweet & Maxwell, 1974).

Foster, B. F., The origin and progress of book-keeping ... (London: John Souter, 1852).

Garcke, E. and Fells, J. M., Factory Accounts ... (London: Crosby Lockwood and Son, 1st ed. 1887).

Handson, Ralph, Analysis or resolution of merchants accompts ... (London: Nicholas Bourne, 3rd ed. 1633).

Hatton, Edward, The merchant's magazine ... (London: Chr. Coningsby, 1695).

Historical Accounting Literature (London: Mansell, 1975).

Johnson, C. (ed.), Dialogus de Scaccario, The Course of the Exchequer ... (London: Thomas Nelson and Sons, 1950).

Johnson, George, Foreign Exchange in Accounts ... (London: Effingham Wilson, 1912).

Jones, John, Diarium mercatoris; or, a key to merchants accounts ... (Gloucester: J. and J. Knapton et al, no date).

Liset, Abraham, Amphithalami, or, the accomptants closet ... (London: Nicholas Bourne, 1660).

Lisle, G., Accounting in theory and practice ... (Edinburgh: William Green and Sons, 1899).

Lisle, G. (ed.), Encyclopaedia of Accounting (Edinburgh: William Green and Sons, 8 vols., 1903-07).

Lundin, R., The fundamental principle and reasons of accompting by debitor and creditor ... (Edinburgh, 1736).

Lundin, R., The reasons for accompting by debitor and creditor ... (Edinburgh, 1707).

McClelland, J., The origins and present organisation of the profession of chartered accountants in Scotland (Glasgow, 1869).

McKerrow, R. B., An Introduction to Bibliography for Literary Students (Oxford: Clarendon Press, 1927).

Mair, John, Book-keeping methodiz'd ... (Edinburgh: T. and W. Ruddimans, 1st ed. 1736).

Mair, John, Book-keeping moderniz'd ... (Edinburgh: A. Kincaird & W. Creech and J. Bell, 1st ed. 1773).

Mellis, John, A briefe instruction ... (London: John Windet, 1588).

Mitchell, William, A new and complete system of book-keeping ... (Philadelphia: Bioren & Madan, 1796).

Murray, D., Chapters in the History of Bookkeeping, Accountancy and Commercial Arithmetic (Glasgow: Jackson, Wylie & Co., 1930).

North, Roger, The gentleman accomptant ... (London: E. Curll, 1714).

Oldcastle, Hugh, A profitable treatyce ... (London: John Gough, 1543).

Pacioli, L., Summa de arithmetica geometria proportioni & proportionalita ... (Venice: Paganino da Paganini, 1494).

Peele, James, The maner and fourme how to keepe a perfecte reconyng ... (London: Richard Grafton, 1553).

Peele, James, The pathe waye to perfectnes in th' accomptes of debitour and creditour ... (London: Thomas Purfoote, 1569).

Petri, Nicolaus, Boeckhouwen op die Italiaensche maniere ... (1576).

Petri, Nicolaus (translated by W. P.), The pathway to knowledge ... (London: William Barley, 1596).

Pixley, F. W., Accountancy ... (London: Pitman, 1908).

Pryce-Jones, J. and Parker, R. H., Accounting in Scotland. A Historical Bibliography (Edinburgh: Institute of Chartered Accountants of Scotland, 2nd ed. 1976).

Snell, Charles, Merchants accompts, in the true Italian manner ... (London: J. Place, 1701).

Snell, Charles, Rules for book-keeping, according to the Italian manner ... (London: John Place, 1701).

Tap, John, The path-way to knowledge ... (London: Tho. Pavier, 1613).

Weddington, John, A breffe instruction and manner, howe to kepe merchantes bokes, of accomptes ... (Antwerp: Petter van Keerbergher, 1567)

Woolf, A. H., A Short History of Accountants and Accountancy (London: Gee & Co., 1912).

Worthington, B., Professional Accountants: an Historical Sketch (London: Gee & Co.).

Yamey, B. S., Edey, H. C. and Thomson, H. W., Accounting in England and Scotland: 1543-1800 (London: Sweet & Maxwell, 1963).

Ympyn, Jan., A notable and very excellente woorke ... (London, 1547).

FOOTNOTES

1. Colinson's book is one of the few works on accounting in English with a Latin or Greek short title. The others are Malynes's Consuetudo: vel, Lex Mercatoria, or, the ancient law-merchant ... , 1656, to which are appended the books by Dafforne and Collins; Liset's Amphithalami, or the accomptants closet ... , 1660; Every's Speculum mercativum. Or the young merchants ... accompts ... (1673); Jones's Diarium mercatoris; or a key to merchants accounts ... (n.d., c. 1700), Hawkins' Clavis commercii: or, the key of commerce ..., (1704) and Browne's Arithmetica infinita ... (1718).

The word Amphithalami used by Liset appears at first sight to be Greek. In fact it is known to occur once in Latin literature, viz, in Vitruvius, de architectura (1st century B.C.), book vi, ch.7 where there is a description of Greek houses. The relevant paragraph may be translated as follows:

> As we pass in, there is the Great Hall in which the ladies sit with the spinning women. Right and left of the recess are the bedchambers, of which one is called the thalamus, the other the amphithalamus. Round the colonnades are the ordinary dining-rooms, the bedrooms, and the privies. This part of the building is called the women's quarter, gynaeconitis.

(I am indebted to Professor Peter Wiseman of the Department of Classics, University of Exeter for this reference.) Dr. G. A. Lee of the University of Nottingham has suggested to me that what Vitruvius actually wrote was antithalamus but: "In any case, it is unlikely that Liset knew anything about the derivation of the word; he probably thought it sounded fine, and used it as meaning 'closet' or 'private chamber'."

"Thalamus" is used in the 12th century Dialogus de Scaccario (Dialogue of the Exchequer) by Richard, Son of Nigel, Treasurer of England and Bishop of London, to refer to the privy Chamber adjoining the hall of the Exchequer: Johnson (1950), p.44.

2. The title of the pamphlet by J. McClelland (1869) includes the words "chartered accountants" not "chartered accountancy" as wrongly transcribed in Pryce-Jones and Parker (1976).